Christian Drumm

Improving Schema Mapping by Exploiting Domain Knowledge

Christian Drumm

Improving Schema Mapping by Exploiting Domain Knowledge

Südwestdeutscher Verlag für Hochschulschriften

Impressum/Imprint (nur für Deutschland/ only for Germany)
Bibliografische Information der Deutschen Nationalbibliothek: Die Deutsche Nationalbibliothek verzeichnet diese Publikation in der Deutschen Nationalbibliografie; detaillierte bibliografische Daten sind im Internet über http://dnb.d-nb.de abrufbar.
Alle in diesem Buch genannten Marken und Produktnamen unterliegen warenzeichen-, markenoder patentrechtlichem Schutz bzw. sind Warenzeichen oder eingetragene Warenzeichen der jeweiligen Inhaber. Die Wiedergabe von Marken, Produktnamen, Gebrauchsnamen, Handelsnamen, Warenbezeichnungen u.s.w. in diesem Werk berechtigt auch ohne besondere Kennzeichnung nicht zu der Annahme, dass solche Namen im Sinne der Warenzeichen- und Markenschutzgesetzgebung als frei zu betrachten wären und daher von jedermann benutzt werden dürften.

Verlag: Südwestdeutscher Verlag für Hochschulschriften Aktiengesellschaft & Co. KG
Dudweiler Landstr. 99, 66123 Saarbrücken, Deutschland
Telefon +49 681 37 20 271-1, Telefax +49 681 37 20 271-0, Email: info@svh-verlag.de
Zugl.: Karlsruhe, Universität Karlsruhe, Diss., 2008

Herstellung in Deutschland:
Schaltungsdienst Lange o.H.G., Berlin
Books on Demand GmbH, Norderstedt
Reha GmbH, Saarbrücken
Amazon Distribution GmbH, Leipzig
ISBN: 978-3-8381-0293-1

Imprint (only for USA, GB)
Bibliographic information published by the Deutsche Nationalbibliothek: The Deutsche Nationalbibliothek lists this publication in the Deutsche Nationalbibliografie; detailed bibliographic data are available in the Internet at http://dnb.d-nb.de.
Any brand names and product names mentioned in this book are subject to trademark, brand or patent protection and are trademarks or registered trademarks of their respective holders. The use of brand names, product names, common names, trade names, product descriptions etc. even without a particular marking in this works is in no way to be construed to mean that such names may be regarded as unrestricted in respect of trademark and brand protection legislation and could thus be used by anyone.

Publisher:
Südwestdeutscher Verlag für Hochschulschriften Aktiengesellschaft & Co. KG
Dudweiler Landstr. 99, 66123 Saarbrücken, Germany
Phone +49 681 37 20 271-1, Fax +49 681 37 20 271-0, Email: info@svh-verlag.de

Copyright © 2009 by the author and Südwestdeutscher Verlag für Hochschulschriften Aktiengesellschaft & Co. KG and licensors
All rights reserved. Saarbrücken 2009

Printed in the U.S.A.
Printed in the U.K. by (see last page)
ISBN: 978-3-8381-0293-1

Mailand oder Madrid - Hauptsache Italien!
Andreas Möller

Abstract

This dissertation addresses the problem of semi-automatically creating schema mappings. The need for developing schema mappings is a pervasive problem in many integration scenarios. Although the problem is well-known and a large body of work exists in the area, the development of schema mappings is today largely performed manually in industrial integration scenarios.

In this thesis an approach for the semi-automatic creation of schema mappings based on a central ontology is developed. The central ontology stores domain as well as integration knowledge. Using this ontology as a basis, schema mappings of high quality can be created automatically.

In particular, this thesis addressed the following questions:

- **Which knowledge is necessary to create schema mappings?** It is obvious that schema information alone is not sufficient to create mapping between complex schemas. The thesis analysis which types of background knowledge are required in order to create a correct mapping between two schemas. This analyses of required background knowledge is not particularly focused towards the automatic creation of schema mappings but also applies to the manual development of schema mappings.

- **How can the necessary background knowledge be collected?** The background knowledge required to create schema mappings is usually not easily accessible. As a result, two approaches for the collection of background knowledge are developed and evaluated in this thesis. A particular focus is placed on enabling the non-intrusive collection of the background knowledge to enable the application of the approaches in productive environments.

- **How can background knowledge be exploited by an automated approach?** In order to exploit background knowledge during the mapping creation, it needs to be available in a machine interpretable format. The thesis shows an approach for the modeling of domain and integration knowledge in an ontology and, based on this, develops a schema mapping approach capable of exploiting the modeled knowledge during the automatic schema mapping creation.

- **Can complex mappings be created automatically?** Most existing approaches focus on the automatic identification of matches between schemas, i.e. identifying corresponding schema elements. However, identifying matching elements is only the first step when creating a schema mapping. The approach developed in this thesis is not only capable of identifying matching schema elements but also able to identify the complex expressions necessary to translate instances of the schemas.

- **Can the mapping quality required for industrial applications be achieved?** Automatic schema mapping approaches will only be used in industrial integration tools if the mapping quality surpasses a certain threshold. The approach developed in this thesis is therefore evaluated using schemas originating from real integration projects in order to assess whether if it is capable of creating mappings of the required quality.

In summary, the results of this thesis show that by exploiting background knowledge automatic schema mapping can be developed to a level where it is applicable in complex industrial scenarios. The novel knowledge collection approaches compliment the mapping approach by presenting non-intrusive methods for collecting the required background knowledge from business users.

I wish to thank ...

... my Supervisor

Rudi Studer

... the Reviewers

Raphael Volz
Anupriya Ankolekar
Andreas Abecker
Jens Lemcke
Kioumars Namiri
Gunther Stuhec
Harald Fuchs
Uwe Kubach
Matthias Born
Ingo Weber

... the Colleagues

Michael Altenhofen, Christian Brelage, Hong-Hai Do, Elmar Dorner, Andreas Friesen, Gregor Hackenbroich, Philipp Kunfermann, Peter Lienhard, Daniel Oberle, Ivan Markovic, Burkhard Neidecker-Lutz, Rainer Ruggaber, Thorsten Sandfuchs, Daniel Scheibli, Kay-Uwe Schmidt, Matthias Schmitt, Irina Selenski, Murray Spork, Axel Spriestersbach, York Sure, Orestis Terzidis, Wolfgang Theilmann, Susan Thomas, Rüdiger Winter

... and last but not least all my friends & my family for their support!

Christian Drumm

Contents

1	**Introduction**	**1**
1.1	Motivation	1
1.2	Examples Scenarios & Requirements	5
1.3	Research Questions	7
1.4	Contribution	8
1.5	Overview	9
I	**Foundations**	**11**
2	**Scenarios & Use Cases**	**13**
2.1	Enterprise Application Integration	13
2.2	Data Migration	16
2.3	Schema Mapping	19
2.4	Summary	22
3	**Challenges for Integration**	**23**
3.1	Running Example	23
3.2	Heterogeneity Layers	24
3.3	Types of Heterogeneity	26
3.3.1	Types of Structural Heterogeneity	26
3.3.2	Types of Semantic Heterogeneity	29
3.4	Resulting Integration Challenges	32
3.4.1	Integration Challenges resulting from Semantic Heterogeneities	33
3.4.2	Integration Challenges resulting from Structural Heterogeneities	34
3.5	The Role of Ontologies in Integration	35
3.6	Summary	38
4	**Definitions**	**39**
4.1	Schema	39
4.2	XML and XML Schema	39

4.3	Ontology	44
4.4	Matching and Mapping	46
4.5	Lifting	48
4.6	Summary	50

II Ontology-based Mapping   51

5 The Mapping Process   53
- 5.1 The Manual Mapping Process ... 53
- 5.2 The Semi-Automatic Mapping Process ... 55
- 5.3 The Ontology-Based Mapping Approach ... 58
  - 5.3.1 Related Work ... 59
  - 5.3.2 Information Capacity Considerations ... 65
- 5.4 Summary ... 65

6 The Role of Background Knowledge   67
- 6.1 Background Knowledge ... 67
  - 6.1.1 Domain Knowledge ... 68
  - 6.1.2 Integration Knowledge ... 68
  - 6.1.3 Relation of Background Knowledge and Heterogeneity Problems ... 74
- 6.2 Collecting Domain Knowledge ... 75
  - 6.2.1 Collection of Usage Characteristics ... 76
  - 6.2.2 Example Data Injection ... 78
- 6.3 Modeling Domain and Integration Knowledge ... 80
  - 6.3.1 Conceptual Modeling of the Domain ... 80
  - 6.3.2 Modeling Integration Knowledge ... 81
  - 6.3.3 Modeling Example Data ... 88
- 6.4 Summary ... 88

7 Lifting   89
- 7.1 Overview ... 89
- 7.2 Matching Algorithms ... 93
  - 7.2.1 Exploitable Schema and Ontology Features ... 93
  - 7.2.2 Similarity Metrics ... 98
  - 7.2.3 Matching Algorithm Details ... 102
- 7.3 Aggregation ... 106
  - 7.3.1 Similarity Matrix Aggregation ... 107
  - 7.3.2 Lifting Extraction ... 108
- 7.4 Summary ... 111

8 Mapping Extraction — 113
- 8.1 Overview — 113
- 8.2 Mapping Categories — 115
  - 8.2.1 Mapping Category Details — 117
  - 8.2.2 Generation of Mapping Code — 122
- 8.3 Mapping Extraction Algorithm — 125
  - 8.3.1 Inferring Matching Schema Entities — 125
  - 8.3.2 Identification of Mapping Categories — 130
- 8.4 Summary — 133

III Implementation and Evaluation — 135

9 Implementation — 137
- 9.1 The OBM Framework — 137
  - 9.1.1 Schema and Ontology Representation — 139
  - 9.1.2 Lifting Representation — 139
  - 9.1.3 Mapping Representation — 139
  - 9.1.4 Implementation Considerations & Optimizations — 140
- 9.2 The Evaluation Toolkit *Evanto* — 142
- 9.3 Summary — 144

10 Evaluation — 145
- 10.1 Industrial State of the Art — 145
  - 10.1.1 Tools supporting B2B Integration — 145
  - 10.1.2 Data Migration Tools — 148
  - 10.1.3 Documentation Tools — 149
- 10.2 Evaluation Approach — 150
  - 10.2.1 Evaluation Scenarios — 151
  - 10.2.2 Master Mappings — 155
  - 10.2.3 Evaluation Ontology — 155
  - 10.2.4 Quality Metrics — 157
- 10.3 Experiments — 158
  - 10.3.1 Schema Reduction — 158
  - 10.3.2 Example Data Injection — 159
  - 10.3.3 Automatic Schema Mapping — 160
  - 10.3.4 Requirements Revisited — 166
- 10.4 Summary — 168

IV Summary and Outlook — 169

11 Summary & Future Work — 171

11.1 Future Work 171
    11.1.1 Knowledge Collection 171
    11.1.2 Automatic Mapping Calculation 173
    11.1.3 Review, Correction & Testing 175
    11.1.4 Iteration & Finalization 176
11.2 Application of the OBM Approach to semantic Web services . . . 176
11.3 Industrial Applications 178
    11.3.1 The SAP NetWeaver Composition Environment 178
    11.3.2 The SAP Migration Workbench 179
    11.3.3 SAP CCTS Modeller Warp 10 180

12 Conclusion   **183**

V Appendix 187

A Questionnaire to Collect Usage Characteristics 189

B Implementation Details of the OBM Framework 197
B.1 The Lifting Package. 198
B.2 The Mapping Package. 198
B.3 The Repository Package. 199
B.4 Used Libraries 199
B.5 Public API 200

C Evanto Details 203

List of Figures

1.1	The scope of different types of Enterprise Application Integration.	2
2.1	A simple B2B interaction.	14
2.2	Excerpt of the XML schema of a SAP IDOC for exchanging purchase orders.	21
3.1	Running example showing two schemas for representing customer data including example instance values.	24
3.2	Heterogeneity layers including some examples of heterogeneity occurring at each layer.	25
4.1	The XML schema representation of the BusinessPartner schema in the running example.	42
4.2	An example instance of the `BusinessPartner` schema.	43
4.3	Example ontology describing the domain of business partners.	45
4.4	Example of a lifting from a source schema to an ontology.	49
5.1	Manual mapping process supported by current tools.	54
5.2	The proposed generic process for the semi-automatic creation of schema mappings.	56
5.3	The steps in the generic semi-automatic mapping process this thesis focuses on.	58
5.4	Schematic overview of the ontology-based schema mapping approach and its alignment to the generic automatic schema mapping process.	59
6.1	A classification of the different types of background knowledge required for the development of correct schema mappings.	68
6.2	Running example including the knowledge necessary to identify matching schema elements.	69
6.3	Alignment of the knowledge collection approaches and the semi-automatic mapping process.	76
6.4	Example of a schema reduction based on usage characteristics collected using a questionnaire.	77

6.5 The idea of Example Data Injection. Example data is manually entered into the business system and exported using the system specific data format. 79
6.6 Example ontology for the domain of business partners. 81
6.7 Example of the approach for the modeling of technical names. . . 83
6.8 Example of the approach for the modeling of default values. . . . 85
6.9 Example of the approach for the modeling of internal or global identifiers. 86
6.10 An example of adding code-list information to the domain ontology. 87
6.11 Example instances of the concept of the example ontology. 88

7.1 Overview of the conceptual architecture of the schema lifting component. 90
7.2 Example of a lifting from a source schema to an ontology. 92
7.3 The aggregation of the matcher results. 107
7.4 Example showing the idea underlying the domain-ontology-based lifting extraction. 109

8.1 Overview of the mapping extraction approach. 114
8.2 The running example including the mapping categories associated to the correspondences. 115
8.3 Example of liftings related through a sub-class relation. 128
8.4 Example of liftings related through inheritance. 129

9.1 Architecture of the OBM Framework. 138
9.2 Excerpt of the serialization format used to store liftings. 140
9.3 Excerpt of the serialization format used to store mappings. 141
9.4 Example of an Evanto script. 143

10.1 The design time tool of the SAP Exchange Infrastructure showing two messages. 147
10.2 Creation of schema mappings in the SAP Migration Workbench. . 149
10.3 A list of possible errors in a schema mapping generated by the invocation of a migration interface in test mode. 150
10.4 Partial graphical representation of the structure and naming of the `BusinessPartner` schema. 153
10.5 Partial graphical representation of the structure and naming of the `DEBMAS` schema. 154
10.6 The results achieved by the OBM Framework using the Technical Names matcher. 162
10.7 The results achieved by the OBM Framework using the combination of the Instance Equality and the Instance Split/Concat matcher. 163
10.8 The results achieved by the OBM Framework using the combination of Technical Names and example data based matchers. 164

LIST OF FIGURES

10.9 The results achieved by the OBM Framework by reusing integration knowledge from related integration scenarios. 166

11.1 Steps of the ontology mapping process discussed in the future work. 171
11.2 The Galaxy Workbench showing a simple process and a schema mapping. 179
11.3 High-level architecture of the CCTS Modeller Warp 10. 181

B.1 Overview of the packages comprising the OBM Framework implementation. 198

C.1 Example of an Evanto script. 204

List of Tables

3.1	Overview of the classification of schematic heterogeneities (based on [SvH05, Wac03].	27
3.2	Overview of the classification of semantic heterogeneities (based on [SvH05, Wac03].	30
3.3	Different types of heterogeneities and how they can be addressed by ontologies.	38
6.1	Types of integration knowledge suitable for an integration into a domain ontology as well as the process step in which they are exploited.	70
6.2	Different types of heterogeneities and the background knowledge required for solving them.	74
7.1	The list of exploitable schema features together with a short explanation of each feature.	94
7.2	The list of exploitable ontology features.	96
8.1	Overview of the identified mapping categories together with a short explanation.	118
8.2	Absolute number of occurrences and occurrence frequency of the different mapping categories in the evaluation scenarios (cf. Section 10.2.1).	122
8.3	Generation of mapping expressions for the different mapping categories.	123
8.4	Required background knowledge for the identification of the different mapping categories. The required type of knowledge is indicated by a ✓ in the table, not required knowledge by a ✗. . . .	131
10.1	The four evaluation scenarios.	152
10.2	Complexity of the schemas used for evaluation in the data migration scenario.	155
10.3	The size of the master mappings in the different evaluation scenarios.	156
10.4	Complexity of the target schema after the reduction	159
10.5	Excerpt of the example data for a customer.	160

Chapter 1

Introduction

This thesis develops automatic schema mapping to a new level where it can be applied in industrial settings. In order to achieve the mapping quality required in an industrial setting, domain knowledge needs to be exploited. The automatic schema mapping approach developed in this thesis exploits domain knowledge during the preprocessing as well as the automatic mapping process and thereby improves the quality of the automatically generated mappings. By using an ontology as a central knowledge base encapsulating the domain knowledge throughout the automatic mapping process, the developed approach is capable of identifying even complex mappings common in industrial scenarios.

1.1 Motivation

In dynamic business environments enterprises are faced with numerous types of integration ranging from organizational integration to application integration. Changing markets and short term business opportunities require enterprises to perform the different types of integration frequently in order to adapt to the evolving business environment. This thesis focuses on the integration challenges at the technical level where schema mapping plays a central role. More precisely, the focus of this thesis is on the two use cases *application integration* and *data migration*.

Application Integration. Bussler [Bus03] identifies three main types of application integration:

1. Application-to-Application (A2A) integration

2. Business-to-Business (B2B) integration

3. Application Service Provider (ASP) integration.

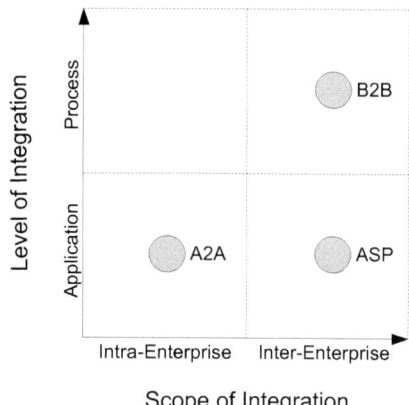

Figure 1.1: The scope of different types of Enterprise Application Integration.

In the context of enterprise applications these types of integration are usually referred to as *Enterprise Application Integration*.

As depicted in Figure 1.1 A2A integration is concerned with the integration of business application within one enterprise whereas B2B integration is concerned with the integration of business applications and business processes across enterprises. Application service provider integration is similar to B2B integration but especially focuses on the integration of applications hosted by a service provider with existing business applications.

Recently the Service Oriented Architecture paradigm [KBS06] together with the Web services technology stack [Wor06a] as the implementation technology has become the standard architecture for Enterprise Application Integration. In this paradigm application functionality is encapsulated using Web services which are described using a Web Services Description Language (WSDL) [Wor01a] description and additional specifications (cf. [The07]). For this thesis it is sufficient to understand that a WSDL definition of a Web service interface includes the specification of a set of operations, messages and data types. The data types used by a service to send and receive information are described as XML Schemas (XSD) [Wor01b] building on top of one another. A message can be divided into parts. Each part is defined by a data type. A general WSDL operation consists of two messages: an input and an output message.[1]

The different Web service specifications only facilitate the technical integration of different Web services. As the Web services used to encapsulate the functionality of different applications are in the general case developed indepen-

---

[1] We abstract from more details of WSDL e.g. the binding and possible behavioral axioms on the operations, since it is irrelevant to what we explain in the following section. The interested reader may refer to the referenced background material.

1.1 Motivation

dently, the input and output message of different services most likely differ in e.g. naming of elements, size, and structure. As the creation of novel applications or functionality based on existing services requires the integration of numerous different services, the heterogeneity of input and output messages results in the need for mappings between them. The need for these mappings also remains in the B2B case when existing B2B message standards (like e.g. EDIFACT [Uni], RosettaNet [Ros07], CIDX [CID] or PIDX [Ame07]) are used as a basis for the message exchange between the partners. Since a large number of B2B message standards and pseudo-standards exist, not all of them are supported by a given business system resulting in the need for message mappings.

Data Migration. Similar problems occur in the area of *Data Migration*. Data Migration is the task of migrating data from one or many data sources to a target application or system. As an example consider the migration of data from an existing legacy application into a new one. Migration of legacy data also requires mappings between the schemas used by the legacy application to represent data and the ones used by the new application. As in the case of Enterprise Application Integration the schema mappings necessary in a data migration project account for a significant amount of the involved development costs. However, in contrast to the Enterprise Application Integration case, these costs cannot be amortized through cost savings during operation. The reason is that Data Migration is typically only performed once. After that the developed mappings are no longer necessary. An additional difference between the scenarios in the area of Data Migration and Enterprise Application Integration is the nature of the involved data. In the Enterprise Application Integration case, data that is especially geared towards data exchange (e.g. a purchase order message) needs to be transmitted. Data Migration requires the exchange of master data (e.g. data concerning customers, suppliers or products) and transactional data (e.g. the production orders related to a certain sales order). The import and export interfaces for these types of data are usually not geared towards interoperability resulting in additional challenges.

Schema Mapping. Today the mappings necessary in different scenarios in the areas of Enterprise Application Integration and Data Migration are largely developed manually using either specialized tools or standard programming languages. However, even the specialized tools only offer rudimentary support for the (semi-) automatic creation of mappings e.g. the automatic creation of a mapping for identical schemas. Additionally, current tools do not capture the knowledge necessary to create mappings between message schemas. This knowledge includes:

Semantics of schema elements: The schemas used for Enterprise Application Integration or Data Migration are very complex. In order to create a mapping between two of them, a developer must know which real-world entities are represented by which schema entities and how the entities of the two schemas are related.

Used communication subset: Although Enterprise Application Integration or Data Migration schemas are very complex, usually only a subset of them is used in a certain project. The reason is that the schemas are an expanded representation of all data that possibly needs to be transmitted in the B2B integration case [Stu07] or stored in the case of standard software. Each integration project only requires a subset of this data. Therefore, only the mapping for the subset used needs to be created. Consequently, a mapping developer needs to understand which subset of the schemas is relevant in the given context.

Customization of standards: In contrast to the fact that usually only a subset of a schema is used, existing standard schemas are usually customized. These customizations include the development of extensions to the standard and also the nonstandard usage of certain parts or elements. An example of such a nonstandard usage of an element would be to store the email address of a contact in an element intended for the storage of free form notes. Consequently, a developer needs to know about these customizations and misuses in order to create correct mappings.

Implementation Details: In the area of Enterprise Application Integration most standard schemas are slightly underspecified, i.e. certain details important for an implementation of the standard are deliberately omitted. As an example consider a schema element that contains the unambiguous identifier of a business partner. Usually an Enterprise Application Integration messaging standard does not enforce the usage of a certain standard for such a element. In the given example this would enable the usage of either the DUNS[2] number, the EIN[3] number or a custom code to identify business partners. A developer needs to know these implementation details in order to create the correct mapping.

The knowledge necessary to create mappings is not integrated and often not available in a machine processable format. Instead it is usually scattered across different documents or only available to a few specialists.

Automating the creation of the mappings necessary both in Enterprise Application Integration and Data Migration would simplify both types of integration by reducing the necessary development efforts. The reduction of the development efforts achieved by an automation of the mapping creation ultimately leads to

---

[2] The Data Universal Numbering System. See http://www.dnb.com/US/duns_update/index.html for details.

[3] The Employer Identification Number. See http://www.irs.gov/businesses/small/article/0,,id=98350,00.html for details.

improved flexibility as necessary Enterprise Application Integration or Data Migration tasks can be performed more easily. Consequently companies would be able to adopt to changing market requirements more quickly by integrating new business partners or replacing legacy applications. Furthermore, schema mappings help to save existing investments in the Enterprise Application Integration case. The reason is that by using mappings legacy applications can be integrated with novel ones in order to provide new functionality.

1.2 Examples Scenarios & Requirements

In order to illustrate the abstract discussion of Enterprise Application Integration and Data Migration provided above, one real world example scenario for each of the two areas is briefly discussed below.

Automation of an Ordering Process between SAP R/3 and non-SAP Systems. The automation of an ordering process is a typical example for a process requiring B2B integration. In order to enable this integration between SAP R/3 and non-SAP systems, mappings between the involved B2B messages need to be created. In the context of SAP R/3 the standard used for B2B integration is SAP IDoc, an SAP specific format for B2B messages. Non-SAP systems typically do not support SAP IDoc but rather use different industry standards for B2B communication. Consequently, mappings between the SAP IDoc message schemas and the ones used by the non-SAP systems need to be developed in a given B2B integration project.

The complexity of B2B messages becomes obvious if a SAP IDoc messages is examined in detail. A purchase order in the SAP IDoc format consists of several hundred elements. Additionally, SAP IDoc messages are rather flat whereas other B2B messaging standards are deeply structured. It is obvious that the development of the necessary mapping requires significant effort.

Data Migration from legacy Systems to SAP Business ByDesign. SAP Business ByDesign[4] is a novel SAP solution for small and medium size enterprises. In order to enable these small and medium size enterprises to use the new solution, a simple approach to the migration of legacy data is required. The main reason is that small and medium enterprises can not afford the cost and time necessary for complex data migration projects. Unfortunately, in the light of this cost requirement the data schemas for master data, e.g. business partner information, are very complex. For example, the schema for storing business partner information in SAP Busines ByDesign consists of over 4500 elements.

---

[4] http://www.sap.com/solutions/sme/businessbydesign/index.epx

As a large variety of possible legacy systems exist, the migration approaches need to be able to cope with previously unknown source systems. Consequently, the migration approach needs to enable a user to i) quickly collect the required integration knowledge and ii) to easily reuse integration knowledge from previous migration projects. In addition, it is quite common that only parts of the functionality offered by SAP Busines ByDesign is supported by the legacy system. Consequently, only mappings for parts of the complex schemas need to be created.

Requirements. The previous examples and discussion highlight the following list of six requirements necessary for an automatic schema mapping approach in an industrial setting.

R1 (Quality): The quality of the resulting mappings is the most important issue for any automatic mapping approach. As schema mapping is a central task in B2B integration and Data Migration, an automatic schema mapping approach will only be applicable in any industrial scenarios if it leads to a significant reduction of the required integration efforts. This significant reduction can only be achieved if both a high accuracy and a high level of completeness are achieved. Consequently, the accuracy and the completeness are used to measure the quality of automatically created mappings.

R2 (Identification of Mappings): In industrial settings an automatic approach not only needs to identify correspondences between schemas, but also must be capable of creating mappings between them. The reason is that creating a correct mapping on the basis of correspondences between schemas still requires significant effort. Consequently, complete mappings need to be proposed by the developed approach. However, creating the complete mapping automatically is not possible in the general case. As a result, the developed approach needs to be able to at least propose an initial template in the cases where the complete mapping rule can not be identified. This initial template can then later on be completed by a user in order to finalize the mapping.

R3 (Complex Mapping Expressions): Although simple direct mappings between schema elements are common, a complete approach needs to be able to create complex mapping rules between schema elements. As a fully automatic creation of the complex mapping rules is also not possible in the general case, at least templates of complex mapping expressions that can easily be completed by a user need to be created.

R4 (Capture and Reuse of Integration Knowledge): Capturing the integration knowledge necessary to create a mapping is essential to the scenarios described earlier. On the one hand it enables developers to query the available integration knowledge, on the other hand this knowledge can be used by the automatic schema mapping approach to increase the quality of the mappings.

R5 (Flexible Execution): As different tools are used to execute mappings in different B2B integration and Data Migration scenarios, the created mapping rules must not be tied to a specific execution environment. Instead, an abstract mapping representation is needed. This abstract representation should be automatically translatable into a concrete syntax for mappings required by the available execution environment.

R6 (Performance): Performance is always an important issue when investigating automatic approaches. Since schema mapping in B2B integration and Data Migration scenarios is a design time or development time task, the required performance is not tightly restricted. However, in order to be usable when integrated into a development tool, the automatic mapping approach should be executable in the area of several minutes on typical mapping problems. The reason is that longer execution times are not suitable for interactive development tools. Generally, quality should be emphasized over performance.

In the remainder of the thesis these requirements are used to direct the development of the automatic mapping approach and also to analyze the applicability of the developed approach in different real-world scenarios.

1.3 Research Questions

In order to develop an automatic mapping approach capable of achieving the requirements mentioned above, the following research questions need to be addressed in this thesis:

Which knowledge is necessary to create schema mappings? It is obvious that schema information alone is not sufficient to create mappings between complex schemas. The thesis analyzes which types of background knowledge are required in order to create a correct mapping between two schemas. This analysis of required background knowledge is not particularly focused towards the automatic creation of schema mappings but also applies to the manual development of schema mappings.

How can the necessary background knowledge be collected? The background knowledge required to create schema mappings is usually not easily accessible. Therefore, two approaches for the collection of background knowledge are developed and evaluated in this thesis. A particular focus is placed on enabling the non-intrusive collection of the background knowledge to enable the application of the approaches in productive environments.

How can background knowledge be exploited? In order to exploit background knowledge during the mapping creation it needs to be available in a machine interpretable format. The thesis shows an approach for the modeling of domain and integration knowledge in an ontology and, based on this, develops a schema mapping approach capable of exploiting the modeled knowledge during the automatic schema mapping creation.

Can complex mappings be created automatically? Most existing approaches focus on the automatic identification of matches between schemas, i.e. identifying corresponding schema elements. However, identifying matching elements is only the first step when creating a schema mapping. The approach developed in this thesis is not only capable of identifying matching schema elements but is also able to identify the complex expressions necessary to translate instances of the schemas.

Can the quality required for industrial applications be achieved?
Automatic schema mapping approaches will only be used in industrial integration tools if the mapping quality surpasses a certain threshold. The approach developed in this thesis is therefore evaluated using schemas originating from real integration projects in order to asses if it is capable of creating mappings of the required quality.

1.4 Contribution

A central feature necessary for the development of an automatic mapping approach capable of coping with the requirements presented above is the exploitation of domain knowledge. Achieving automatic mapping results of high quality is only possible if even complex mapping rules can be created automatically. The prerequisite for generating mappings containing complex mapping rules is a detailed knowledge of different facets of the domain. The schema mapping approach developed in this thesis focuses on the exploitation of domain knowledge. The domain knowledge required is usually not easily accessible, therefore methods for the capturing of the required knowledge also need to be developed. The following paragraph summarizes the contributions of this thesis.

> 1. The main contribution of the thesis is an ontology-based schema mapping approach. By exploiting existing domain knowledge of integration experts, which is encapsulated in an ontology, this approach is capable of automatically creating high quality schema mappings. Furthermore, the mapping algorithms developed in this thesis will be tailored towards the exploitation of integration knowledge modeled in the domain ontology. Consequently the developed approach can easily be adapted to different scenarios by exchanging the used domain ontology.
>
> 2. The second contribution is a set of novel approaches for the capturing of existing user knowledge, which is required for the creation of schema mappings. These approaches are especially tailored towards embedding them into the process of creating schema mappings and therefore only require a minimal manual effort.

1.5 Overview

The remainder of this thesis is organized as follows: Part I provides the foundations of the thesis. In Chapter 2 the integration scenarios, namely Enterprise Application Integration and Data Migration, that are the basis of this thesis, are analyzed in detail. After that, the central task in these scenarios, namely schema mapping, is discussed. The discussion of the schema mapping task focuses on the common requirements of both integration scenarios and abstracts from their specific details. Following this the challenges faced in integration are analyzed and categorized in Chapter 3. In addition, Chapter 3 discusses why ontologies are a suitable tool for solving these integration challenges. Part I closes by providing definitions of the important terms used in the remainder of the thesis.

Parts II and III represent the main contribution of the thesis. In Part II the ontology-based schema mapping approach is developed while in Part III the implementation and the evaluation of the approach is described.

Part II starts by introducing a generic schema matching process as seen from the users point of view in Chapter 5 and by introducing the ontology-based mapping approach. This chapter also provides a detailed overview of the research related to the ontology-based mapping approach. Following this, the role of background knowledge for the development of schema mapping is studied in Chapter 6. In the Chapters 7 and 8 the details of the ontology-based mapping approach are developed.

After this Part III describes the implementation details of the ontology-based mapping approach in Chapter 9, while Chapter 10 provides a detailed evaluation of the schema mapping approach. The performed evaluation is based on real-world Data Migration scenarios encountered during the work at SAP Research.

The thesis closes with Part IV by providing an outlook on future work in the area of schema mapping in Chapter 11. Following this, possible industrial applications of the schema mapping approach developed in this thesis are presented. Finally, Chapter 12 summarizes the presented work.

Some parts of this thesis are based on the following contributions that have previously been published in different journals, books and conference or workshop proceedings: [Dru04], [DK05], [DLN06], [DSDR07], [Dru07], [DLO07], [WMD07] and [WMD08].

Part I
Foundations

Chapter 2
Scenarios & Use Cases

This chapter investigates different industrial scenarios in the two areas Enterprise Application Integration and Data Migration in more detail. For the scenarios in each of the two areas the currently available solutions as well as the problems and limitations of these solutions are described. In addition, possible improvements over the current state of the art are identified.[1]

Based on the analysis of the different scenarios it becomes obvious that the task of developing *schema mappings* is in the center of solving the integration problem in the different scenarios. The common properties of the introduced scenarios in the two areas of Enterprise Application Integration and B2B integration are used throughout the thesis to guide the development of an approach capable of solving the schema mapping task semi-automatically. In Part III of the thesis the scenarios introduced in this chapter are revisited again as they are the basis for evaluating the developed approach.

2.1 Enterprise Application Integration

The goal of Enterprise Application Integration is automating the execution of business processes across the boundaries of different applications. As an example of a typical business process requiring Enterprise Application Integration, consider the procurement process depicted in Figure 2.1. In this process the company A wants to buy certain goods from company B. The overall process necessary to complete this transaction consists of several process steps involving both partners. First a "Request for Quotation" message is sent from company A to company B. Company B processes this message internally, possibly also involving different business systems, and replies with a "Quote Response" message. If A accepts the quotation of B it sends a "Purchase Order" message in the next step and the process continues. As the two systems involved in the process were

---
[1]Note that this discussion in not tied to specific implementation technologies. It rather abstracts from implementation details in order to identify the essential underlying problems.

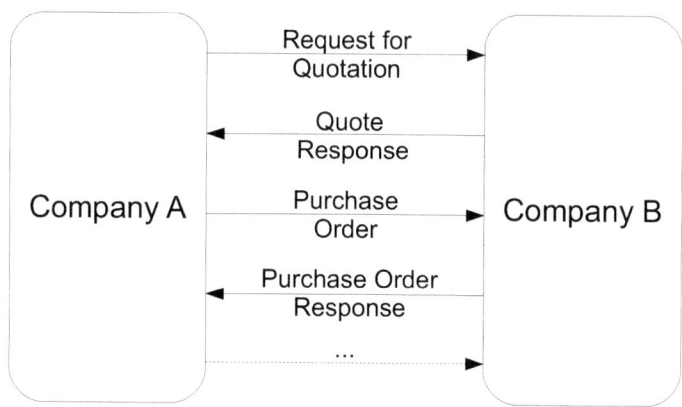

Figure 2.1: A simple B2B interaction.

most likely developed independently, they most certainly use different schemas to describe the sent messages. Consequently mappings between theses schemas are necessary to enable the integration of the systems.

Using this simple example as a basis the main difference between the three types of Enterprise Application Integration, namely

- Application-to-Application (A2A) integration
- Business-to-Business (B2B) integration
- Application Service Provider integration

identified by Bussler [Bus03] can easily be shown. In the case of Application-to-Application (A2A) integration there would only be one company owning both systems. Consequently, the integration does not require creating mappings but would theoretically also be possible by changing one of the two systems in order to enable interoperability.[2] In the context of B2B or Application Service Provider integration changing the involved systems is usually not an option as they are not controlled by one partner. Therefore, the creation of schema mappings is necessary to enable interoperability in these cases.

Integration Challenges. Common to each of the three types of Enterprise Application Integration is that they have to cope with heterogeneities on different levels ranging from heterogeneities in the supported communication technologies

---

[2]However, in real A2A integration projects usually the involved systems are also not changed and, therefore, schema mappings are required in order to enable interoperability.

2.1 Enterprise Application Integration

to heterogeneities on the semantic level[3]. However, solving the heterogeneities on the different levels becomes much more difficult across company boundaries as a consensus needs to be reached on each level of heterogeneity. This thesis focuses on Enterprise Application Integration across company boundaries. In these cases the integration problems have to be solved at the mapping level as changing either of the involved systems is usually not possible. If the two types of Enterprise Application Integration that cross company boundaries, namely B2B integration and Application Service Provider integration, are examined in more detail their main difference becomes obvious. While Application Service Provider integration aims at integrating single applications, B2B integration aims at the integration of whole business processes. It is common that complex business processes already cross the boundaries of several applications inside one company. This feature possibly adds another layer of complexity to B2B integration since also the systems within one company are usually already heterogeneous. Consequently, only scenarios in the area of B2B integration are considered in the following as they expose all integration problems related to the more general area of Enterprise Application Integration. As an example of a concrete B2B integration scenario consider the automation of the purchasing process between a SAP and an Oracle system or the automation of the invoicing process between a legacy system and a SAP system.

In order to overcome the heterogeneity problems related to B2B integration numerous B2B messaging standards (e.g. RosettaNet [Ros07], CIDX [CID] or PIDX [Ame07]) have been developed. However, a large number of B2B messaging standards and pseudo-standards exist and these standards themselves are rather heterogeneous. Therefore, B2B integration on the basis of B2B messaging standards requires solving the same problems as in the more general case.

The Service Oriented Architecture paradigm [KBS06] together with the Web services technology stack [Wor06a] as the implementation technology has become the standard architecture for Enterprise Application Integration and in particular for B2B integration. Note that in general most scenarios in the area of B2B integration which are implemented using the Service Oriented Architecture paradigm not only require a mapping between the message schemas used by different Web services but also between the operations offered by them. This aspect of B2B integration is usually referred to as *process mediation* [CDS$^+$04]. However, since this thesis focuses on automatic schema mapping, the process mediation aspect of B2B integration will not be further discussed.

Opportunities. Today the mappings necessary for B2B integration are developed manually using either specialized tools or standard programming lan-

---

[3]For a detailed discussion of the different levels of heterogeneity and their related problems see Chapter 3.

guages.[4] Due to the complexity of typical B2B messages the manual development of mappings requires significant development efforts. Consequently, current approaches to B2B integration are not flexible enough to enable B2B integration even in short-term business relationships. The required flexibility could be achieved by the (semi-)automatic creation of the required message mapping. Creating message mappings (semi-)automatically would significantly reduce the necessary development effort for each mapping. However, such an automatic schema mapping would need to create mappings of a high quality. If an automatic approach creates too many wrong mapping rules, removing or fixing these wrong parts quickly becomes more effort than creating the mapping from scratch and renders an automatic approach useless (cf. requirements R1, R2 and R3).

Also, an integrated representation of the knowledge necessary to create a message mapping in a machine processable format would be beneficial (cf. requirement R4). Instead of browsing through a large number of documents or data bases in order to find the information necessary to create a mapping, such a knowledge base would enable the integrated querying of the available integration knowledge. In addition to supporting a developer when creating message mappings, this integration knowledge base could be exploited by a automatic mapping approach to create high quality mappings.

2.2 Data Migration

A different problem area where schema mappings play a central role is Data Migration. The goal of Data Migration is to migrate data between one or many data sources and a target application or system. An example of a characteristic scenario in the area of Data Migration is the introduction of SAP Enterprise Resource Planning (ERP) software in order to replace several existing legacy applications. As the legacy applications and the new one most likely use different schemas to store data a mapping between these different schemas is necessary.

Similar scenarios in the area of Data Migration aiming at replacing existing legacy applications are quite common in industry. Especially the recent focus of large enterprise software companies on small and medium enterprises requires solutions for these Data Migration scenarios. As small and medium enterprises typically already have some kind of business software in place, existing data needs to be migrated whenever new applications are introduced.

As mentioned above the common goal in the different scenarios in the area of Data Migration is to migrate data between different data sources. The data sources in the migration scenario can be divided into two categories: data sources providing the data that is migrated and data source receiving this data. After

---

[4] A comprehensive review of tools currently available commercially for to support B2B integration is presented in Section 10.1.

2.2 Data Migration

the migration is performed the data sources that provided the data are usually no longer used.

Integration Challenges. The key differentiator between scenarios in the area of Data Migration compared to B2B integration is the nature of the data that is exchanged. While in a B2B integration usually only transactional data is exchanged, three types of data need to be migrated in a typical Data Migration scenario:

1. **Basic Master Data.** This type of master data does not depend on the existence of other data. It can therefore be migrated without taking other data into account. Examples of this type of master data are product data and business partner data.

2. **Dependent Master Data.** This type of master data does depend on other master data. Therefore it can only be migrated as soon as all the master data it depends on hast been migrated. An example of dependent master data is the bill of materials that requires among other the existence of product master data.

3. **Transactional Data.** Transactional data, like e.g. previously received purchase orders or already sent invoice notifications, has to be treated specially during the migration. First, it depends on the existence of the master data and, second, creating transactional data in the system usually triggers a business process. However, this is usually not wanted during Data Migration. As an example, consider entering a purchase order into the system. In certain industries this might automatically create a production order to start the production of the ordered goods. When migrating existing purchase orders, creating a new production order is certainly unwanted as this would result in a duplicate production order for one single purchase order. Therefore transactional data has to be specially treated during Data Migration.

In comparison to B2B integration, the import and export interfaces for these types of data are usually not geared towards fostering the interoperability of systems. Consequently, the schemas describing the export formats are typically very close to the technical implementation of the system. They usually only contain technical names and are undocumented, making an understanding of the formats difficult even for a human. Furthermore, in order to enable the migration of dependent master data and transactional data special migration services are necessary. These migration services need to be offered by the target system to enable the creation of dependent master data and transactional data without causing unwanted side effects.

Besides this, two additional major differences exist between scenarios in the areas of B2B integration and Data Migration. First, it is quite common in Data Migration projects that implementation details of the target system are known in detail while only very limited knowledge of the source system exists. There are different reasons for this situation. In the case of legacy system migration, the knowledge is usually not available due to lacking documentation and expertise. In the case of competitor system migration, legal constraints prevent software vendors from gaining detailed knowledge about implementation details of the competitor systems. However, this information is necessary in order to be able to migrate the necessary data. Second, a Data Migration project usually requires the creation of mappings for several similar schemas. As an example consider basic master data like customers, suppliers and employees. It is very likely that the schemas describing this data in one system contain large similar parts (e.g. address data and banking information).

Opportunities. The development of the necessary schema mappings accounts for a significant amount of the involved development efforts. In contrast to the B2B integration case these costs cannot be amortized in the Data Migration case through cost savings during operation. The reason is that Data Migration is only performed once. After all data in the legacy system has been migrated the legacy systems will no longer be operated. Therefore reducing the development efforts associated to schema mapping is beneficial also in Data Migration scenarios.

Again automating the creation of the necessary mappings could significantly reduce the costs related to Data Migration (cf. requirements R1, R2, R3). In addition, an integrated representation of the knowledge necessary to create the mappings involved in a Data Migration project would also be beneficial in order to support reuse of this knowledge in future migration projects (cf.. requirement R4). Although Data Migration for one particular legacy system is only performed once, three types of future migration projects are possible:

- Migration projects inside one company aiming at the migration of similar legacy systems to one specific target system.

- Migration projects inside one company aiming at the migration of similar legacy systems to one type of target system.

- Migration projects in different companies aiming at the migration of different legacy systems to one type of target system.

While the first two types of future projects might be common in big companies with a large number of business systems, the third type is of special interest for service providers supporting the Data Migration for different clients. In each of the three cases, an integrated representation of the available knowledge would simplify future projects by i) allowing users to query this knowledge and by ii) allowing software tools to exploit this knowledge. Additionally, the special properties of the Data Migration scenarios should be taken into account. The in-depth knowledge of the target schemas need to be exploited in order to compensate for the lack of knowledge about the source schemas. Furthermore, the property of the Data Migration scenarios that numerous mappings between similar schemas need to be created also need to be exploited by supporting the reuse of previously created mappings.

2.3 Schema Mapping

From the discussion in the previous sections it is obvious that the central task required in B2B integration and Data Migration is the development of a *schema mapping*. The goal of this task is, given two schemas, a source and a target schema, to create the mapping rules necessary to transform an instance of the source schema into an instance of the target schema.

Generally, the task of developing a schema mapping involves two steps:

1. Identifying correspondences between the source and the target schema

2. Creating the mapping rules for the correspondences identified in the first step.

Identifying Correspondences. In order to enable an identification of corresponding schema entities a developer needs to understand the semantics of the schema entities, i.e. which real-world entities are represented by which schema entities. In addition to this, a developer also needs knowledge regarding the used communication subset and possible customizations of the schemas. Knowledge regarding the used communication subset is important since in a particular integration project usually only a subset of the supported complexity of a schema is required. Therefore, a mapping only needs to be created for the used subset which leads to a complexity reduction for the resulting mapping. Customizations of schemas include the extension of them as well as the nonstandard usage of certain schema entities. Consequently, this knowledge is important to correctly identify corresponding entities.

Creating Mapping Rules. After corresponding entities have been identified a mapping rule needs to be created for each correspondence in order to create a final schema mapping. An example of such a mapping rule is the *move* of the contents of the source to the target entity. While this simple type of mapping rule occurs in about 36% of the cases, more complex mapping rules are required for about 64% of the correspondences.[5] Consequently, the creation of the mapping

---

[5] A detailed analysis of the occurrence frequency of different types of mapping rules is given in Section 8.

rules accounts for a significant part of the effort necessary in the development of schema mapping. In order to create the mapping rules, detailed knowledge regarding implementation details is necessary. The required knowledge includes, for example, which code lists are used to represent the values of certain schema elements and how to translate between them.

Note that the mapping rules, and consequently also the schema mappings, are in the general case uni-directional. Therefore, a different schema mapping is necessary to translate schema A into schema B than to translate schema B into schema A. The reason is that some mapping rules (e.g. the calculation of a sum) are not reversible.

Manual Mapping Development. The manual development of the schema mappings required in B2B integration or Data Migration is a tedious and error-prone task due to the complexity of the schemas in industrial integration scenarios. Features of these schemas are:

Complexity: The schemas usually consist of several hundred up to several thousand message elements. Furthermore, flexible constraints at the schema entity level allow for a very large number of possible implementations of given schemas.

Structure: The structuring of the schemas ranges from very flat structures to deeply nested ones.

Element Naming: Schema entity names range from verbose names over technical names to cryptic abbreviations.

Data Types: The data types of the schema elements range from the usage of very specific data types to the usage of generic data types like string for the elements.

Specification: Usually standard schemas (i.e. schemas defined by B2B messaging standards) are underspecified allowing different incompatible implementations of the standard.

As an example, consider the excerpt of the B2B message schema depicted in Figure 2.2. The figure shows a short excerpt of a schema used in SAP systems for exchanging purchase orders. The root element of this schema is the element with the name ORDER05. The structure of the root element is defined by a sequence of complex elements. An example of such a complex element is the element with the name IDOC. The IDOC element contains, for example, the optional element MANDT. Note that in the case of the MANDT element no short documentation text is attached. Furthermore, the possible values of the MANDT element are restricted to strings of length three. Already this short excerpt exhibits most of the features mentioned above.

2.3 Schema Mapping

```xml
<xsd:schema xmlns:xsd = "http://www.w3.org/2001/XMLSchema" >
  <xsd:element name = "ORDERS05" >
    <xsd:annotation>
      <xsd:documentation> Purchasing/Sales </xsd:documentation>
    </xsd:annotation>
    <xsd:complexType>
      <xsd:sequence>
        <xsd:element name = "IDOC" >
          <xsd:complexType>
            <xsd:sequence>
              <xsd:element name = "EDI_DC40" >
                <xsd:annotation>
                  <xsd:documentation>
                    IDoc Control Record
                  </xsd:documentation>
                </xsd:annotation>
                <xsd:complexType>
                  <xsd:sequence>
                    <xsd:element name = "TABNAM" type = "xsd:string"
                      fixed = "EDI_DC40" >
                      <xsd:annotation>
                        <xsd:documentation>
                          Name of table structure
                        </xsd:documentation>
                      </xsd:annotation>
                    </xsd:element>
                    <xsd:element name = "MANDT" minOccurs = "0" >
                      <xsd:annotation>
                        </xsd:documentation>
                      </xsd:annotation>
                      <xsd:simpleType>
                        <xsd:restriction base = "xsd:string" >
                          <xsd:maxLength value = "3" />
                        </xsd:restriction>
                      </xsd:simpleType>
                    </xsd:element>
                    <xsd:element name = "DOCNUM" minOccurs = "0" >
...
    </xsd:complexType>
  </xsd:element>
</xsd:schema>
```

Figure 2.2: Excerpt of the XML schema of a SAP IDOC for exchanging purchase orders.

Furthermore, current tools used to develop schema mapping in B2B integration and data migration projects only provide basic support for the reuse of existing mappings or fragments of them. Reuse in current integration solutions is usually restricted to a template based approach, enabling a user to create mapping templates for recurring schema fragments manually. Automatic support for a reuse of existing mappings and existing mapping fragments is normally not available. However, the reuse of existing mappings as well as fragments of them is seen as a very promising approach, especially in the context of B2B messages [RB01].

2.4 Summary

This chapter presented different use cases in the areas of B2B integration and Data Migration. The central task in all presented use cases is the development of schema mappings. This task consists of two complex steps. First matching schema entities need to be identified in the source and the target schema, second mapping rules need to be created for the identified correspondences. Consequently, performing the development of schema mappings manually requires high development efforts and is error prone.

Chapter 3
Challenges for Integration

This section introduces and classifies the challenges faced when integrating heterogeneous systems. The chapter first introduces a running example (Section 3.1). Next, the different heterogeneity layers existing in different integration scenarios are introduced (Section 3.2). On this basis the types of heterogeneities existing in these layers (Section 3.3) as well as the integration challenges resulting from these types of heterogeneities (Section 3.4) are discussed. The chapter closes by presenting how ontologies can be applied to solve the different integration challenges (Section 3.5).

3.1 Running Example

This section introduces an example that is used in subsequent sections to illustrate different types of heterogeneities and the resulting integration challenges. Furthermore, this example is used as a running example throughout the remainder of the thesis.

The running example originates from the area of Data Migration and is presented in Figure 3.1. The **DEBMAS** schema depicted in the Figure 3.1 describes the data format used by a legacy system to represent a customer. The structure of this example schema, as well as the element names, are inspired by the schemas used in SAP R/3. In contrast to this, the **BusinessPartner** schema describes the data format used by a target system to describe business partners. The structure and naming of the **BusinessPartner** schema has been inspired by the one used in SAP Business ByDesign. The set of business partners described by the **BusinessPartner** schema includes customers, suppliers and employees. The values in parentheses show example element values for one customer instance. Furthermore, the dotted lines indicate corresponding elements in the two schemas. For example, the **ANRED** element in the source schema corresponds to the **FormOfAddressCode** element in the target schema as they contain the same semantic information, namely the form of address. However, it is obvious that

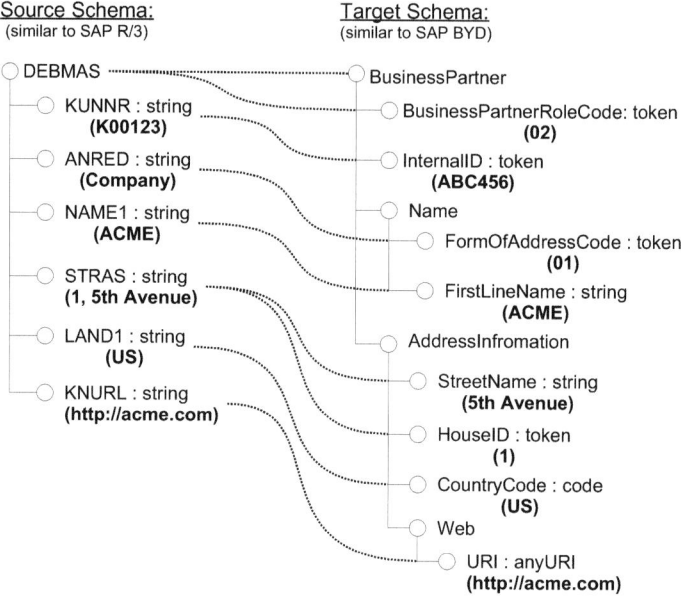

Figure 3.1: Running example showing two schemas for representing customer data including example instance values.

detecting this correspondence and determining a mapping rule to transform values of the ANRED element to those of the FormOfAddressCode element remains a challenge as the former uses a textual representation whereas the latter utilizes specific codes. Another example of a correspondence between the two schemas is the complex correspondence between the source element STRAS and the target elements StreetName and HouseID. In this case, the value of the former element needs to be split in order to form valid entries of the latter two elements.

3.2 Heterogeneity Layers

Approaches aiming to integrate heterogeneous systems usually have to deal with heterogeneities on different levels. Sheth et al. [SK93, KS00, NVS+06] identified four layers on which heterogeneities can occur. These layers are depicted in Figure 3.2 together with some examples of the kind of heterogeneities occurring on the respective layers.

System Heterogeneities: The system heterogeneities constitute the lowest layer of possible heterogeneities. They consist of differences in the underlying hardware platform, the used operation system, the supported commu-

3.2 Heterogeneity Layers

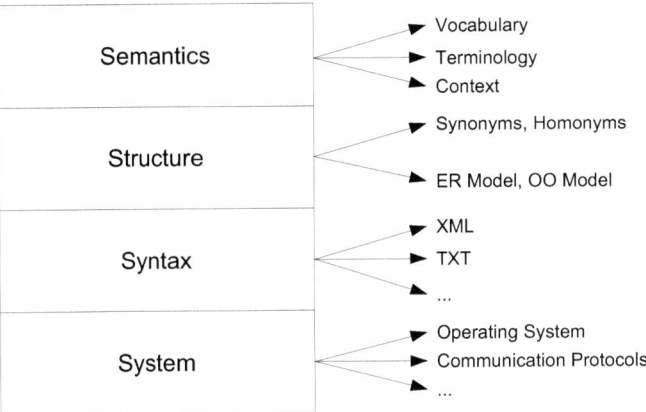

Figure 3.2: Heterogeneity layers including some examples of heterogeneity occurring at each layer.

nication protocols, the used database system management system and so on.

Syntactic Heterogeneities: The second layer of heterogeneity is formed by the syntactic heterogeneities. Heterogeneities on this layer are caused by the usage of different representation formats to store data. Examples of such representation formats are plain text files or XML files.

Structural Heterogeneities: The third layer consists of the structural heterogeneities. Structural heterogeneities occur when different data models are used for representing the data. Additionally, in the cases when the same data model is used, structural heterogeneities occur because the same data usually can be modeled differently in the data model.

Semantic Heterogeneities: The topmost layer of heterogeneities consists of the semantic heterogeneities. They are caused by interpreting the available information differently in different contexts or by the usage of different vocabularies and taxonomies. As a simple example of semantic heterogeneities consider the string "DE". In different contexts this string could either be interpreted as an abbreviation for "Deutschland" or as an abbreviation for "Delaware".

In the different scenarios introduced in Chapter 2 XML is the standard syntax for exchanging data. The main advantage of XML in these scenarios is that heterogeneities on the system and syntax level are automatically resolved. As a result, this thesis focuses on heterogeneities on the structural and semantic layers, respectively. In order to understand the challenges arising from the heterogeneities on these levels, the following subsections introduce a classification of possible heterogeneities on the structural and semantic level.

Note that the classification presented above does not take inconsistent and redundant [Wac03] data into account. Inconsistent and redundant data occurs whenever two data sources contain information about the same real-world entities, e.g. the same customer with different identifiers [SPR07]. As these problems cannot be solved by a schema mapping approach but rather require an independent data cleansing step, the integration challenges originating from inconsistent and redundant data are not further discussed in this chapter.

3.3 Types of Heterogeneity

Wache [Wac03] presents a comprehensive classification of structural and semantic heterogeneities. The following section uses this classification as a basis to investigate structural and semantic heterogeneities in more detail. Based on the classification introduced by Wache, examples of the described heterogeneities related to the areas of B2B integration and Data Migration are presented. Note that the investigation of structural and semantic heterogeneities in the following is based on the assumption that two information sources need to be integrated. In the use cases introduced in the previous section these two sources are either two message schemas or a message schema and an ontology. However, the following discussion is not limited to these kind of data but is e.g. also valid in the context of database schema integration.

3.3.1 Types of Structural Heterogeneity

According to the classification introduced by Wache [Wac03] the structural heterogeneities can be divided into two classes, *data model heterogeneity* and *schematic heterogeneity*.

Data Model Heterogeneity

Data model heterogeneities are caused by the usage of different data models, e.g. a relational data model versus an object-oriented one. In the running example the effects of data model heterogeneities are visible at the level of the schema structures. The rather flat structure of the DEBMAS schema originates from the underlying relational data model whereas the deeply nested structure of the BusinessPartner schema originates from the underlying XML Schema data model.

3.3 Types of Heterogeneity

Table 3.1: Overview of the classification of schematic heterogeneities (based on [SvH05, Wac03].

Nr.	Heterogeneity Type	Characteristic
	H1 - Schematic Bilateral Heterogeneities	
H1.1	Bilateral Naming	Usage of different names for schema entities.
H1.2	Bilateral Data Type	Usage of different data types for schema entities.
H1.3	Bilateral Integrity	Assignment of different integrity constraints to schema entities.
	H2 - Schematic Multilateral Heterogeneities	
H2.1	Multilateral Property	Representation of real-world entities using different sets of properties.
H2.2	Multilateral Entity	Representation of real-world entities as different sets of schema entities.
H2.3	Missing Information	Information is present in one schema and missing in the other.
	H3 - Schematic Meta-level Heterogeneities	
H3.1	Data-Attribute	Usage of different modeling primitives to represent the same information.
H3.2	Data-Entity	Usage of different modeling primitives to represent the same information.
H3.3	Attribute-Entity	Usage of different modeling primitives to represent the same information.

Schematic Heterogeneity

Even if the same data model is used, information can still be represented differently resulting in schematic heterogeneities. An example of such a heterogeneity in the object-oriented data model is the modeling of an address as a set of attributes or as an independent class.

The schematic heterogeneities can be further divided into three categories: i) the *bilateral heterogeneities*, ii) the *multilateral heterogeneities* and iii) the *meta-level heterogeneities*. This classification is presented in Table 3.1. The table shows the three categories of schematic heterogeneities and how these classes can be further divided into subcategories. For each category its main characteristic is highlighted in the table.

Bilateral Heterogeneities. The bilateral heterogeneities are heterogeneities that occur directly between two schema entities. As shown by Table 3.1 they can be further divided into *naming* heterogeneities, *data type* heterogeneities and *integrity constraint* heterogeneities.

Naming heterogeneities occur due to the usage of synonyms or homonyms as the names of schema entities. The usage of synonyms results in different names for related schema entities whereas homonyms result in the usage of the same name for unrelated schema entities. In addition to this, the usage of technical names and the usage of different languages also lead to naming heterogeneities. As an example of a complex naming heterogeneity, consider the schema entity named KUNNR in the short running example in Figure 3.1. KUNNR is an abbreviation for the word "Kundennummer", the German translation of "customer code". In the running example the entity KUNNR corresponds to the entity InternalID, since in the target system the customer code is used as an internal identifier for a particular customer.

Data type heterogeneities occur when directly related schema entities use different data types to encode the data. Such a heterogeneity exists in the running example between the schema entities LAND1 and CountryCode. While the former uses the data type string to represent the country in which an address is located, the latter uses the data type code.

Finally, the integrity constraint heterogeneities refer to the usage of different integrity constraints for schema entities. The integrity constraint heterogeneities include the usages of different default values for schema entities as well as the presence of conflicting integrity constraints related to schema entities. Note that some schema languages as e.g. XML Schema only allow to express some types of integrity constraint directly (e.g. occurrence restrictions) and rather use the data type system in order to express others. Therefore these types of heterogeneities might in some cases be hidden inside the data type heterogeneities introduced before. As an example, consider a schema entity with possible values 00, 01 and 02. This restriction is in XML Schema specified as a restriction on a data type rather than as a constraint of the element.

According to Wache [Wac03] integrity constraint heterogeneities are usually closely related to semantic heterogeneities (cf. Section 3.3.2). The *Employee Number* is an example of such a situation. While the integrity constraint in one schema could be that this must be a nine digit integer number, the integrity constraint in another schema could be a letter followed by a 6 digit number. The underlying reason for this constraint heterogeneity is a semantic representation heterogeneity. While in the first schema the *Social Security Number*[1] of a person is used as a unique identifier, the second schema expects the usage of a custom numbering schema. Consequently the need for solving constraint heterogeneities usually also involves the need for solving semantic heterogeneities. Furthermore, Wache [Wac03] states that if the data integrity constraints cannot be resolved, usually also the related semantic heterogeneities cannot be resolved.

---

[1] A 9-digit number used in the US for taxation purposes (cf. http://en.wikipedia.org/wiki/Social_Security_number).

Multilateral Heterogeneities. In contrast to the bilateral heterogeneities the multilateral heterogeneities occur when multiple entities of one information source are related to multiple entities in an other information source. The multilateral heterogeneities can again be further divided into *multilateral property correspondences*, *multilateral entity correspondences* and *missing value* heterogeneities.

Multilateral property correspondences refer to a situation where a real world entity is represented in one information source using a different set of properties as in the other. In principle one to many $(1:n)$, many to one $(m:1)$ and many to many $(m:n)$ correspondences between properties are possible. As an example of an $1:n$ property correspondence consider the schema entities `STRAS`, `StreetName` and `HouseID` in the running example. In the source schema the `STRAS` schema entity represents the street name and the house number as one string whereas this information is split across the `StreetName` and `HouseID` entities in the target schema.

Multilateral entity correspondences differ from the previously mentioned ones because they refer to a situation where a set of real world entities is modeled as two sets of entities with different cardinality in two information sources. As in the case of multilateral property correspondences, $1:n$, $m:1$ and $m:n$ entity correspondences exist. As an example of an $1:n$ entity correspondence consider the situation where one system is only capable of storing different telephone numbers while another system differentiates between landline telephone numbers and mobile phone numbers.

Finally, missing value heterogeneities refer to the situation where information contained in one information source is simply missing in the other one.

Meta-level Heterogeneities. Finally, the metal-level heterogeneities are caused by the usage of different modeling primitives in the same data model to represent the same information. Wache [Wac03] further divides the meta-level heterogeneities into *data-attribute correspondences*, *data-entity correspondences* and *attribute-entity correspondences*. This categorization is based on the basic modeling primitives data, attributes and entities which are in some form present in all data modeling formalisms. Data-attribute correspondences are concerned with the situation where information is modeled as data in one information source and as an attribute in an other information source. Similarly data-entity and attribute-entity correspondences are defined.

3.3.2 Types of Semantic Heterogeneity

The top layer of the heterogeneities introduced in Section 3.2 are the semantic heterogeneities. Even when the structural heterogeneities between two information sources have been eliminated, there could still exist semantic heterogeneities. According to the classification introduced by Wache they can be divided into two

Table 3.2: Overview of the classification of semantic heterogeneities (based on [SvH05, Wac03].

Nr.	Heterogeneity Type	Characteristic
H4 - Semantic Data Heterogeneities		
H4.1	Scaling & Value Range	Different scales or abstractions are used.
H4.2	Representation	Different symbols to represent semantically equivalent information, and vice versa.
H4.3	Surjective Mapping	No bijective mapping exists between different value sets.
H5 - Semantic Domain Heterogeneities		
H5.1	Subsumption	A class in one conceptualization subsumes all classes of another conceptualization.
H5.2	Overlap	The classes in different conceptualizations only partially overlap.
H5.3	Aggregation	Two conceptualizations use different levels of abstraction.
H5.5	Incompatibility	The classes in two conceptualizations are incompatible.

classes, the *data heterogeneities* and the *domain heterogeneities* (see Table 3.2). This subsection will investigate the semantic heterogeneities in more detail.

Semantic Data Heterogeneities

Semantic data heterogeneities originate from the usage of different encodings for the data stored in the information sources. They consist of the *scaling* and *value range* heterogeneities, the *representation* heterogeneities and the *surjective mappings*.

Scaling & Value Range Heterogeneities. This type of semantic heterogeneities originates from the usage of different scales to represent the same properties. Popular examples of scaling heterogeneities are the encoding of a length using either "centimeter" or "inch" as the basic unit, or the encoding of weight using either "gram" or "ounce" as a basic unit. Value range heterogeneities occur when different abstractions of the same underlying scale are used.

Representation Heterogeneities. In contrast to the previous heterogeneity, representation heterogeneity occurs when different symbols are used to represent semantically equivalent information or vice versa. As an example for the first case consider different date representation standards. According to ISO 8601

3.3 Types of Heterogeneity

[Intb] January 2nd 2007 is represented as 2007-01-02 whereas the same date is commonly represented as 01/02/2007 in the US.

Surjective Mappings. In contrast to the previous two heterogeneities where a bijective mapping between the different data values exists the surjective mapping heterogeneity occurs when a value set needs to be mapped to a different one of smaller cardinality. In this case no bijective mapping of the data values is possible and information is lost during the mapping. As an example of a surjective mapping heterogeneity, consider an approval code of a purchase order. While this code in the first system can take the values "Approval Not Necessary", "Approved", "Rejected" and "In Revision" the second system only supports the values "Approved" and "Rejected." Consequently, a surjective mapping between the different values is required. Note that an injective mapping would not pose any problems as no information is lost by this mapping.

Semantic Domain Heterogeneities

In contrast to the semantic data heterogeneities the semantic domain heterogeneities are caused by a different abstraction of the real world entities in the conceptualization used by different information sources. Consequently they occur between classes of objects in a conceptualization and not between attributes of these classes. The types of semantic domain heterogeneities are therefore classified according to the relation of the real world entities represented by the classes in the used conceptualization. In [Wac03] Wache identifies four types of semantic domain heterogeneities: i) domain *subsumption*, ii) domain *overlap*, iii) *aggregation* and iv) domain *inconsistency*.

Subsumption. A domain subsumption heterogeneity occurs when the instances of a class in the conceptualization used by one information source includes all the instances of a class in the conceptualization used by the other information source. This type of heterogeneity occurs in the running example. While the **DEBMAS** schema is only capable of representing information regarding entities of the class "customer", the **BusinessPartner** schema is capable of representing information regarding entities of the class of "business partners". The class "business partner" subsumes the classes like e.g. "customer", "vendor" or "employee" as all instances of the later three classes are also instances of the class "business partner".

Overlap. In contrast to the domain subsumption heterogeneity, a domain overlap heterogeneity occurs when the classes from two conceptualizations only partially overlap. This situation is equivalent to the one that some instances of one class are also instances of an other class while some are not. An example of such an overlap can be found when investigating the classes of "Customers" and "Employees". Most likely there are some customers that are also employees, but there will also be customers that are not employees and vice versa.

Aggregation. Closely related to the two types of semantic domain heterogeneities mentioned before is the domain aggregation heterogeneity. Domain aggregation heterogeneities occur when the conceptualizations used by different data sources represent data using different levels of abstractions. This in turn leads to different aggregation of the data. According to [SvH05] domain aggregation heterogeneities are in many cases related to domain subsumption heterogeneities.

Incompatibility. In contrast to the previously mentioned heterogeneities incompatibility is not concerned with related but with unrelated classes of objects. A domain inconsistency heterogeneity occurs when two classes originating from two different conceptualization do not share any instances. This information is very useful as it allows to exclude certain incorrect relationships between different data sources.

Note the difference between incompatibility heterogeneities (H5.5) and missing information heterogeneities (H2.3). While the former refers to a situation where two classes do not share any instances, the latter refers to a situation where only properties are missing in one class that are available in the other. The two classes can in the latter case still share common instances.

3.4 Resulting Integration Challenges

As already identified in Section 2 the common task in the two use cases is the creation of schema mappings. These mappings are used to translate data corresponding to a source schema into data corresponding to a target schema. It is obvious from the discussions in the previous sections that, even though the use cases in this thesis are only concerned with heterogeneities on the schematic and semantic layer, still many types of heterogeneity exist. These heterogeneities obviously result in challenges closely related to the two steps comprising the creation of schema mappings:

- The identification of related schema entities
- The creation of correct mappings functions.

Furthermore, the multilateral and meta-level heterogeneities are responsible for increasing the complexity of the creation of mappings as they enlarge the search space for mappings significantly.

3.4 Resulting Integration Challenges   33

Besides that it is important to note that the heterogeneities described in the previous section often occur in combination. For example it is common that a naming and a data type (cf. schema entities KUNNR and InternalID in the running example) or a naming and different multi-lateral heterogeneities occur together (cf. schema entities STRAS, StreetName and HouseID in the running example). This situation results in further challenges when creating schema mappings.

This sections investigates the integration challenges originating from the different heterogeneities in detail and relates them to the steps in the schema mapping task.

3.4.1 Integration Challenges resulting from Semantic Heterogeneities

The main integration challenge resulting from semantic domain heterogeneities is the identification of related classes in the conceptualization used by different information sources. As usually no direct correspondence between classes in the conceptualization and schemas used in B2B communication exist, semantic heterogeneities result in a need to identify related schemas and/or schemas fragments. Depending on the type of semantic domain heterogeneity present in a given situation different cases are possible. A subsumption relation between the classes in two different information sources for example can lead to a mapping between several schemas of one information source and one schema of the other. The reason is that in the case of a subsumption heterogeneity one information source might use several schemas to represent information that is in the other information source represented using one schema.[2] In order to detect this correspondence background knowledge regarding the relation of the different classes in the conceptualization is required.

In contrast to this, the integration challenges resulting from semantic data heterogeneities (H4) are not related to the identification of related schemas or fragments of them but rather to the creation of mapping rules. In the context of scaling and value range heterogeneities (H4.1) the main problem is the identification of the correct function capable of translating between the data represented in different scales. For most commonly used scales (e.g. inches and meters to represent length) the required functions exist and only need to be identified. However, in some cases necessary translation function might need to be created first. An example of such a case is the usage of Social Security Numbers versus a custom numbering schema to unambiguously identify employees. In this case no standard function capable of the translation exists, and, therefore, a new translation func-

---
[2]As an example of this situation consider an information source representing customers, vendors and employees as separate schemas whereas a second information source represents them in one business partner schema.

tion needs to be created. The same is true for the representation heterogeneities (H4.2). In the case of surjective mappings a custom translation function almost always needs to be developed.

In all cases described above detailed domain and implementation knowledge is necessary to identify or create the required translation functions as usually the information on used scales, value ranges or data representations is not part of the schema information. Most B2B messaging standards, for example, deliberately do not require the usage of certain scales or representations to enable more flexible usage. Instead the schemas described in some B2B messaging standards contain entities to store information regarding the used scales, value ranges or data representation. However, not all standards offer such schema entities. Consequently the used scales, value ranges and representations can in general only be determined using additional background knowledge, instance data or a combination of both.

3.4.2 Integration Challenges resulting from Structural Heterogeneities

Focusing on the bilateral naming heterogeneities (H1.1) first, it is obvious that they result in challenges for identifying related schema entities. The usage of different languages, abbreviations, technical names and domain or context specific terminology hinders the identification of related schema entities. Again, additional knowledge like dictionaries, descriptions of the used naming rules or documentation is necessary to cope with this problem. The data type and integrity constraint heterogeneities (H1.3) result in challenges for the creation of correct mapping rules. In the case of simple data type heterogeneities (H1.2), e.g. the usage of a string data type versus the usage of an integer data type, usually no additional mapping functions are required. However, in the case of conflicting integrity constraints usually complex mapping functions are necessary. The reason for this is that integrity constraint heterogeneities (H1.3) are often closely related to semantic heterogeneities (cf. sec. 3.3.1).

The multilateral heterogeneities (H2) result in problems for the identification of related schema entities as well as in problem for the creation of the necessary mapping rules. Due to the multilateral heterogeneities not only single schema entities but sets of schema entities can be related. Firstly, these sets of related schema entities from the two schemas need to be identified. As multilateral heterogeneities usually occur in combination with bilateral heterogeneities, the schema entities part of the sets are named differently, have different data types and different associated integrity constraints, the identification of related sets of elements is not straightforward. Once related elements have been identified, the creation of the mapping function again is difficult. As an example consider a simple case where the content of the elements `Street` and `HouseNumber` in one schema needs to be concatenated and mapped onto the element `Street` of a second schema. In order to create the correct mapping function it is necessary to know "What is the required delimiter between the values?", "Which element needs to be the first one, which the second one?".[3] Without additional background knowledge it is not possible to generate the correct mapping functions

In contrast to the previous heterogeneities that occur between the schema entities of the same type (e.g. attributes) the meta-level heterogeneities (H3) occur between different types of schema entities. Consequently it is not sufficient to compare schema entities of the same type to identify correspondences. Besides this, the meta-level heterogeneities often occur in combination with bilateral heterogeneities (H1).

3.5 The Role of Ontologies in Integration

As the simple examples given in the previous section show, the presented integration challenges can only be solved by exploiting domain specific background knowledge in addition to the information contained in the schemas. In the scenarios presented in Chapter 2 the domain specific background knowledge is either not documented or only available in human readable format and distributed across different documents and or systems. As no integrated representation of the background knowledge exists, it is difficult to exploit the knowledge in an automatic schema mapping approach.

Ontologies enable representing knowledge in a machine and human understandable format. Therefore ontologies have become a popular research topic in areas like information integration and retrieval or knowledge management. According to the definition given by Studer et al. in [SBF98] an ontology is a *formal, explicit specification of a shared conceptualization.*[4] The different properties required for an ontology by this definition are:

- **formal:** an ontology should be specified in an machine readable language

- **explicit:** the used concepts and the restrictions on them should be explicitly defined

- **shared:** the knowledge captured in an ontology should be shared, i.e. consensual knowledge of more than one individual

- **conceptualization:** an ontology provides an abstract model of some fragment of the real world.

---

[3] In the USA the house number usually precedes the street name while in Germany the correct order is the other way around.

[4] This definition of ontology is an extension of the one provided by Gruber [Gru93]. Gruber defined an ontology as an *explicit specification of a conceptualization.*

These properties of ontologies enable the usage of ontologies for a number of different purposes in the context of the integration use cases investigated in this thesis. First, ontologies can be used to integrate the available background knowledge from different sources and store it in a machine interpretable format. Second, ontologies can help to cope with semantic heterogeneities. Third, ontologies can provide a conceptualization of the domain that is easily understandable by humans.

Ontologies in Information Integration. As the integration challenges presented in the previous section show, additional background knowledge is necessary to create mappings between different schemas. Today this knowledge is either distributed across different documents and systems, or not even documented. In the second case the knowledge necessary to create the mappings can only be obtained by detailed system analysis on the source code level or by interviewing the developers of the system. As a result the knowledge is not accessible to support the semi-automatic creation of schema mappings. Therefore current approaches rely heavily on general purpose dictionaries and thesauri like e.g. WordNet [Fel98] to cope with the integration challenges posed by the different structural and semantic heterogeneities. However, the usage of general purpose dictionaries and thesauri is bound to fail as already the simple example given in Section 3.3.1 for bilateral naming heterogeneities show.

Integrating the knowledge currently distributed across different documents into one (or possibly a set of connected) ontologies would enable the exploitation of this knowledge in automatic schema mapping algorithms. In contrast to general purpose dictionaries, ontologies integrating domain specific knowledge provide information specially tailored toward the current integration problem. When an integration problem in a different domain (e.g. B2B integration in the chemical industry instead of the automotive industry) needs to be solved, the ontology used in the integration process is changed. The result will be that the schema mapping algorithms exploiting this knowledge are automatically exploiting knowledge suitable for the current situation without manual tuning.

A nice additional advantage of integrating the necessary integration knowledge in one ontology is that this ontology can also be used to provide an integrated documentation to human users. Instead of having to browse through different documents to find the required information, a user uses the ontology as a single integrated information source for the integration knowledge. In addition, the integration ontology can then be augmented by additional information like e.g. example instances for important concepts to facilitate human understanding.

Schematic & Semantic heterogeneities. In addition to the information integration aspect mentioned in the previous section ontologies can also help to cope with schematic and semantic heterogeneities. Instead of relying on general

3.5 The Role of Ontologies in Integration

purpose thesauri or dictionaries to identify semantic heterogeneities, the conceptual model of the domain includes the taxonomic information necessary to identify semantic heterogeneities. As an example consider the concepts business partners and employees again. A general purpose thesaurus might suggest, that these two classes are overlapping. However, if the ontology states, that in the given domain an employee is a subclass of business partner, all employees are subsumed by the class business partner.

An overview of the types of heterogeneities that can be addressed by integrating the suitable knowledge in an ontology is given in Table 3.3. The table is divided into schematic and semantic heterogeneities. A detailed description on how different types of knowledge are modeled in an ontology in order to enable to cope with different types of heterogeneity is given in Part II. In the subsequent paragraphs a high level overview of how the different heterogeneities can be addressed is given.

Bilateral naming heterogeneities can be addressed in an ontology by modeling the different naming used for elements in different contexts. To illustrate this idea consider the form of address in the running example. In the source system this element is named **ANRED** while it is named `FormOfAddressCode` in the target system. In order to address this heterogeneity in an ontology both names together with the context, e.g. source and target system, in which they are valid need to be modelled in the ontology. Bilateral data type heterogeneities can also be addressed by an ontology. By modeling the compatibility of different data types it is possible to identify compatible schema elements. In contrast to the previous two types, solving heterogeneities of integrity constraints can only partially be facilitated by an ontology. If is, for example, possible to model default values for certain schema elements in the ontology to enable the solving conflicting default values. In contrast integrity constraint heterogeneities resulting from different value ranges for schema elements need to be solved by mapping rules. Multilateral property and entity heterogeneities can again be addressed. While solving the former can be facilitated by providing different modeling alternatives in the ontology, solving the latter can be facilitated by modeling the relations of concepts in the ontology. The modeling of possible default values, i.e. possible values of schema elements if the corresponding information is missing in the source, enables solving the missing information heterogeneities. Finally, also the meta-level heterogeneities can be addressed e.g. providing information regarding code lists which provide a translation between entities and values in the ontology.

Semantic data heterogeneities can only partially be solved using domain knowledge in an ontology. While e.g. semantic representation heterogeneities can be solved by providing different modeling alternatives in the ontology, scaling and value range heterogeneities need to be solved through dedicated mapping functions. In contrast to that, domain knowledge modeled in an ontology facilitates identifying and solving semantic domain heterogeneities.

Table 3.3: Different types of heterogeneities and how they can be addressed by ontologies.

Nr.	Heterogeneity	Addressable?	Approach
Schematic Heterogeneities			
H1.1	Bilateral Naming	yes	Modeling the different naming of schema elements in different contexts
H1.2	Bilateral Data Type	yes	Modeling of compatibility of different data types
H1.3	Bilateral Integrity	partially	Integrity constraints partially need to be handled outside the ontology
H2.1	Multilateral Property	yes	Providing different modeling alternatives
H2.2	Multilateral Entity	yes	Different types of relations (e.g. subclass) of concepts in the domain
H2.3	Missing Information	yes	Modeling of possible default values
H3	Meta-level	yes	Modeling of domain knowledge like e.g. code list
Semantic Heterogeneities			
H4	Data Heterogeneity	partially	Providing different modeling alternatives
H5	Domain Heterogeneity	yes	Different types of relations (e.g. subclass or disjunction) of concepts in the domain

3.6 Summary

This chapter discussed the integration challenges arising from different types of heterogeneities. First, a running example that will be used throughout this thesis was introduced. After that the different layers on which heterogeneity can occur were introduced. The following discussion focused on the structural and semantic layers as they are the relevant ones for the use cases presented in Chapter 2. The different types of heterogeneities existing on the structural and semantic layer were classified and further detailed in subsequent sections. Finally, the role of ontologies for solving the schematic and semantic heterogeneities was discussed.

Chapter 4

Definitions

Some of the essential terms necessary for the understanding of this thesis have already been informally introduced and used in the previous chapters. This chapter now aims at providing formal definitions for all important terms used throughout the remainder of the thesis. In order to foster a thorough understanding of these terms not only the abstract definition but also concrete examples will be presented.

4.1 Schema

In computer science a schema is a formal description of the structure of data. A schema describes how data is stored, accessed and interpreted by applications. For different domains, numerous different schema languages have been developed. For the purpose of this thesis, a schema S is defined as follows:

Definition 4.1.1 (Schema). *A schema S is defined as a structure consisting of*

- *one or several sets of named entities and*
- *one or several sets of relations defined upon these entities.*

This rather general definition of a schema is further restricted in the following sections to define special types of schemas.

4.2 XML and XML Schema

XML [Wor03] is currently the predominant format for exchanging data on the web. XML documents are usually modeled as node-labelled trees. Furthermore, the structure of a valid XML document can be specified by a schema. For XML a number of schema languages with different properties exist. Examples of proposed XML schema languages are XML Schema [Wor01b], RELAX NG [The02] and DTD [Wor06b]. However, XML Schema (XSD) is by far the most prominent of these schema languages.

In order to develop an approach that is independent from the peculiarities of the different schema languages, we will use the following formal definition of XML and XML schema. The definitions presented below are derived from the ones presented in [MLM01, MLMK05].

Definition 4.2.1 (XML Schema). *A XML schema is defined as a structure*

$$S := (N, T, St, \pi)$$

where N is a finite set of non-terminal symbols, T is a set of terminal symbols consisting of the set $\bar{T}$ of terminal names, i.e. element and attribute names, and the set $\bar{\tau}$ of atomic data types, St is a set of start symbols with $St \subset N$. Furthermore, π is a set of production rules of the form $X \rightarrow \mathbf{a}\, RE$, with $X \in N$, $a \in T$ and RE is a regular expression of the form

$$RE := \epsilon | \tau | n | (RE) | RE, RE | RE^? | RE^+ | RE^*$$

where ϵ denotes the empty expression, $\tau \in \bar{\tau}$ and $n \in N$.

Note that the set $\bar{\tau}$ of atomic data types contains the set of primitive XML data types as defined in [Wor04b]. Furthermore the notation "," denotes concatenation, "$a^?$" zero or one occurrence, "a^*" zero to unlimited occurrence of the terminal symbol a. Additionally "a^+" denotes "a, a^*".

In order to simplify the later discussion the *root entities* of a XML schema as well as the auxiliary function *doc* need to be defined. The set of *root entities* Ro of a XML schema is defined as the set $Ro = \{r \in \bar{T} \mid \exists\, X \rightarrow \mathbf{r}\, RE,\ X \in St\}$. This means that the set Ro contains all the terminal symbols r for which a production rule $X \rightarrow \mathbf{r}\, RE$ exists in π with $X \in St$. The auxiliary function $doc(t), t \in T$ is a function that returns the optional short text annotation of a schema entity or $\emptyset$ if no short text annotation is defined for an entity.

Furthermore it is important to note that a terminal symbol $a \in T$ does not unambiguously identify an entity in an XML schema. As any $a \in T$ can occur in multiple production rules, a schema entity can only be identified unambiguously by a sequence of $(a_1, \ldots, a_n)$ of terminal symbols for which production rules

$$X_1 \rightarrow a_1\, RE_1$$
$$\vdots$$
$$X_n \rightarrow a_n\, RE_n$$

exist in π with $X_1 \in St$ and RE_i contains X_{i+1}. To simplify the future discussion the set E of all sequences of terminal symbols possible based on π is defined for each XML Schema. The set E is in the following referred to as the set of all schema entities.

4.2 XML and XML Schema

Example. The following example shows how the `BusinessPartner` schema in the running example can be represented using the previous definition. Figure 4.1 contains a listing of the `BusinessPartner` schema in XML schema notation. Using the definition above, this schema can be encoded as $S := (N, T, St, \pi)$ where:[1]

$N = \{$bp, bpt, bprc, iid, name, add, nt, foac, fln, ait, sn, hid, cc, web, ut, tdt, sdt, cdt, udt$\}$

$T = \{$BusinessPartner, BusinessPartnerRoleCode, InternalID, Name, AddressInformation, FromOfAddressCode, FirstLineName, StreetName, HouseID, CountryCode, Web, URI, token, string, code, anyURI$\}$

$St = \{$bp$\}$

$\pi = \{$bp $\rightarrow$ BusinessPartner(bpt), bpt $\rightarrow$ (bprc, iid, name, add),
bprc $\rightarrow$ BusinessPartnerRoleCode(tdt), iid $\rightarrow$ InternalID(tdt),
name $\rightarrow$ Name(nt), add $\rightarrow$ AddressInformation(ait), nt $\rightarrow$ (foac, fln),
foac $\rightarrow$ FormOfAddressCode(tdt), fln $\rightarrow$ FirstLineName(sdt),
ait $\rightarrow$ (sn, hid, cc, web), sn $\rightarrow$ StreetName(sdt), hid $\rightarrow$ HouseID(tdt),
cc $\rightarrow$ CountryCode(cdt), web $\rightarrow$ Web(ut), ut $\rightarrow$ URI(udt),
tdt $\rightarrow$ token(ϵ), sdt $\rightarrow$ string(ϵ), cdr $\rightarrow$ code(ϵ),
udt $\rightarrow$ anyURI(ϵ)$\}$

Next, the term XML document is defined based on the definition of XML schema given before.

Definition 4.2.2 (XML Document). *A XML Document D is a structure*

$$D := (E, <, r, \lambda)$$

where E is a set of nodes, $<$ a child relation between nodes, $r \in E$ a root node and $\lambda : E \rightarrow T$ a labeling function.

Using these definitions of XML schema and XML documents it is now possible to define validity of a XML document against a XML schema. A XML document D is *valid instance* of a XML schema S iff an *Interpretation I* against the XML schema S exists such that:

- $\forall e \in E : I(e) \in N$

- $\forall e \in E$ with children $e_0, e_1, \ldots, e_n$ there exists a production rule $X \rightarrow \mathbf{a}RE$ in π such that

    - $I(e) = X$

---
[1]Note further that $T = \{\bar{T}, \bar{\tau}\}$ with $\bar{\tau} = \{$token, string, code, anyURI$\}$

```
<schema xmlns = "http://www.w3.org/2001/XMLSchema" >
  <element name = "BusinessPartner" type = "BusinessPartType" />

  <complexType name = "BusinessPartType" >
    <sequence>
      <element name = "BusinessPartnerRoleCode" type = "token" />
      <element name = "InternalID" type = "token" />
      <element name = "Name" type = "NameType" />
      <element name = "AddressInformation" type = "AddInfoType" />
    </sequence>
  </complexType>

  <complexType name = "NameType" >
    <sequence>
      <element name = "FormOfAddressCode" type = "token" />
      <element name = "FirstLineName" type = "string" />
    </sequence>
  </complexType>

  <complexType name = "AddInfoType" >
    <sequence>
      <element name = "StreetName" type = "string" />
      <element name = "HouseID" type = "token" />
      <element name = "CountryCode" type = "code" />
      <element name = "Web" type = "WebType" />
    </sequence>
  </complexType>

  <complexType name = "WebType" >
    <sequence>
      <element name = "URI" type = "anyURI" />
    </sequence>
  </complexType>
</schema>
```

Figure 4.1: The XML schema representation of the BusinessPartner schema in the running example.

4.2 XML and XML Schema

- $\lambda(e) = \mathbf{a}$
- $I(e_0), I(e_1), \ldots, I(e_n)$ matches RE

Example. This example shows how parts of an instance of the `BusinessPartner` schema in the running example are represented using the previous definition. The running example in Figure 3.1 contains some instance values in parenthesis. The XML representation of these instance values, excluding the `AddressInformation` part, is shown in the listing in Figure 4.2.

```
<BusinessPartner>
    <BusinessPartnerRoleCode> 02 </BusinessPartnerRoleCode>
    <InternalID> ABC456 </InternalID>

    <Name >
        <FormOfAddressCode> 01 </FormOfAddressCode >
        <FirstLineName> ACME </FirstLineName >
    </Name >
    ...
</BusinessPartner>
```

Figure 4.2: An example instance of the `BusinessPartner` schema.

The XML document shown in Figure 4.2 can be represented as $D = (E, <, r, \lambda, \eta)$ where:

$E =$ {BusinessPartner, BusinessPartnerRoleCode, InternalID, Name, FormOfAddressCode, FirstLineName, 02, ABC456, 01, ACME}

$< =$ {(BusinessPartner, BusinessPartnerRoleCode), (BusinessPartner, InternalID), (BusinessPartner, Name), (Name, FormOfAddressCode), (Name, FirstLineName), (BusinessPartnerRoleCode, 02), (InternalID, ABC456), (FormOfAddressCode, 01), (FirstLineName, ACME)}

$r =$ BusinessPartner

$\lambda =$ {{BusinessPartner, BusinessPartnerRoleCode, InternalID, Name, FormOfAddressCode, FirstLineName} $\rightarrow$ id, {02, ABC456, 01} $\rightarrow$ token, {ACME} $\rightarrow$ string}

Using the following interpretation I it is obvious that D is a valid instance of the schema S presented in the previous example.

$$I = \{(\text{BusinessPartner}, \text{bp}), (\text{BusinessPartnerRoleCode}, \text{bprc}), (\text{InternalID}, \text{iid}) \\ (\text{Name}, \text{name}), (\text{FormOfAddressCode}, \text{foac}), (\text{FirstLineName}, \text{fln}), (02, \text{tdt}), \\ (\text{ABC456}, \text{tdt}), (01, \text{tdt}), (\text{ACME}, \text{sdt})\}$$

4.3 Ontology

In Section 3.5 we defined an ontology according to [SBF98] as a formal, explicit specification of a shared conceptualization. This section now introduces a formal definition of the term ontology. The definition given below extends the definition by Stumme et al. [SEH+04] and is a versatile algebraic notion of ontologies that abstracts from individual languages such as W3C's OWL [Wor04a], F-Logic [KLW95]. Furthermore, the UML notation introduced by Brockmans in [BHHS06], will be used in the following to visualize ontologies in the presented notation.

Definition 4.3.1 (Ontology). *An ontology O is a structure*

$$O := (C, R, A, T, I, V, \alpha, \leq_C, \sigma_R, \sigma_A, \sigma_\alpha, i_C, i_R, i_a)$$

where C is a set of concepts aligned in a hierarchy $\leq_C$, R is a set of relations, A is a set of attributes, T is a set of data types, I is the set of all instances, V is the set of all data values, α is the set of annotation relations, $\sigma_R : R \to C \times C$ is the signature of R, $\sigma_A : A \to C \times T$ is the signature of A and $\sigma_\alpha : \alpha \to (C \cup R \cup A) \times I$ is the signature of α. Furthermore, the function $i_C : C \to \mathfrak{P}(I)$ defines the instances of concepts, $i_R : R \to \mathfrak{P}(I \times I)$ the instances of relations and $i_A : A \to \mathfrak{P}(I \times V)$ the instances of attributes.

In addition the domain and range of a relation $r \in R$ are defined as $dom(r) := \pi_1(\sigma_R(r))$ and $range(r) := \pi_2(\sigma_R(r))$ respectively.

This definition of ontology formalizes the intentional aspect of a domain, i.e. the assertions on concepts, relations, attributes, data types and how they are related as well as the extensional aspect of a domain, i.e. assertion on instances of concepts and relations. Furthermore, it is important to note that the annotation relations α present in the ontology definition are more than simple string annotations. Instead the annotation relations in α enable linking concepts, relations and attributes to instances making it possible to create complex annotations for all the entities in an ontology. The annotation relations α are in a later part of the thesis (cf. Chapter 6) used to link integration knowledge to the conceptual model of a domain.

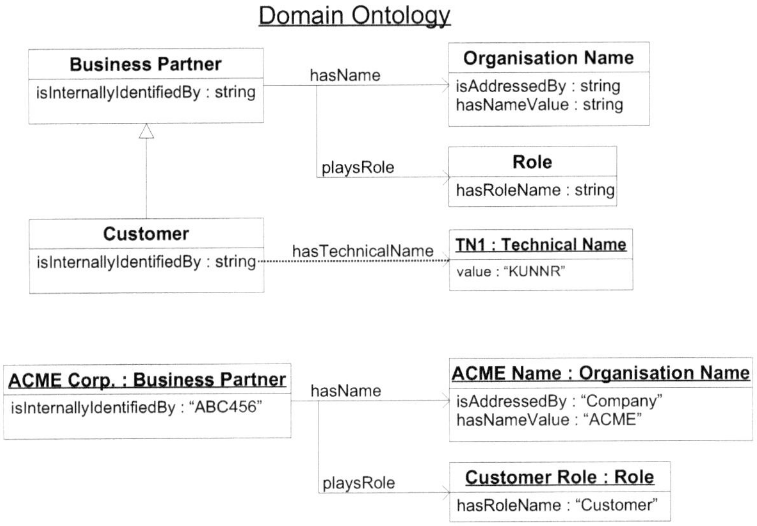

4.3 Ontology

Domain Ontology

[Figure: UML diagram showing Business Partner (isInternallyIdentifiedBy : string) with hasName relation to Organisation Name (isAddressedBy : string, hasNameValue : string), playsRole relation to Role (hasRoleName : string). Customer (isInternallyIdentifiedBy : string) is a subclass of Business Partner, with hasTechnicalName annotation to TN1 : Technical Name (value : "KUNNR"). Instance level: ACME Corp. : Business Partner (isInternallyIdentifiedBy : "ABC456") hasName ACME Name : Organisation Name (isAddressedBy : "Company", hasNameValue : "ACME"), playsRole Customer Role : Role (hasRoleName : "Customer").]

Figure 4.3: Example ontology describing the domain of business partners.

Example. In order to show how an ontology is represented using the previous definition, again the running example introduced in Section 3.1 is used. Figure 4.3 shows a small example ontology in UML notation. The ontology describes the domain of business partners as presented in the running example. The example ontology contains a number of concepts, like e.g. *BusinessParner, Customer* and *Role*, which are aligned in a hierarchy. In this case the concept *Customer* is a subconcept of *BusinessPartner*. Additionally it contains a number of relations, e.g. *hasName*, and a number of attributes, e.g. *isAddressedBy* and *hasNameValue*. Besides these intentional aspects, i.e. assertions regarding concepts, relations and attributes, the ontology also contains extension aspects, i.e. assertions regarding instances and data values. Examples of instances in Figure 4.3 are *ACME Corp.* and *ACME Name*, examples of data values *ABC456* and *ACME*. Furthermore the example ontology also contains one annotation relation called *hasTechnicalName*. This annotation relation links the concept *Customer* to the instance *TN1*. The idea underlying the *hasTechnicalName* annotation relation is to link information how a concept is represented in a schema to the ontology. The details of this idea are described in Section 6.3.

Using the previous definition, this ontology can be represented as $O := (C, R, A, T, I, V, \alpha, \leq_C, \sigma_R, \sigma_A, \sigma_\alpha, i_C, i_R, i_a)$ with:

$C = \{\text{BusinessPartner}, \text{Customer}, \text{OrganisationName}, \text{Role}, \text{TechnicalName}\}$
$R = \{\text{hasName}, \text{playsRole}\}$

$A = \{\text{isInternallyIdentifiedBy}, \text{isAddressedBy}, \text{hasNameValue}, ...\}$

$T = \{\text{string}\}$

$I = \{\text{ACME Corp.}, \text{ACME Name}, \text{Customer Role}, \text{TN1}\}$

$V = \{\text{ABC456}, \text{Company}, \text{ACME}, \text{Customer}, \text{KUNNR}\}$

$\alpha = \{\text{hasTechnicalName}\}$

$\leq_C = \{(\text{Customer}, \text{BusinessPartner})\}$

$\sigma_R = \{\text{hasName} \rightarrow (\text{BusinessPartner}, \text{OrganisationName}),$
$\quad\quad \text{playsRole} \rightarrow (\text{BusinessPartner}, \text{Role}), ...\}$

$\sigma_A = \{\text{isInternallyIdentifiedBy} \rightarrow (\text{BusinessPartner}, \text{string}),$
$\quad\quad \text{hasNameValue} \rightarrow (\text{OrganisationName}, \text{string}), ...\}$

$\sigma_\alpha = \{\text{hasTechnicalName} \rightarrow (\text{isInternallyIdentifiedBy}, \text{TN1})\}$

$i_C = \{\text{Customer} \rightarrow \{\text{ACME Corp.}\}, \text{OrganisationName} \rightarrow \{\text{ACME Name}\}, ...\}$

$i_R = \{\text{hasName} \rightarrow \{(\text{ACME Corp.}, \text{ACME Name})\}, \text{playsRole} \rightarrow \{(\text{ACME Corp.}, \text{Customer Role})\}\}$

$i_A = \{\text{isInternallyIdentifiedBy} \rightarrow \{(\text{ACME Corp.}, \text{ABC456})\}, ...\}$

4.4 Matching and Mapping

As mentioned in Chapter 2, solving different integration scenarios requires solving two independent tasks. First, corresponding elements in the involved schemas need to be identified. The process of identifying these correspondences is called *Matching*. Second, the necessary mapping rules for the translation of data instances need to be created based on the identified correspondences. In this section, the terms related to these two tasks are formally defined based on the definitions provided above.

Definition 4.4.1 (Matching). *Matching is the process of identifying corresponding elements in two schemas, the source schema S_S and the target schema S_T. The result of this process, which can either be executed manually, semi-automatically or fully automatic, is a set Mat of matches mat_i between the two structures. Each match mat_i contains the corresponding entities of the source structure $e_{S_S,k}, \ldots, e_{S_S,l}$ and the target structure $e_{S_T,q}, \ldots, e_{S_T,r}$.*

$$Mat_{S_S \rightarrow S_T} := \{mat_1, \ldots, mat_n\}$$
$$mat_i := (e_{S_S,k}, \ldots, e_{S_S,l}, e_{S_T,q}, \ldots, e_{S_T,r})$$

Note that this definition does not restrict the type of the involved structures. Matching can for example be performed between two XML schemas, two ontologies or a XML schema and an ontology. Furthermore the definition does not

4.4 Matching and Mapping

restrict the number of involved source or target schema entities. Consequently it allows $1:n$, $m:1$ and $m:n$ relations between entities of the source and the target schema.[2]

Example. Again the running example is used to illustrate this definition. The matching schema elements in the running (represented by dotted lines in Figure 3.1) can be represented as:

$$Mat_{S_S \rightarrow S_T} = \{(\text{DEBMAS}, \text{BusinessPartner}, \text{BusinessPartnerRoleCode}),$$
$$(\text{KUNNR}, \text{InternalID}), (\text{ANRED}, \text{FormOfAddressCode}),$$
$$(\text{NAME1}, \text{FirstLineName}), (\text{STRAS}, \text{StreetName}, \text{HouseID}),$$
$$(\text{LAND1}, \text{CountryCode}), (\text{KNURL}, \text{URI})\}$$

Definition 4.4.2 (Mapping). *A mapping M between two schemas S_S and S_T is an extension of a matching. It is defined as a set of mapping elements m. Each mapping element relates entities of the source structure $e_{S_S,k}, \ldots, e_{S_S,l}$ to entities of the target structure $e_{S_T,q}, \ldots, e_{S_T,r}$ using a mapping rule mapexp. The mapping rule specifies how the involved entities are related.*

$$M_{S_S \rightarrow S_T} := \{m_1, \ldots, m_m\}$$
$$m_j := (e_{S_S,k}, \ldots, e_{S_S,l}, e_{S_T,q}, \ldots, e_{S_T,r}, mapexp_j)$$
$$:= (mat_j, mapexp) \quad \text{with } mat_j \in Mat_{S_S \rightarrow S_T}$$

Note that the type of mapping rules used to define a mapping is not further restricted in the previous definition for two reasons. First, the mapping rules depend on the involved structures. In the case of an ontology mapping different mapping expressions are necessary than in the case of a XML Schema mapping. Second, the mapping rules depend on the execution environment responsible for executing the mapping during runtime.

One consequence of not restricting the mapping rules is that a mapping is unidirectional. This is indicated by the arrow form S to T in the definition above. The definition of a mapping between two schemas as being unidirectional is chosen deliberately as real mappings occurring in the different integration scenarios presented in Chapter 2 often contain mapping rules like the calculation of sums for which no inverse mapping rule exists. Furthermore, the definition of a mapping given above does not restrict the relation between entities of the source and the target schema to be $1:1$, but rather allows for $m:n$ relations. Restricting mappings to $1:1$ mappings between entities of the source and target structure simplifies the mapping elements to $m_j = (e_{S,k}, e_{T,l}, mapexp_j)$.

---

[2] Note that a match mat_i does not define how the source entities $e_{S_S,k}, \ldots, e_{S_S,l}$ correspond to the target entities $e_{S_S,l}, e_{S_T,q}$. The mapping expression (cf. subsequent definition) defining the relation of the entities in detail is not part of a match mat_i.

Example. The following example illustrate the definition of a mapping. Instead of concrete mapping rules this example uses so called mapping categories. This mapping categories are introduced in Section 8.2. For the purpose of this example it is sufficient to understand, that mapping categories (e.g. *Move*, *Split* or *Code-Value-Mapping*) are abstractions of concrete mapping rules. For example, the mapping category *Split* which is associated to the matching element (STRAS, StreetName, HouseID) states that the string value of the source schema element *STRAS* needs to be split into the target schema elements *StreetName* and `HouseID` without further detailing the concrete algorithm.

$$
\begin{aligned}
M_{S_S \to S_T} = \quad & \{(\text{DEBMAS}, \text{BusinessPartner}, \texttt{Create-Instance}) \\
& (\text{DEBMAS}, \text{BusinessPartnerRoleCode}, \texttt{Default}), \\
& (\text{KUNNR}, \text{InternalID}, \texttt{Internal-ID}), \\
& (\text{ANRED}, \text{FormOfAddressCode}, \texttt{Code-Value-Mapping}), \\
& (\text{NAME1}, \text{FirstLineName}, \texttt{Move}), \\
& (\text{STRAS}, \text{StreetName}, \text{HouseID}, \texttt{Split}), \\
& (\text{LAND1}, \text{CountryCode}, \texttt{Move}), (\text{KNURL}, \text{URI}, \texttt{Move})\}
\end{aligned}
$$

The general definition of mapping given above can now be further restricted to define for example the term XML schema mapping as follows.

Definition 4.4.3 (XML Schema Mapping). *A mapping between two XML schemas S_S and S_T is as set of mapping elements $m_j = (e_{S,k}, e_{T,l}, mapexp_j)$ as defined in Definition 4.4.2 where each mapping element relates entities of the source XML schema S_S to entities of the target XML schema S_T.*

$$
\begin{aligned}
M_{S_S \to S_T} &:= \{(e_{S_S,i}, \ldots, e_{S_S,j}, e_{S_T,m}, \ldots, e_{S_T,n}, mapexp_j)\} \\
e_{S_S,x} &\in S_S \\
e_{S_T,y} &\in S_T
\end{aligned}
$$

4.5 Lifting

A special kind of matching that will be frequently used throughout the thesis is the matching between a schema and an ontology. This special kind of matching is denoted with the term *lifting* in the remainder of the thesis. Based on the previous definitions, a lifting can be defined as:

Definition 4.5.1 (Lifting). *A lifting $L_{S \to O}$ from a schema S to an ontology O is a matching with:*

$$
\begin{aligned}
L_{S \to O} &= \{(e_{S,i}, \ldots, e_{S,j}, e_{O,m})\} \\
e_{S,i}, \ldots, e_{S,j} &\in S \\
e_{O,m} &\in C \cup R \cup A
\end{aligned}
$$

4.5 Lifting

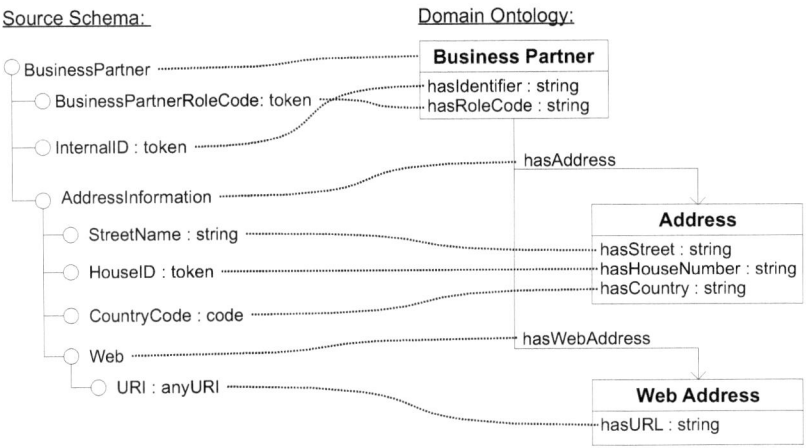

Figure 4.4: Example of a lifting from a source schema to an ontology.

Note that the given definition of lifting restricts the target entities in a match $mat_i = (e_{S,i}, \ldots, e_{S,j}, e_{O,m})$ to one ontology entity, namely $e_{O,m}$. The reason for this restriction is that in the mapping approach introduced in this thesis[3] it is assumed that each schema entity corresponds to exactly one ontology entity.

discusses the notion of information capacity and the relation to the presented approach in detail.

Example. To illustrate the definition of lifting given above the schema and domain ontology depicted in Figure 4.5 are used as an example. The lifting between the schema and the domain ontology is depicted by dotted lines in the figure. Using the above definition this lifting can be represented as:

$L_{S \to O} = $ {(BusinessPartner, Business Partner)
(BusinessPartnerRoleCode, hasRoleCode),
(InternalID, hasIdentifier), (AddressInformation, hasAddress),
(StreetName, hasStreet), (HouseID, hasHouseNumber),
(CountryCode, hasCountry), (Web, hasWebAddress),
(URI, hasURL)}

Again, this definition can be specialized to define, for example, the term XML schema lifting.

---

[3] See Section 5.3 for a detailed description of the Ontology-based Mapping Approach introduced in this thesis.

Definition 4.5.2 (XML Schema Lifting). *A XML schema lifting $L_{S \to O}$ from a XML schema S to an ontology O is a matching with:*

$$\begin{aligned}
L_{S \to O} &:= \{l_1, \ldots, l_n\} \\
l_i &:= (e_{S,i}, \ldots, e_{S,j}, e_{O,m}) \\
e_{S,i}, \ldots, e_{S,j} &\in T_S \\
e_{O,m} &\in C \cup R \cup A
\end{aligned}$$

4.6 Summary

This section introduced formal definitions of the relevant term used throughout the remainder of this thesis. Based on the definitions of the terms schema, XML schema and ontology, the terms matching and mapping were defined. In addition, the term lifting which is a special matching between a schema and an ontology was introduced.

Part II

Ontology-based Mapping

Chapter 5

The Mapping Process

This chapter now focuses on the process of developing schema mappings. First a generic schema mapping process for the manual development of schema mappings is introduced (Section 5.1). On its basis a novel process for the semi-automatic development of mappings is defined (Section 5.2). The process presented below takes a user-centric view of the automatic schema mapping process. In particular the process steps of the overall process in which domain knowledge plays an important role are identified and analyzed in detail. Additionally, this chapter highlights which parts of the presented process are addressed by this thesis. As well, this chapter provides a high-level overview of the proposed schema mapping approach (Section 5.3) together with a detailed analysis of related research.

5.1 The Manual Mapping Process

The process supported by state of the art industrial solutions (like e.g. the SAP Exchange Infrastructure [SO05])[1] for the manual development of schema mappings is depicted in Figure 5.1. From a user point of view this process consists of 5 main steps.

Step 1 (Preprocessing): The first step is a preprocessing step. In this step the schemas as well as possibly instance data is prepared for the usage in a given mapping tool. Depending on the capabilities of the mapping tool and the integration task at hand this step could consist of establishing a connection to a database, exporting XML schemas and instance data from a certain system or even include the reverse engineering of database schemas.

Step 2 (Import): The second step is the import of the prepared schemas and instance data into the mapping tool.

---
[1] See Section 10.1 for a detailed review of state of the art industrial solutions.

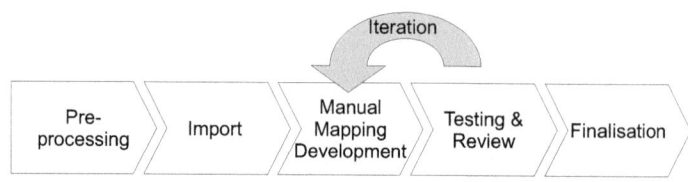

Figure 5.1: Manual mapping process supported by current tools.

Step 3 (Mapping Development): The third step is the development of the mapping. Using the interface provided by the given mapping tool, a user analyses the two schemas, identifies corresponding elements in the source and the target schema and creates the required mapping rules manually. Depending on the mapping tool, the mapping rules are either developed using a graphical metaphor or using a programming language.

Step 4 (Testing and Review): After the creation of the mapping it is usually tested using example data. Depending on the results of the test a revision of the mapping might become necessary. In this case an iteration of the third and fourth step is performed until the test results indicate the correctness of the mapping.

Step 5 (Finalization): The last step is the finalization of the created mapping. After this step, the mapping is available for future execution.

Note that the complexity of the preprocessing step varies largely depending on the type of integration project at hand. In a B2B integration project the schemas of the sent and received messages are usually available beforehand. In contrast to that extracting data schemas from legacy applications in the case of a data migration project might already require significant efforts. The reason is that the legacy application often do not offer an interface for exporting the schemas used to store data. Therefore manual work is required to extract the schemas.

Furthermore, it is important to note that not all process steps need to be executed by the same person. For example, the preprocessing and import of the schemas could be performed by a different person than the one performing the actual schema mapping development. However, some integration knowledge gained in the preprocessing step is also necessary for the mapping development. Consequently there is a need for knowledge sharing between the different steps of the manual schema mapping process.

Tasks requiring background knowledge. The manual mapping process introduced above requires detailed background knowledge from a user in order to allow the completion of the three main steps, namely the *Preprocessing*, the *Mapping Development* and the *Testing and Review*. During preprocessing, detailed technical knowledge regarding the systems involved in the integration project is necessary. Only if this knowledge is available the user is capable of exporting the legacy system schemas in a Data Migration project or identify the relevant parts of a given B2B message in a B2B integration project. The mapping development step also requires detailed knowledge regarding the involved schemas, e.g. which real world entities are represented by which schema entities, as well as knowledge regarding implementation details, e.g. encoding schemas used for certain schema entities.[2] Finally, the testing and review of the developed mappings requires detailed domain knowledge. Although it is possible to automatically test parts of a mapping using example data, a final soundness check of a mapping can only be performed by a user. Even if a mapping is technically correct, i.e. a source schema instance is transformed into a valid target schema instance by the proposed mapping, the mapping could still be incorrect. In the running example introduced in Section 3.1, the `NAME1` element could be mapped to the `StreetName` element and the `STRAS` element to the `FirstLineName` element without violating any integrity constraints. Still this mapping is obviously not correct.

As the discussion above shows, background knowledge is central to the task of developing schema mappings. Nevertheless this knowledge is currently not captured by the available tools. Consequently, the available background knowledge can neither be accessed centrally by a user nor can it be exploited to automate parts of the mapping development. In the following section the manual mapping development process is extended in order to support an automation of the mapping development.

5.2 The Semi-Automatic Mapping Process

The mapping process proposed in this thesis to allow the semi-automatic development of schema mappings is depicted in Figure 5.2. It extends the one presented in the previous section by adding an additional step for collecting knowledge from the user and by replacing the manual mapping development with an automated step. The processes steps forming the semi-automatic mapping process are:

Step 1 (Knowledge Collection): In contrast to the manual mapping process, the first step is a knowledge collection step. The purpose of this step is to non-intrusively collect as much information about the involved system as possible prior to starting the schema mapping in order to effectively support the automatic mapping step later on. Examples of the collected information could include meta data about the involved systems, like e.g.

---

[2] A detailed list of the different types of background knowledge necessary to develop a schema mapping is given in Chapter 6.

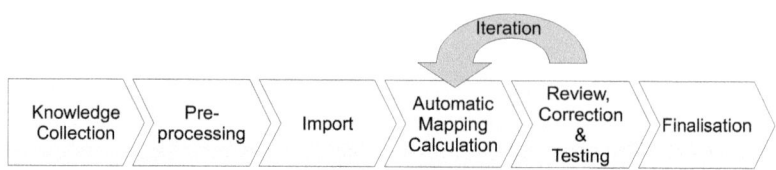

Figure 5.2: The proposed generic process for the semi-automatic creation of schema mappings.

information regarding its vendor or its version, or usage characteristics of these systems.

Step 2 (**Preprocessing**): The second step is the preprocessing of the data to prepare it for the usage in the given mapping tool. This step is identical to the preprocessing step in the manual mapping development process.

Step 3 (**Import**): As in the manual mapping process, the step following the preprocessing is the import of the data into the semi-automatic mapping tool.

Step 4 (**Automatic Mapping Calculation**): After the required data has been imported into the mapping tool, a first mapping is calculated by the mapping tool using the automatic mapping algorithms. This algorithm exploits the available information, like e.g. schema information or background knowledge, and suggests a mapping between the source and the target schema on the basis of this information. Details concerning the automatic mapping algorithms including the exploited information are provided in the subsequent sections.

Step 5 (**Review, Correction & Testing**): The mapping created in the previous step is reviewed, corrected and tested by a user. Depending on the review and test results an iteration of the automatic mapping calculation and the review phase is possible.

Step 6 (**Finalization**): Again, the last step is the finalization of the created mapping. After this step the mapping is available for future execution.

The development of the semi-automatic mapping process presented above is driven by two observations. Firstly, the integration of human knowledge about i) the systems involved into the mapping process and ii) peculiarities of a given integration task improves the results achieved by automatic mapping algorithms significantly (cf. [Do06, Ehr06]). Therefore, the mapping approaches proposed by Do [Do06] and Ehrig [Ehr06] require, for example, the selection of features used for similarity computation or the configuration of matching algorithms in

5.2 The Semi-Automatic Mapping Process

order to adjust the approaches to the integration task at hand. The focus of the *Knowledge Collection* step in the presented process is to non-intrusively collect the necessary information for tuning the automatic mapping calculation without requiring detailed knowledge about the underlying mapping algorithms. A detailed description of possible approaches for collecting domain knowledge from users is provided in Section 6.2.

Secondly, it is obvious that in production environments the results of automatic schema mapping algorithms will not immediately be deployed. Instead, the mapping created by automatic approaches has to be carefully examined, completed and tested by a user. This part of the process might involve an iterative execution of the mapping algorithms on parts or the complete schema. Consequently the process enables an iteration of the *Automatic Mapping Calculation* after the *Review, Correction and Testing* step. Note that in case of an iteration over these two steps decisions taken in the review and correction step should influence the next execution of the automatic mapping calculation. For example, it is intuitively obvious that user declined matches should not be proposed again in the next run whereas user verified matches should have higher significance than automatically created ones. Furthermore, decisions taken in the Review and Correction step could also help to improve future mappings in the same domain. However, possible approaches to optimize the iteration between the Review and Correction step and the Automatic Mapping Calculation step as well as knowledge collection from decisions taken in the Review and Correction step are not investigated in this thesis.

Note, that the process presented above is agnostic regarding the method used for automatically calculating schema mappings in Step 4 of the process. Especially, the process does not require the availability of machine processable domain knowledge. Existing schema matching systems could easily be adopted to support this generic process. The ontology-based mapping approach which is developed in this thesis nevertheless fits nicely into the proposed process steps.

The remainder of this thesis focuses on the the first and the fourth step in the proposed generic process for the semi-automatic generation of schema mappings (cf. Figure 5.3). The reason is that these two steps are the main steps influencing the quality of an automatically generated schema mapping. Furthermore, these two steps are independent from the used integration tools. In contrast to that the preprocessing, import and finalization steps are tool specific and have no influence on the quality of the generated schema mappings. The step of reviewing, correcting and testing schema mappings is already well supported in commercially available integration tools and is consequently not in the focus of this thesis.[3]

---
[3]For an example of a commercially available tool supporting the Reviewing, Correcting and Testing step see Section 10.1.2.

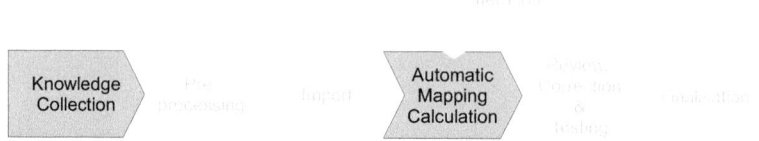

Figure 5.3: The steps in the generic semi-automatic mapping process this thesis focuses on.

5.3 The Ontology-Based Mapping Approach

This section provides a high-level overview of the <u>O</u>ntology-<u>B</u>ased <u>M</u>apping (OBM) approach pursued in this thesis. The OBM approach introduced below is one possible implementation of the automatic mapping calculation in the fourth step of the mapping process. Detailed descriptions of the individual steps compromising the overall approach are presented in subsequent chapters.

Figure 5.4 depicts a schematic overview of the proposed ontology-based mapping approach. For each of the individual steps the inputs and outputs are shown. The idea underlying this approach is that lifting the source and the target schema to the domain ontology exploiting the encapsulated knowledge is easier than creating a mapping between the two schemas directly. This idea gives rise to essentially three steps:

Step 1: *Lifting* the source schema S_1 to the domain ontology

Step 2: *Lifting* the target schema S_2 to the domain ontology

Step 3: *Extracting* the schema mapping $M_{S_1 \to S_2}$ based on the two liftings $L_{S_1 \to O}$ and $L_{S_2 \to O}$ and on the domain ontology O.

The proposed approach divides the problem of developing a schema mapping for two schemas S_1 and S_2 into two sub-problems: i) the lifting of the two schemas to a domain ontology and ii) the extraction of a schema mapping based on two liftings and a domain ontology. Details on how the lifting of schemas is performed are given in Chapter 7 while details on the extraction of mappings are given in Chapter 8.

Note that the lifting of the target schema might not be necessary in all scenarios requiring schema mapping. As an example, consider a Data Migration scenario as described in Section 2.2. It is quite common in Data Migration projects that multiple source systems containing similar data are migrated into one target system. In this case the target schema is fixed for a certain set of mappings and only the source schema changes. Consequently, the lifting of the target system only needs to be performed once and can be reused afterwards.

5.3 The Ontology-Based Mapping Approach

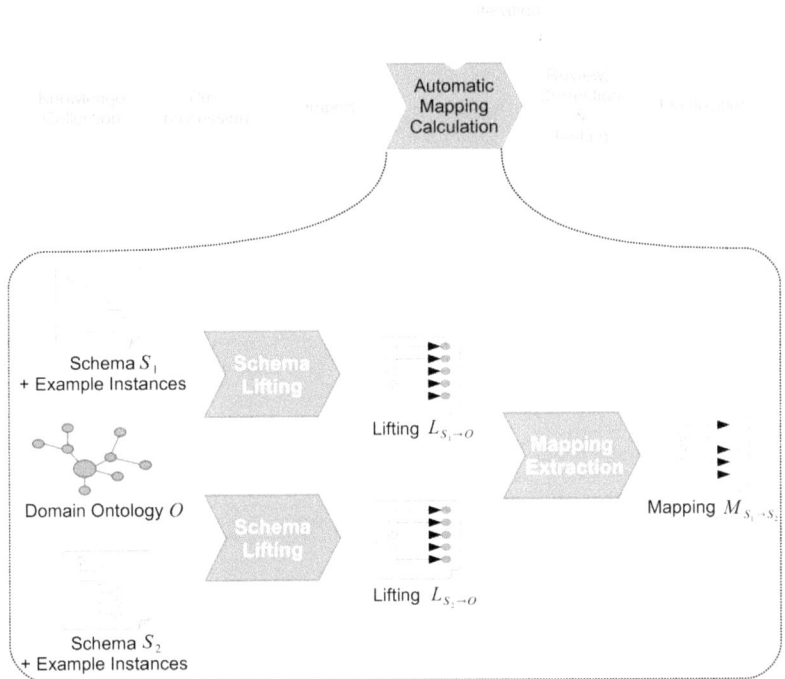

Figure 5.4: Schematic overview of the ontology-based schema mapping approach and its alignment to the generic automatic schema mapping process.

Furthermore, it is important to note that this thesis does not focus on the creation of a domain ontology. Instead, only how additional integration knowledge can be added to an existing domain ontology in a non-intrusive fashion is discussed in Section 6.3. As a basis for adding integration knowledge this thesis assumes the availability of a domain ontology containing a conceptual model of the domain. This is a valid assumption as more and more companies investigate possible applications of semantic Web technologies and numerous projects focus on the creation of domain ontologies for business domains.

5.3.1 Related Work

This subsection reviews the research in different areas that is related to the OBM approach. Related research mainly originates from two areas, namely i) research in the area of automatic schema matching and mapping and ii) research in the area of ontology matching and merging. In addition to that, existing work in the area of conceptual re-engineering is also related to the OBM approach. Consequently, a brief overview over existing work in this area is also presented.

Schema Matching & Mapping

The recent book by Euzenat and Shvaiko [ES07] provides a comprehensive overview of current schema matching and mapping systems. Among the large body of work in the schema mapping area only those approaches that are the closest to OBM are mentioned here. To date, only a few matching approaches address the task of finding not only matches between schemas but also mappings. Each of the known approaches that support the creation of mappings is briefly discussed below. For each approach the main difference to the OBM approach is highlighted.

DIKE. DIKE [PTU00] is a system aiming to support the creation of collaborative information systems. Based on a set of data bases the DIKE system creates a central global schema enabling integrated access to the set of data bases. During the matching step DIKE is able to detect semantic relationships, like synonymy and homonymy, between schema entities using WordNet [Fel98]. Furthermore, DIKE is also capable of detecting similarities between sub-schemas and schema fragments.

The main difference between DIKE and the OBM approach is, that DIKE does not detect complex mappings between schemas but rather only the semantic relationships between terms based on the relationship[4] information available in WordNet [Fel98].

iMap. The iMap [DLD$^+$04] system uses machine learning to infer complex mappings between two data bases based on a set of matchers. The matchers implemented in iMap mainly exploit instance information in order to infer complex relations between different attributes of the data bases. In addition to instance information iMap exploits some domain knowledge in the form of constraints which originate either from the data base schemas or are supplied by the user. As well, past mapping results and so-called overlapping data is exploited. The idea underlying overlapping data is to identify shared instances in the source and target data base in order to create mappings of higher quality.

In addition to the schema mapping part iMap also provides an *explanation component*. The goal of this component is to explain to a user why iMap suggested a particular mapping and thereby enables a user to adjust the iMap system to a particular mapping problem as well as to correct wrong mappings more quickly.

---
[4]For each term WordNet contains information regarding e.g. synonyms or hyponyms of the term.

5.3 The Ontology-Based Mapping Approach

The main difference between iMap and the OBM approach is that the OBM approach does not try to identify a complex schema mapping on the basis of unrelated instance data but rather uses specific example data instances. In addition, the OBM approach exploits an ontology during schema mapping. This ontology combines domain knowledge with integration knowledge and therefore enables the OBM approach to identify complex mapping expressions that cannot be identified by iMap.

Mapping System by Xu and Embley. In [XE03] Xu and Embley present a system capable of discovering complex mappings between schemas. In order to identify complex mappings their system exploits three types of information. First, WordNet is used to identify terminological relationships between schema entities. Second, data value characteristics calculated on the basis of unrelated instance data are used to identify matches between schema entities. Third, simple domain ontologies are used in order to suggest complex matches between schema entities. The set of complex mapping operations the system is able to identify is restricted to i) split and concatenations operations on strings, ii) union and selection operations on sets of related elements and iii) one particular type of structural heterogeneity, namely data-entity correspondences (cf. Section 3.3.1).

Again, a major difference between the OBM approach and the system developed by Xu and Embley is that the OBM approach uses specific example data in order to identify complex mappings. The usage of this example data together with the domain ontology enables OBM to identify much more complex mapping expressions between schema entities.

Although Xu and Embley also apply ontologies to the mapping problem their usage of ontologies differs significantly form the one in the OBM approach. In their systems only very small ontologies are used to model a particular subdomain, like e.g. the different types of phone numbers. This small ontologies are then only used to identify a particular kind of relation between the concepts by directly associating matchers to concepts in the ontology.

Clio & HepToX. The two systems Clio [HHH+05] and HepToX [BCL+05] have similar goals. Starting from a set of correspondences provided by either the user or a (semi-)automatic matching component, Clio and HepToX try to infer query mappings in order to enable a querying of the integrated schemas as well as a transformation of instances of one schema to instances of the other. While Clio is a generic tool capable of supporting different data sources and query languages, HepToX is specially tailored towards XML and the XQuery language.

Unlike these prototypes, OBM exploits domain knowledge to identify mapping expressions and complex matches. Example instance data combined with domain knowledge enable the detection of complex matches between two schemas which can not be identified using Clio and HepToX approaches.

COMA & COMA++. COMA [DR02] and its further development COMA++ are systems enabling the flexible combination of different schema matching approaches. In contrast to the systems discussed above, COMA++ is not capable of identifying complex mappings between schemas but rather focuses on identifying matches between schemas. Nevertheless, COMA++ is mentioned here as its conceptual architecture, which enables the flexible combination of different matching algorithms, inspired the design of many other schema mapping and ontology mapping approaches.

COMA++ provides a set of structure-based and string-similarity-based matching algorithms which can be executed independently on the input schemas. In addition previous match results can be reused using a specific reuse-oriented matcher. The results of the individual matchers are combined using different strategies like e.g. maximum, weighted average or minimum. COMA++ also features a sophisticated graphical user interface that enables users to interact with the tool and also features rich functionality for an evaluation of matching results.

The basic architecture of the OBM approach is based on the one suggested by Do and Rahm for COMA++. However the main differences between the OBM approach and COMA++ are that i) COMA++ is not able to identify complex mappings between schemas, ii) does not exploit instance information and iii) does not exploit domain and integration knowledge.

QuickMig. The work most closely related to the OBM approach is our previous work QuickMig [DSDR07]. QuickMig introduces an approach for non-intrusively collecting domain knowledge during a data migration project based on a questionnaire and specialized example data instances. Based on the specialized example instances, dedicated matchers capable of identifying matches and the corresponding complex mapping categories with high quality are available.

While we utilize the QuickMig architecture for OBM, OBM extends QuickMig significantly in several areas. First, OBM exploits not only schema and instance information but also integration knowledge modeled in an ontology during matching. Second, by exploiting the integration knowledge OBM is capable of identifying complex mapping expressions the instance based matchers of QuickMig are not able to identify. Third, OBM uses a two-step approach for creating the final mapping instead of directly mapping two schemas. This enables an integrated reuse of integration knowledge collected in previous integration projects.

Ontology Matching & Merging

The recent report on the results of the Ontology Alignment Evaluation Initiative 2007 [EIM+07] provides a comprehensive overview of the performance of different ontology matching systems on a predefined set of ontology matching tasks. Again,

5.3 The Ontology-Based Mapping Approach

only those approaches among the existing work in the ontology mapping area that are the closest to OBM are mentioned below.

MapOnto. MapOnto [ABM05] uses a similar approach as Clio and HepToX. Based on a set of simple matches between a schema and an ontology, MapOnto tries to create the mapping expressions. The simple matches can either be provided manually by a user or they are created using other schema matching approaches. The result of the MapOnto system is a set of complex formulas in a subset of first-order logic describing the mapping from the schema to the ontology

As the MapOnto approach is similar to Clio and HepToX also the main differenced between MapOnto and the OBM approach are quite similar. Unlike MapOnto the OBM approach exploits domain knowledge to identify complex matches and the corresponding mapping expressions. Furthermore, the OBM approach does not require an initial set of matches between the schemas as MapOnto does. In addition to that the OBM approach also exploits example instance data combined with domain knowledge which enables the detection of complex mappings between two schemas which can not be identified using MapOnto.

NOM and QOM. NOM (Naive Ontology Mapping) and QOM (Quick Ontology Mapping) are two approaches to ontology mapping which are part of the FOAM framework [Ehr06]. Similar to COMA++ the NOM tool enables the combination of different matching algorithms exploiting linguistic, structural and instance-based features to identify matches between two ontologies. In addition to COMA++ the NOM tool also exploits ontological knowledge like e.g. inheritance relationships between concepts and attributes.

QOM extends NOM in order to enable an efficient matching between two ontologies. QOM restricts the matching algorithms provided by NOM in order to improve efficiency on the expense of matching quality.

The major difference between the OBM approach and QOM is the ability of the OBM approach to identify complex mappings between schemas. NOM and QOM only try to identify matches between ontologies. In contrast to NOM and QOM which only exploit knowledge contained in the matched ontologies, the OBM approach explicitly exploits background knowledge in the form of a domain ontology augmented with integration knowledge. Finally, the OBM approach exploits specific example data and not just unrelated instances.

Falcon-AO. Falcon-AO [JHCQ05] is a system for matching of OWL ontologies. It sequentially applies linguistic and structural matching algorithms in order to calculate a matching between the input ontologies. The linguistic matching uses a TF-IDF-based similarity metric [CRF03] in order to calculate the similarity of entities based on their names and annotations. If the linguistic matching identifies matches with high confidence, these matches are directly returned. Otherwise the structural matcher tries to identify further matches.

Again the major difference between Falcon-AO and the OBM approach is the capability to identify complex mappings between schemas. As well, Falcon-AO neither exploits background knowledge nor instance data.

Conceptual Re-engineering

Conceptual re-engineering subsumes existing work on the extraction of conceptual models from existing development artifacts as well as on mapping between different representation formats. As the OBM approach lifts existing schemas to an existing ontology, these approaches are also related to the OBM approach.

Examples of the first type of conceptual re-engineering are the work by Hainaut on extracting entity relationship models from existing databases [Hai91] or work on the migration of relational data bases to object-oriented ones by Behm et al. [BGD97]. In both cases a fixed set of patterns and tight user interaction is used to extract the conceptual models. This is similar to the *lifting* step in the OBM approach where a set of matchers is used to infer matches between different models, namely the input schemas and the ontology. However, the main difference is that in the OBM approach the ontology is given and the relation between the ontology and the schemas needs to be inferred while in the work described previously, the models are created on the basis of existing artifacts. In addition, no user interaction is required in the lifting step of the OBM approach.

Similar work has been performed in the Semantic Web community. The goal of this work has been to match various different data formats such as XML schemas and instances to different Semantic Web ontology-formats. The main idea underlying this effort was to bootstrap the Semantic Web by enabling the automatic transformation of existing data. Battle [Bat04] describes an approach enabling a round tripping between XML and RDF. Based on an XML Schema a fixed set of transformations is used to create RDF for XML instance data. Other authors [BA05, FZT04] focus on the creation of OWL ontologies based on XML schemas. However, all these approaches are based on fixed transformations. In contrast to them the OBM approach does not aim at creating ad-hoc ontologies based on XML schemas. Instead the OBM approach links different existing schemas to an existing domain ontology in order to create a mapping between the schemas.

The Harmonise framework presented in [DFRW02] uses manually created mappings between XML schemas and a domain ontology to enable runtime interoperability of systems. In contrast to this the OBM approach uses the domain ontology only during design-time for mapping creation without focussing on a particular runtime architecture. The mappings generated using the OBM approach can be executed afterwards using existing integration middleware.

5.3.2 Information Capacity Considerations.

As the OBM approach relies on a central ontology containing the domain and integration knowledge some considerations regarding the required information capacity of this ontology are necessary. Miller et al. [MIR93] define the *information capacity* of a schema S as the set of possible instances $\hat{I}(S)$ of the schema. Based on this definition of information capacity they define the notion of *information capacity preserving mappings*. Given two schemas S_1 and S_2 and the set of all valid instances of these schemas $\hat{I}(S_1)$ and $\hat{I}(S_2)$ Miller et al. define that an information capacity preserving mapping between the instances of the two schemas S_1 and S_2 is a total, injective function $m : \hat{I}(S_1) \rightarrow \hat{I}(S_2)$. This means that an information capacity preserving mapping translates any instance of a schema S_1 in a valid instance of schema S_2 without losing information. As a counterexample of a information capacity preserving mapping, consider a mapping in which a particular source schema entity is not mapped to any target schema entity. Such a mapping would relate different source schema instances[5] to the same target schema instance. Consequently, this mapping would not be information capacity preserving. Furthermore, Miller et al. define that if m is an information capacity preserving mapping, then S_2 *dominates* S_1 via m which is denoted by $S_1 \preceq S_2$.

Based on these definitions Miller et al. observe that integration approaches relying on a global schema S_G need to satisfy the following property: The global schema S_G must dominate the union of the schemas $S_1, ..., S_j$ that need to be integrated, i.e. $S_1 \cup ... \cup S_j \preceq S_G$.

This statement is also true in case of the ontology-based mapping approach introduced above. In order to allow this approach to achieve results of high quality, the domain ontology used in a particular integration scenario needs to dominate the schemas in this scenario regarding their information capacity. Consequently the further discussions in this thesis assume that the ontology used as a central part of the proposed approach dominates the schemas with respect to its information capacity.

5.4 Summary

In this section the generic mapping process supported by current integration tools was described. Based on this analysis an extension of the generic process supporting the semi-automatic calculation of schema mappings was introduced. On the basis of the semi-automatic mapping process, a high-level overview of the proposed ontology-based mapping approach was given. Finally, the relevant related work in the areas schema matching and mapping as well as in the area

---

[5]Namely those instances of the source schema that only differ in the not mapped schema entity.)

of ontology matching and merging was reviewed. In the following chapters the individual steps compromising the OBM approach are described in more detail.

Chapter 6

The Role of Background Knowledge

This chapter investigates the role of background knowledge in more detail. First, Section 6.1 introduces and classifies different types of available background knowledge and investigates their relation to the different types of heterogeneities introduced in Section 3.3. Next, two novel approaches for the collection of domain knowledge are presented. The unique feature of these approaches is that they can be used as an integrated part of a mapping process. Finally, Section 6.3 presents the approach developed in this thesis for augmenting a domain ontology with additional background knowledge.

6.1 Background Knowledge

In this section different types of background knowledge are introduced. They are useful or necessary to develop the schema mapping required in complex integration scenarios like B2B integration or Data Migration. Some of the domain knowledge is closely related to solving the different types of heterogeneities presented in Chapter 3. Consequently, this section also revisits these heterogeneities and shows which types of domain knowledge are required or helpful in solving certain types of heterogeneities.

Figure 6.1 shows a high level classification of the background knowledge required for the development of schema mappings. The available background knowledge necessary to create a correct mapping in an integration project can in general be divided into two types:

- *domain knowledge*
- *integration knowledge.*

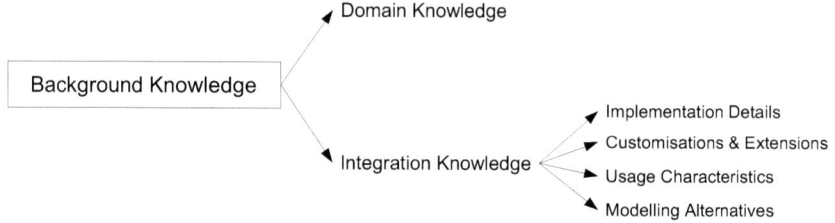

Figure 6.1: A classification of the different types of background knowledge required for the development of correct schema mappings.

While the domain knowledge consists of the relevant entities in the domain, their relations and attributes, the integration knowledge is related to details of the systems or messaging standards that need to be integrated in a given project.

6.1.1 Domain Knowledge

The first step in the creation of a mapping is the identification of matching schema entities. Identifying matching schema entities requires an understanding of the relation of the real world entities represented by certain schemas or schema entities. The domain knowledge contains exactly this type of information. As an example consider the two schemas in our running example. Figure 6.2 shows an excerpt of the two schemas together with the knowledge necessary to identify corresponding schema elements. The source schema in the running example represents a customer while the target schema represents a business partner. Without the domain knowledge that, in this particular context, a customer is a kind of business partner, it is not possible to identify that the schema element `DEBMAS` and `BusinessPartner` match. Details on how domain knowledge can be captured and exploited during the mapping process is presented in subsequent chapters.

6.1.2 Integration Knowledge

The domain knowledge only represents one part of the knowledge necessary to create schema mappings in B2B integration or data migration projects. A large part of the necessary information, namely the integration knowledge, is still missing. The necessary integration knowledge to create correct schema mappings can be divided into four groups (cf. Figure 6.1) of knowledge:

- *implementation details* of a certain system or messaging standard
- *customizations and extensions* applied to a certain system or messaging standard

6.1 Background Knowledge

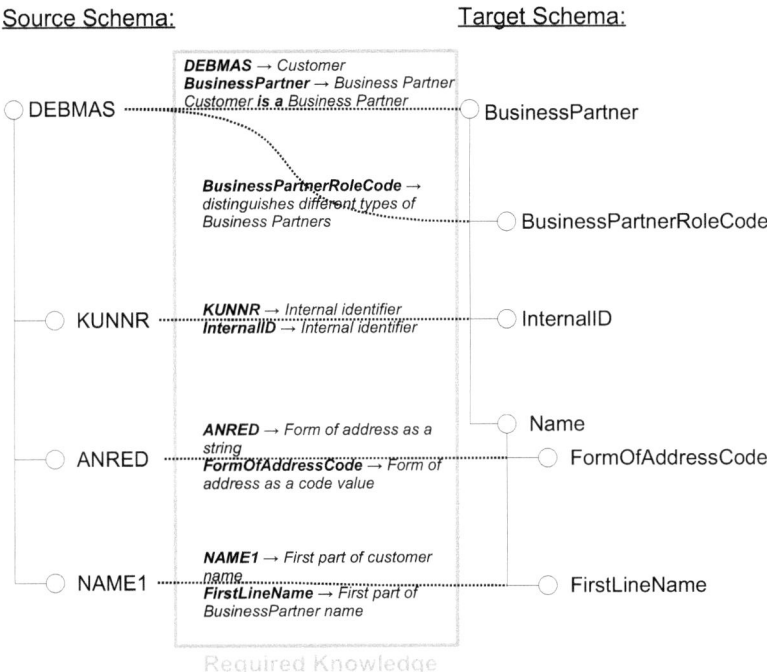

Figure 6.2: Running example including the knowledge necessary to identify matching schema elements.

- *usage characteristics* of a system or messaging standard
- common *modeling alternatives* for certain types of information.

This integration knowledge is today usually only captured in the documentation of business systems or even not captured at all. Consequently, it is not available in a machine processable format to support the semi-automatic development of schema mappings.

Note that not all types of integration knowledge presented above are suitable for being integrated into a domain ontology. Table 6.1 provides an overview of which types of knowledge are suitable for this integration. As well, the table shows in which process step the knowledge can beneficially be exploited.

Knowledge about implementation details, customizations, extensions and common modeling alternatives can be exploited beneficially during the process of creating a mapping. The knowledge regarding implementation details, customizations and extensions should be integrated into the domain ontology as this knowledge depends on the domain and the current context. In contrast

Table 6.1: Types of integration knowledge suitable for an integration into a domain ontology as well as the process step in which they are exploited.

Type of Knowledge	Integrated into Ontology	Exploited during
Implementation Details	Yes	Mapping Creation
Customizations & Extensions	Yes	Mapping Creation
Common Modeling Alternatives	No	Mapping Creation
Usage Characteristics	No	Preprocessing

to this knowledge regarding well-known modeling alternatives can be used to develop specific matching algorithms (cf. [DSDR07]). Consequently, this knowledge should not be part of the domain ontology. Knowledge regarding usage characteristics should also not be integrated into the domain ontology. Instead, this knowledge can be used to reduce the complexity of the mapping problem during the preprocessing step of the semi-automatic schema mapping process.

A detailed description of how the different types of integration knowledge can be exploited during the different steps of an automatic schema mapping approach is presented in Chapters 7 and 8. In the following subsections, the different types of integration knowledge will be discussed in more detail.

Implementation Details

Implementation details are an important part of the background knowledge necessary to create mappings in integration scenarios. Implementation details of a system are usually known to developers responsible for the development, maintenance or extensions of a system. In the context of B2B integration information similar to implementation details of systems is available in the documentation related to certain B2B messaging standards. However, usually the information regarding implementation details is not captured in a machine processable format. In addition, this information is usually not available in an integrated set of documents but rather split across several unrelated documents.

The implementation details relevant for the creation of message mappings can be divided into the four categories listed below.

- *Naming* of schema elements and applied *naming conventions*
- *Encoding scheme* used to encode certain values
- *Required* element set and possible *default values*
- *Data type* and *integrity constraints*.

In the following paragraphs each of these categories is briefly described.

6.1 Background Knowledge

Naming & Naming Conventions. Understanding the naming conventions used in a schema and which real world entities are designated using a certain name is the basic knowledge necessary to identify matching schema entities. As an example consider the ANRED element in the running example introduced in Section 3.1. Without the knowledge that in this particular case the element name ANRED is an abbreviated form of the German noun "Anrede" which can have the meaning of "form of address" in the English language, it is not possible to identify a match between the schema entities ANRED and FormOfAddressCode.

The level of detail of the knowledge required to identify related schema elements largely depends on the involved schemas. While some common B2B messaging standards like e.g. RosettaNet[1] or CIDX[2] use verbose element names which provide first hints regarding matching schema entities, others like SAP IDOC use cryptical names which makes the identification of matching entities much more complex.

Used encoding scheme. The knowledge of the used encoding scheme is necessary to create the correct mapping rule for matching elements. As an example consider again the schema elements ANRED and FormOfAddressCode. Creating a correct mapping rule requires the knowledge of how the different possible values of the ANRED element are translated to allowed values for the FormOfAddressCode element.

Depending on the system at hand, encoding of data values can either be based on standardized code lists, like e.g. the ISO standard for country codes [Inta], and standardized data formats, e.g. the ISO standard for representing date information [Intb] or depend on the implementation of the system. Furthermore, a mapping rule can only be created if an algorithm for the conversion between different encoding schemes exists.

Mandatory schema elements and default values. Large B2B messaging standards as well as database schemas usually are built up from a small set of mandatory elements and a large set of optional elements. In the running example the element BusinessPartnerRoleCode is a mandatory one. This element describes the role (i.e. supplier, customer or employee) of a business partner. The schema element specifying the role of a business partner is required for any valid instance of a business partner. In contrast to this, the elements KNURL and URI are optional. The rationale is that there might be some business partners where this kind of information is not available. Consequently, the information is not mandatory for a valid instance of a business partner.

---

[1] Details concerning the RosettaNet standard are given online at http://www.rosettanet.org.

[2] Details concerning the CIDX standard can be found online at http://www.cidx.org.

Closely related to information on mandatory and optional elements is information concerning possible default values. In some cases default values exist for mandatory elements. As an example, consider the `FormOfAddress` element in the running example. This is a mandatory element but can also be defaulted to a special value, e.g. `00` in the example. The meaning of the default value is that an unspecific form of address will be used when communicating with this business partner.

The knowledge of mandatory elements and possible default values for certain elements is essential when developing mappings between different schemas. The reason is that all mandatory elements of a target schema either need to be part of a mapping expression or need to be created and initialized with suitable default values in order to create a valid mapping.

Data type and integrity constraints. Finally, data type and integrity constraints are knowledge required to create valid schema mappings. Although these types of constraints can be specified on the schema level, concrete implementations of a certain messaging standard or system might require further restrictions. In the running example this could, for example, be true in the case of the `InternalID`. The `BusinessPartner` schema only requires this element to be of type `token`. However, in one implementation using this schema to store business partner information, a valid identification number for a business partner might consist of two upper case letters followed by four numbers while in another implementation a valid identification number might consist of 6 arbitrary characters. In order to create a valid mapping, this information regarding these underlying implementation details must be available to the user.

Customizations & Extensions

Closely related to implementation details is the knowledge concerning customizations and extensions applied to a system or messaging standard. Customizations and extensions are usually necessary to allow the usage of a system or messaging standard in a context with special requirements which are not covered by the existing versions of the system or messaging standard. As an example, consider the email address of a business partner. Using the schemas in the running example this information can not be stored. Consequently, a customization of the schema is required to enable the storing of email addresses for business partners. This customization can be performed using two approaches: either by using extension mechanisms which are provided by most currently available messaging standards and business software systems, or by misusing unused parts of a schema or system (cf. previous subsection). An example of a misuse would be storing the email address in an unused schema element, e.g. an element allowing to add free form text. While the usage of dedicated customization and extension mechanisms allows for adaptation while retaining compatibility with the standard, misusing

6.1 Background Knowledge

unused parts of a schema or systems might result in in-compatibilities between two independent implementations of the same system or messaging standard.

In both cases, a developer creating a schema mapping needs to know about performed customizations and extensions in order to be able to create a valid mapping.

Usage Characteristics

The schemas used in industrial integration projects are very large. This complexity partially originates from the fact that B2B messaging standards and standard software aims to support a large number of possible usage scenarios resulting in a large number of possibly necessary data [Stu07]. However, the complete complexity of these schemas or messaging standards is usually not exploited in a given implementation. Consequently, it is only necessary to create mapping rules for the used schema entities in a given integration project. In the context of data migration projects the legacy systems typically do not support the same complexity as the target system. Therefore, mappings are only necessary for certain parts of the schemas describing the data. Similar situations occur in the context of B2B integration. Usually only a subset of the information supported by a given B2B messaging standard is required or available in a certain integration scenario. As a result only a mapping for parts of the involved messaging standards are necessary.

Note that in the OBM approach, the information regarding usage characteristics is not exploited during the semi-automatic creation of schema mappings. Instead, it will be exploited during the preparation step of the schema mapping process in order to reduce the complexity of the schema mapping problem. Details on how this complexity reduction based on known usage characteristics is performed are presented in Section 6.2.1.

Well-known Modeling Alternatives

For some types of data a set of well-known modeling alternatives exist. As an example, consider the modeling of the street address in the running example. The **DEBMAS** schema stores the street address, consisting of the street name and the house number, as one string in the element **STRAS**. As well, the **STRAS** element uses a representation of a street address in which the house number precedes the street name. This representation is common in the USA while in Germany the street name usually preceds the house number. In contrast to this, the **BusinessPartner** schema stores the same information in two separate elements, namely the elements **StreetName** and **HouseID**. Other examples of data with well-known modeling alternatives are date and time information and telephone numbers.

Table 6.2: Different types of heterogeneities and the background knowledge required for solving them.

Heterogeneity	Background Knowledge
Schematic Heterogeneities	
Bilateral Naming	Naming of schema elements and applied naming conventions.
Bilateral Data Type	Data types used in schemas.
Bilateral Integrity	Integrity constraints related to schema elements.
Multilateral Property & Entity Correspondence	Detailed domain knowledge.
Missing Information	Usage characteristics.
Meta-level	Detailed domain and integration knowledge.
Semantic Heterogeneities	
Domain	Detailed domain knowledge
Data	Used encoding schemas, possible default values, used data types and integrity constraints.

Information regarding well known modeling alternatives for certain types of data is valuable information for the identification of matching schema entities as well as for the creation of correct mapping rules.

6.1.3 Relation of Background Knowledge and Heterogeneity Problems

It is obvious that some types of the domain knowledge introduced above are directly related to certain types of heterogeneity. An overview of how the different types of heterogeneities are related to different types of background knowledge is given in Table 6.2. The following paragraphs describe this relation in more detail.

Schematic Heterogeneities. The relation between the bilateral schematic heterogeneities and different types of background knowledge is straight forward. In order to solve bilateral naming heterogeneities knowledge regarding the naming of schema elements and the naming conventions applied in the source and the target schema are necessary. The same direct relation exists in the case of bilateral data type heterogeneities. In order to solve these heterogeneities knowledge regarding the data types used in the two schemas is required. Solving bilateral integrity heterogeneities requires knowledge about the integrity constraints related to certain elements in the source and target schema.

Solving multilateral schematic heterogeneities is more complex than solving the bilateral ones. While the knowledge about usage characteristics of the source and the target schemas is useful information for solving the missing information heterogeneities, solving multilateral schematic heterogeneities usually requires detailed domain knowledge. As an example consider again the multilateral entity heterogeneity where one system represents "Customers" and "Suppliers" as different schemas and the other system as one "BusinessPartner" schema. To solve this heterogeneity the domain knowledge that "Customers" and "Suppliers" are different types of "BusinessPartners" is required.

In order to solve meta-level heterogeneities detailed domain and integration knowledge is required. For example, in the case of data-attribute and data-entity correspondences, information regarding possible data instances and how this data can be represented as attributes or entities is required. To illustrate a data-entity correspondence, consider again a system using one "BusinessPartner" schema to represent customer and supplier information and an other one using two independent schemas. In this case the "BusinessPartner" schema contains a "BusinessPartnerRole" element that takes different values whenever an instance of the "BusinessPartner" schema represents a customer of a supplier. In order to solve this heterogeneity, knowledge about which values of the "BusinessPartnerRole" element represent a customer and which represent a supplier is required.

Semantic Heterogeneities. As presented in Section 3.2 the semantic heterogeneities can be divided into the semantic domain and the semantic data heterogeneities. Solving semantic domain heterogeneities requires detailed domain knowledge captured in the domain ontology. Integration knowledge is not helpful for solving this type of heterogeneity. In contrast to this, the integration knowledge is essential for solving the semantic data heterogeneities. The scaling and value range, the representation as well as the surjective mapping heterogeneities require knowledge regarding used encoding scheme for data values, possible default values and data type and integrity constraints. This is exactly the type of knowledge provided by the information regarding implementation details.

6.2 Collecting Domain Knowledge

Even though the different types of background knowledge introduced in the previous sections are necessary to create valid schema mappings, background knowledge is often not easily accessible. The reasons for this are manifold and mostly related to system evolution and outdated documentation. Business software usually evolves over time. New functionality is added and existing functionality is modified. As documentation needs to be updated manually, the documentation is often not up to date with the system functionality. In addition developers involved in the design of a particular system and with detailed knowledge of certain functionality of the system may no longer be available.

Figure 6.3: Alignment of the knowledge collection approaches and the semi-automatic mapping process.

Consequently, two challenges arise for semi-automatic mapping approaches trying to exploit background knowledge in a mapping process. First, the necessary domain knowledge needs to be collected and second, it has to be exploited during the mapping step. In the following subsections, two novel approaches are introduced for the collection of integration knowledge during the knowledge collection step (cf. Figure 6.3) in the semi-automatic mapping process. The approaches are:

- Collection of usage characteristics
- Example data injection.

Both approaches were first introduced in [DSDR07]. Each of them is explained in detail in the following subsections. However, before detailing the two approaches, it is important to note that they are not mutually exclusive. Instead, they focus on different aspects of background knowledge. While the approach to the collection of usage characteristics aims at identifying unused parts of schemas ,the example data injection aims at collecting information regarding implementation details, customizations and modeling alternatives.

Common to both approaches is that they do not rely on detailed user knowledge regarding implementation details, usage characteristics or customizations. Instead, the approaches aim at deducting valuable background knowledge from the knowledge necessary to use a given system. Consequently, these approaches enable to partially overcome the problems posed by a lack of detailed knowledge about the systems involved in an integration project.

6.2.1 Collection of Usage Characteristics

The goal behind the collection of usage characteristics is a complexity reduction of the mapping problem. Detailed knowledge regarding which parts of a schema are relevant in the current integration scenario reduces the complexity of the mapping problem as no mapping rules need to be created for unused schema entities. Thus the collection of usage characteristics is beneficial for both manual and semi-automatic mapping creation. While a complexity reduction of the mapping

6.2 Collecting Domain Knowledge

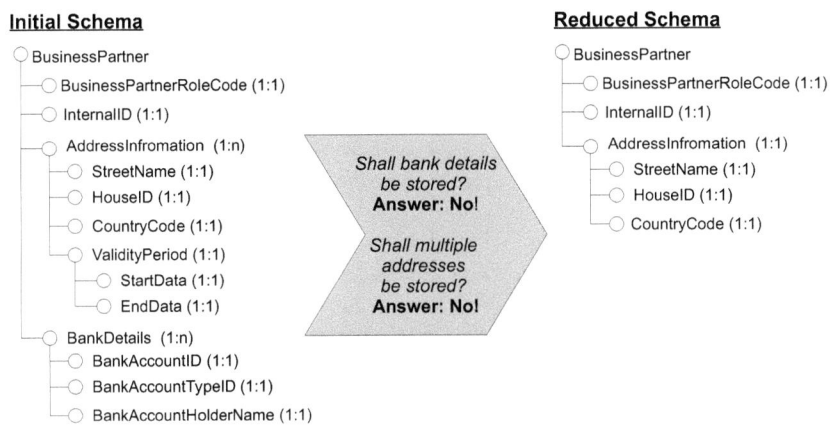

Figure 6.4: Example of a schema reduction based on usage characteristics collected using a questionnaire.

problem leads to reduced development efforts in the case of manual mapping development, the benefits are twofold in the semi-automatic case. First, the complexity reduction reduces the possibility for the suggestion of wrong mappings and consequently improves the quality of automatic approaches. Second, the effort for the manual review of the proposed mapping is also reduced.

The proposed approach to collect usage characteristics of a given schema is based on an (electronic) questionnaire. The questionnaire consists of questions that a business user of a system can answer easily. Each question in the questionnaire is related to a specific capability of a system or messaging standard. As an example, consider a system that stores customer data. This specific system is capable of storing banking information as well as multiple addresses (e.g. different billing and delivery addresses or time-dependent address information) for each customer. A questionnaire to identify usage characteristics would for example contain questions like: "Shall bank account data be stored for a customer?" or "Shall multiple addresses be stored for each customer?". Such types of questions can easily be answered by business users as they know if, e.g., bank account data needs to be stored for each customer.

Based on the answers to the questionnaire, relevant parts of the source and target schema respectively can be identified. If for example the questions used in the example above are answered with "no", the `BankDetails` sub-structure of the target schema can be removed and the `Address` sub-structure can be simplified. The complexity reduction that can already be achieved in this basic example is depicted in Figure 6.4

One important feature of this approach is that the mapping between the reduced schema and the original schema can be generated automatically. As both the original schema and the questionnaire including all possible answers, are known in advance, the schema reduction and the mappings between the original and the reduced schema resulting from certain answers to the questionnaire can be created in advance and stored together with the questionnaire. As development of the mappings is performed during the development of the questionnaire no additional matching effort arises from the schema reduction in a given integration project.

Note that a given questionnaire is only applicable to collect the usage characteristics for a specific schema or for a specific set of related schemas. Therefore, the creation of a specific questionnaire requires additional development effort. As a result, the creation of such questionnaires only makes sense if they can be reused across several integration projects. In the context of data migration scenarios, this reuse can easily be achieved. If the company developing a new business software provides questionnaires related to the schemas required in the majority of migration projects, these questionnaires can be reused in numerous migration projects. In the context of B2B integration, questionnaires will have to be developed by the creators of B2B messaging standards in order to enable the reuse across different integration projects.

6.2.2 Example Data Injection

The second approach developed to infer background knowledge from user knowledge is the injection of example data. As an example of the underlying idea consider the user of a legacy application for managing customer data. Even though this user has no idea of how customer data is stored in the underlying data base the user is still capable of creating, updating and deleting customer data using the (graphical) user interface of the system. The goal of the *Example Data Injection* approach is to use this knowledge to gain precise information of which schema entities are used to store which kind of information.

The main idea underlying the Example Data Injection is depicted in Figure 6.5. The approach consists of three steps. First, a specific example data instance is provided to a user in a human understandable format e.g. plain text. In the second step, a business user enters the provided information into the system using the well-known user interface. An instance with well known instance values is thereby created inside the legacy system. Note that creating the example instance in these legacy systems can be done quickly by business users, since entering this kind of information into the system is their day to day business. Finally, the newly created example instance is exported from the system and can later on be exploited during the semi-automatic mapping process. Note that the export of the example instance might require an expert knowing at least some technical details of the involved system. However, as the ability to access or export data from existing systems is a prerequisite to enabling integration, this requirement is no limitation of the Example Data Injection.

6.2 Collecting Domain Knowledge

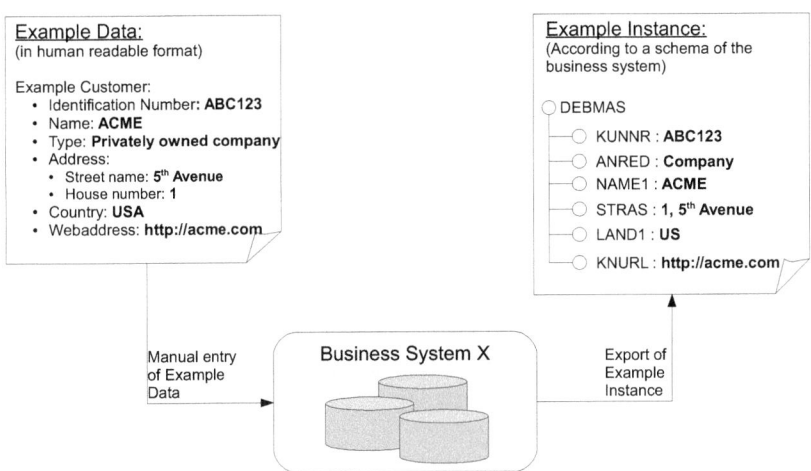

Figure 6.5: The idea of Example Data Injection. Example data is manually entered into the business system and exported using the system specific data format.

In the case of B2B integration example data needs to be injected in both, the source and the target system. In contrast to this, specific example instances aiming to support the Data Migration can already be delivered as part of a specialized integration tool (cf. Section 10.1.2). Therefore, the corresponding example data instance only needs to be created in the source system.

As the simple example in Figure 6.5 already shows, the Example Data Injection can be used to easily collect integration knowledge. While the meaning of the schema element KUNNR might not have been known before, by using the exported example instance it becomes clear that this element stores the identification number of the customer. However, the example also shows some of the problems related to the approach of Example Data Injection. Some elements of the resulting example instance might contain a concatenation of several values like in the case of the STRAS element in the figure. Furthermore, some of the instance data might be represented using a specific code value. An example for this case is the LAND1 element in the figure. It contains the code value "US" to represent the country in which the address is related. In general all the types of heterogeneities introduces in Chapter 3 can occur in the example instances resulting from the Example Data Injection approach.

Various previous schema matching approaches also make use of instance data [BM02, DLD+04, DDH01, DMDH02, HHH+05, LC00, NHT+02]. However, they mostly apply sophisticated statistical or machine learning approaches to unrelated instances available in source and target systems in order to identify matching elements. Unfortunately, similar instances, such as phone and fax numbers typically result in wrong matches, e.g. between customer and supplier phone and fax numbers as reported in [DDH01].

In contrast to these approaches the injection of example data results in one specific instance being available in the format specified by the source and the target schema. Instead of comparing unrelated instances, the matching algorithms can exploit instances based on the same data to identify related schema elements.

The evaluation of the presented approach to the collection of usage characteristics and the Example Data Injection in Chapter 10 shows that both approaches enable a significant improvement of the quality achieved by semi-automatic schema matching approaches. Furthermore, the evaluation shows that the example data should consist of unique values as this improves the accuracy of the semi-automatic schema matching approaches.

6.3 Modeling Domain and Integration Knowledge

One of the requirements of the different integration scenarios presented in Section 2 is the capturing and reuse of integration knowledge. The format in which the knowledge is captured should enable the usages of this knowledge by both, humans and machines. This sharing of knowledge is one of the feature offered by ontologies [Hep07]. Consequently, ontologies where chosen as the central component for storing integration knowledge in the OBM approach.

This section focuses on describing the approach used in this thesis for the modeling of domain and integration knowledge in order to support the requirements of the different integration scenarios. Based on a brief introduction on the conceptual modeling of a domain this section shows how additional integration knowledge can be added to the domain ontology.

6.3.1 Conceptual Modeling of the Domain

According to the definition of an ontology in [SBF98] an ontology is a formal, explicit specification of a shared conceptualization. This definition already states that one main goal of an ontology is to provide a conceptual model of a domain. In order to achieve this goal it is important that the ontology encapsulating the domain knowledge is not modeled according to the technical details of a certain system but rather according to the human understanding of the entities in a domain.

As an example of a conceptual model consider the small excerpt of an ontology depicted in Figure 6.6. This ontology models the domain of business partners, the domain the running example is located in. The ontology consists of the set of concepts Business Partner, Supplier, Customer, Address, Name and Web

6.3 Modeling Domain and Integration Knowledge

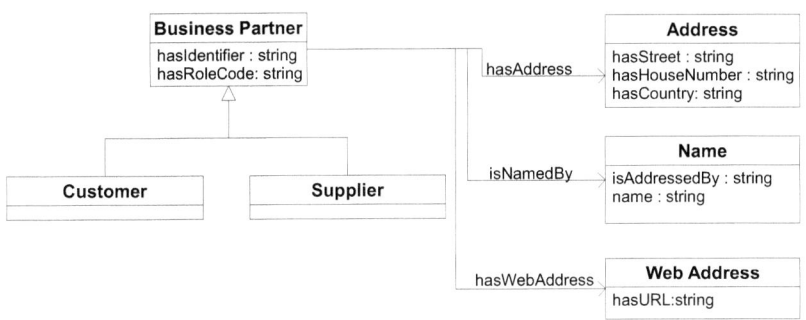

Figure 6.6: Example ontology for the domain of business partners.

Address. Supplier and Customer are sub-concepts of Business Partner. The relations hasAddress and isNamedBy link the concept Business Partner to the concepts Address and Name respectively. In addition, several attributes of the different concepts, like e.g. the hasIdentifier attribute of the concept Business Partner, are shown. The conceptualization used in this ontology conveys, for example, the information that two types of business partners exist, namely customers and suppliers, and that both share some common properties.

The difference between a conceptual model and modeling the technical details of a certain system becomes obvious when revisiting the schemas of the running example in Section 3.1. The DEBMAS schema is a very flat structure. Modeling this schema in an ontology would result in one concept with a large number of attributes. Furthermore, it would not become obvious how this schema is related to others schemas in the legacy system. Similar problems occur if the BusinessPartner schema is modeled. Even though this schema contains more structural information, modeling it as an ontology would result in a concept Business Partner with an attribute hasBusinessPartnerRole. Depending on the values of this attribute instances of the concept would represent customers or suppliers. This again is different from the conceptualization used by humans.

Even though a conceptual domain model, as captured by an ontology, already provides valuable knowledge for the creation of schema mappings, large parts of the required background knowledge, namely the integration knowledge, is still missing (cf. Section 6.1.3). The next subsection introduces an approach for modeling the missing integration knowledge.

6.3.2 Modeling Integration Knowledge

In order to allow the automatic creation of high quality schema mappings based on a central ontology as proposed by the OBM approach it is necessary to augment the domain ontology with additional integration knowledge. This section focuses on the approach developed in this thesis to augment conceptual models with integration knowledge.

The goal of the presented approach for modeling domain knowledge is to:

1. Relate *integration knowledge* to the conceptual domain model without cluttering the domain model and

2. To link the integration knowledge to a *context* in which it is valid.

The importance of these two goals is illustrated by the following example. First consider the ontology presented in Figure 6.6. One possibility to express that the concept `Business Partner` is represented by the schema element named `DEBMAS` would be the following. An additional relation named `hasTechnicalName` is added to the concept `Business Partner`. Using this relation the concept `Business Partner` is linked to some concept named `DEBMAS`. The major drawback of this approach is that it is no longer clear which attributes belong to the conceptual model and which are used to augment it with additional integration knowledge. Consequently, the model would be hard to understand for humans as integration and domain knowledge are interwoven. Furthermore, an exploitation of the integration knowledge during automatic schema mapping would also be more difficult. As a result, the goal of an approach to the modeling of integration knowledge should be to keep the integration knowledge separated from the conceptual model. Nevertheless, the integration knowledge should still be connected to the domain model in order to facilitate a usage of this knowledge by humans.

As a second example consider the `InternalID` element in our running example. Besides representing the system internal identifier of a business partner, the element name `InternalID` could also be used to represent internal identifiers of addresses or pieces of material. In order to disambiguate such cases contextual information is necessary. Examples of possible context information include the vendor, type and version of a system in which a particular implementation detail is present or the country or industry in which the system is used.

The following subsections show how the complex annotation available in the used notion of ontology (cf. Section 4.3) enable the augmentation of a conceptual domain model with additional integration knowledge while achieving the two goals described above. To illustrate the modeling of different types of integration knowledge the example ontology introduced in Figure 6.6 is used as a basis. This ontology represents the conceptual model of the running example. For each of the different types of integration knowledge a small excerpt of this ontology is used to provide an example for the modeling.

Modeling Technical Names

This section shows how the knowledge regarding technical names used in given systems can be modeled using the annotation relations. The approach is depicted

6.3 Modeling Domain and Integration Knowledge

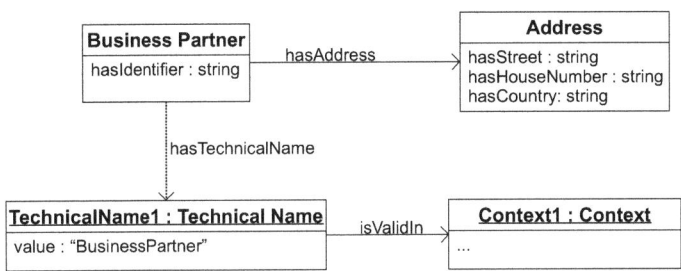

Figure 6.7: Example of the approach for the modeling of technical names.

in Figure 6.7. In order to model technical names a new concept named Technical Name and a new annotation relation named hasTechnicalName are defined in the OBM approach. The concept Technical Name consists of one attribute named value that is of type string and one relation named isValidIn that relates a technical name to the context in which it is valid. In order to associate the information regarding a particular technical name to an entity in the ontology, an instance of the concept Technical Name is created and linked to the ontology entity using the hasTechnicalName annotation relation.

In Figure 6.7 this approach is shown for the concept Business Partner in the example ontology. The instance TechnicalName1 of the concept Technical Name is linked to the concept Business Partner using the annotation relation hasTechnicalName. The value of the value attribute is "BusinessPartner", which is the technical name used in a particular system to represent business partner data. Furthermore, the validity of the TechnicalName1 is restricted to a particular context through linking it to an instance of the concept Context. Using the definition introduced in Section 4.3 this example can be represented as $O := (C, R, A, T, I, V, \alpha, \leq_C, \sigma_R, \sigma_A, \sigma_\alpha, i_C, i_R, i_a)$ with:

$C =$ {Business Partner, Address, **Technical Name, Context**}

$R =$ {hasAddress, **isValidIn**}

$A =$ {hasIdentifier, hasStreet, hasHouseNumber, hasCountry, **value**}

$T =$ {string}

$I =$ {TechnicalName1, Context1}

$V =$ {BusinessPartner}

$\alpha =$ {**hasTechnicalName**}

$\leq_C =$ {}

$\sigma_R =$ {hasAddress → (Business Partner, Address),
isValidIn → (Technical Name, Context)}

$$\sigma_A = \{\text{hasIdentifier} \to (\text{BusinessPartner}, \text{string}),$$
$$\text{value} \to (\textbf{Technical Name}, \text{string}), ...\}$$
$$\sigma_\alpha = \{\textbf{hasTechnicalName} \to (\text{Business Partner}, \text{TechnicalName1})\}$$
$$i_C = \{\textbf{Technical Name} \to \{\text{TechnicalName1}\}, \textbf{Context} \to \{Context1\}\}$$
$$i_R = \{\textbf{isValidIn} \to \{(\text{TechnicalName1}, \text{Context1})\}\}$$
$$i_A = \{\textbf{value} \to \{(\text{TechnicalName1}, \text{BusinessParter})\}, ...\}$$

In the above example the concepts, relations and attributes introduced by the OBM approach to enable the modeling of technical names are printed in bold font.

As shown in this example, annotation relations allow to link concepts, relations and attributes to instances of concepts. Thus the usage of annotation properties allows the creation of complex assertions about concepts, relation and attributes in the ontology. These complex annotation relations can be used to achieve the two goals mentioned above when augmenting a domain model with integration knowledge. Through the usage of annotation relations the differentiation between the conceptual domain model and the information knowledge is made explicit. The domain model consists of the concepts, relations and attributes while the integration knowledge is part of the annotations. Note that some additional concepts need to be created in the domain ontology to use the instances of these concepts in the complex annotations. However, these concepts can easily be separated from the domain knowledge by e.g. using a special concept as a super-concept of all of them.

Note that by using the approach introduced above, each ontology entity can be associated with an unlimited number of technical names. However, only one additional instance of the concept `Context` is needed when technical names for a previously unknown system are added. Note further that details concerning the modeling of the concept `Context` are deliberately omitted here as numerous different approaches exist for the modeling of context (cf. e.g. [WSC+07]).

Modeling Default Values

Recall from Section 6.1.2 that default values are used to provide values for mandatory schema elements if no mapping exists. Possible default values are modeled similar to the way technical names are modeled.

In order to model default values the OBM approach introduces a new concept named `Default Value` and a new annotation property named `hasDefaultValue`. Note that the attribute `value` of the concept `Default Value` is of type `string`. The generic data type `string` is used as it enables the representation of any possibly required value. An example of modeling default value information is given in Figure 6.8. It shows how the default value for the role code of a

6.3 Modeling Domain and Integration Knowledge

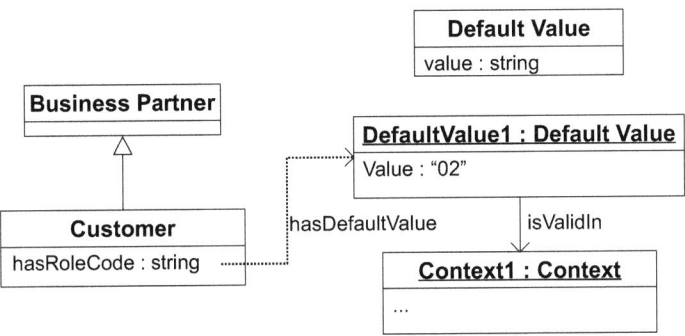

Figure 6.8: Example of the approach for the modeling of default values.

customer is modeled using the `DefaultValue1` instance as well as an instance of the concept `Context`. More formally this example can be represented as $O := (C, R, A, T, I, V, \alpha, \leq_C, \sigma_R, \sigma_A, \sigma_\alpha, i_C, i_R, i_a)$ with:

$C =$ {Business Partner, Customer, **Default Value, Context**}
$R =$ {**isValidIn**}
$A =$ {hasRoleCode, **value**}
$T =$ {string}
$I =$ {DefaultValue1, Context1}
$V =$ {02}
$\alpha =$ {**hasDefaultValue**}
$\leq_C =$ {(Business Partner, Customer)}
$\sigma_R =$ {**isValidIn** → (**Default Value, Context**)}
$\sigma_A =$ {hasRoleCode → (Customer, string),
 value → (**Default Value**, string), ...}
$\sigma_\alpha =$ {**hasDefaultValue** → (hasRoleCode, **DefaultValue1**)}
$i_C =$ {**Default Value** → {DefaultValue1}, **Context** → {Context1}, ...}
$i_R =$ {**isValidIn** → {(DefaultValue1, Context1)}}
$i_A =$ {**value** → {(DefaultValue1, 02)}, ...}

Again the concepts, relations and attributes introduced by the OBM approach for modeling default values are printed in bold font.

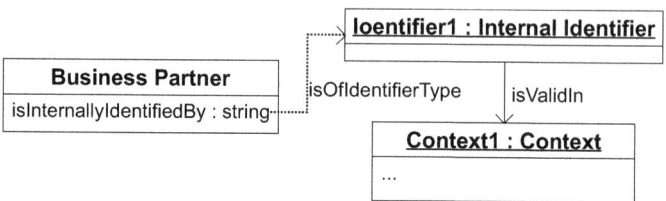

Figure 6.9: Example of the approach for the modeling of internal or global identifiers.

Internal & Global Identifiers

Information concerning internal and global identifiers is modeled similar to the previous types of knowledge. The OBM approach introduces the two concepts Internal Identifier and Global Identifier in order to model this knowledge. Using instances of these concepts which are linked using the annotation relation isOfIdentifierType and the annotation relation isOfIdentifierType respectively, the attributes representing special identifiers can be marked. An example of this approach is depicted in Figure 6.9. The formal representation of this example is omitted since it is very similar to the one presented above.

Modeling Code List Information

Information concerning code lists used to represent the data of certain elements can also be modeled similarly to the previous types of integration knowledge. However, when modeling code lists, additional information like the agency that manages the code-list and possible code-list values also need to be represented.

Figure 6.10 shows an example of how the code-list information for the hasRoleCode attribute of the concept customer in the example ontology can be modeled. Again, an instance of the concept Code List is linked to the concept Customer using the annotation property usesCodeList and the instance is linked to the context in which it is valid. In addition to that two new concepts, namely Agency and Code are introduced. The concept Agency is used to model the agency which is responsible for a certain code list, while the concept Code is used to represent mappings between code values and the information represented by a given code value. In the example a proprietary SAP code list for representing the roles of business partners is modeled together with some example code values. The example shows how the correspondence between the code values 01 and 02 and the information they represent (Supplier and Customer) is modeled using the proposed approach. This example can be represented as an ontology

6.3 Modeling Domain and Integration Knowledge

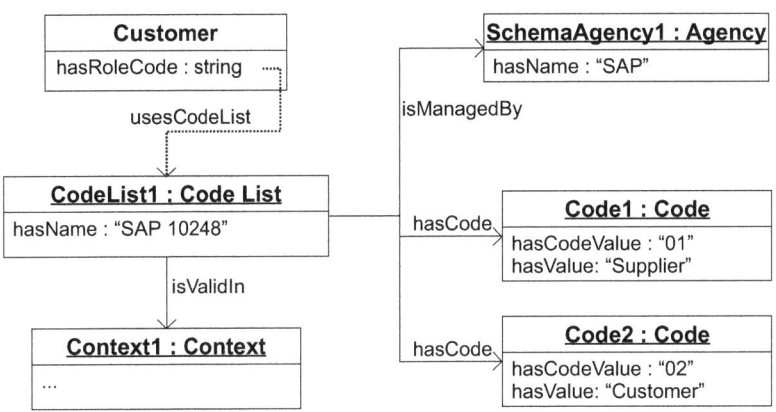

Figure 6.10: An example of adding code-list information to the domain ontology.

$O := (C, R, A, T, I, V, \alpha, \leq_C, \sigma_R, \sigma_A, \sigma_\alpha, i_C, i_R, i_a)$ with:

$C =$ {Customer, **Code List**, **Schema Agency**, **Code**, **Context**}
$R =$ {**isManagedBy**, **isValidIn**, **hasCode**}
$A =$ {hasRoleCode, **hasName**, hasCodeValue, **hasValue**}
$T =$ {string}
$I =$ {CodeList1, Context1, SchemaAgency1, Code1, Code2}
$V =$ {SAP 10248, SAP, 01, Supplier, 02, Customer}
$\alpha =$ {**usesCodeList**}
$\leq_C =$ {}
$\sigma_R =$ {**isManagedBy** → (**Code List**, **Agency**),
   isValidIn → (**Code List**, **Context**),
   hasCode → (**Code List**, **Code**)}
$\sigma_A =$ {hasRoleCode → (Customer, string),
   hasName → (**CodeList**, string), ...}
$\sigma_\alpha =$ {**usesCodeList** → (Customer, CodeList1)}
$i_C =$ {**Code List** → {CodeList1}, **Context** → {Context1},
   Agency → {SchemaAgency1}, **Code** → {Code1}, ...}
$i_R =$ {**isValidIn** → {(TechnicalName1, Context1)},
   isManagedBy → {(CodeList1, SchemaAgency1)}, ...}
$i_A =$ {**value** → {(TechnicalName1, BusinessParter)},
   hasCodeValue → {(Code1, 01)},
   hasValue → {(Code1, Supplier)}, ...}

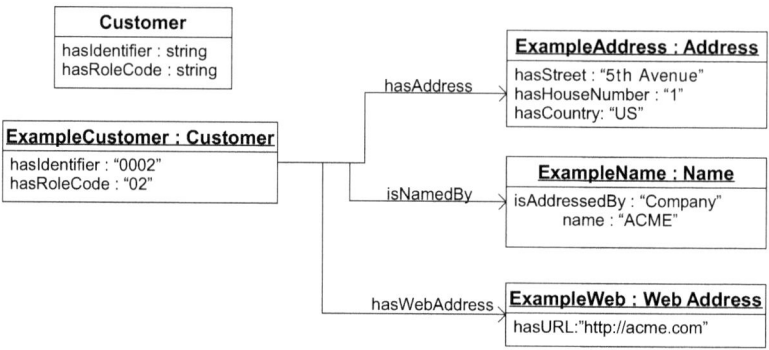

Figure 6.11: Example instances of the concept of the example ontology.

6.3.3 Modeling Example Data

In contrast to the previously described integration knowledge, example data is modeled as part of the domain ontology. The reason is that the availability of an example instance for the concepts modeled in an ontology facilitates understanding of these concepts. In contrast to the integration knowledge, which adds concepts, relations and attributes, an example instance shows possible values for the concepts, relations and attributes in the domain knowledge. This information can help a human user to understand the intended meaning of the elements of the conceptual model. Consequently, it does not need to be separated from the domain model.

In the ontology example data is represented by simply creating instances of the concepts. Figure 6.11 shows example instances for the concepts in the example ontology.

6.4 Summary

In this section the role of background knowledge for the development of schema mappings was investigated in detail. First, a classification of the available background knowledge, namely domain knowledge and integration knowledge, was presented. Next, the relation of the different types of background knowledge to the different types of heterogeneity introduces in Section 3.3 was discussed. Finally, the approach used in this thesis for augmenting an domain model with additional integration knowledge was presented.

Chapter 7

Lifting

The first and second step of the Ontology-Based Mapping (OBM) approach (cf. Figure 5.4) require the lifting of schema entities to entities of the domain ontology. First, this chapter gives an overview of the overall lifting approach. Next, different methods for calculating the similarity of schema and ontology entities (Section 7.2) as well as options for their combination (Section 7.3) are discussed. In this discussion a focus is set on how the background knowledge modeled in the domain ontology can be exploited during the lifting process.

7.1 Overview

In this section the different building blocks comprising the lifting approach are further detailed. The conceptual architecture of the lifting component together with its alignment to the overall Ontology-Based Mapping approach is depicted in Figure 7.1. The architecture is based on the general approach for composite matchers introduced in [DR02]. This architecture, which is the basis of the COMA system, introduces the idea of independently executing matching algorithms, storing their results in a similarity matrix, and aggregating these results in order to extract a mapping. This generic approach is adapted to the problem of creating a lifting from a schema to an ontology resulting in the following three steps:

1. First the input data, i.e. the set of input schemas $\{S_1, ..., S_k\}$ possibly together with corresponding example instance data and the domain ontology O are parsed into an internal representation.

2. In the second step the three-dimensional similarity matrix m_{sim} is calculated for each schema S_i in the set of input schemas using different matching algorithms. The resulting similarity matrix is of dimension $m \times n \times p$ where m is the number of schema entities in the schema $S_i \in$, n the number of

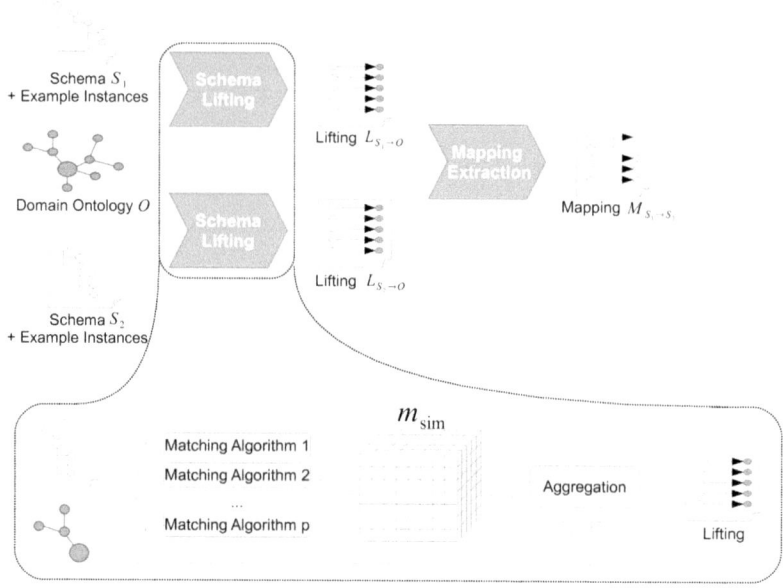

Figure 7.1: Overview of the conceptual architecture of the schema lifting component.

entities in the ontology O and p the number of different matching algorithms. After this step the similarity matrix m_{sim} contains for each pair of schema entity $s_k \in S_i$ and ontology entity $o_j \in O$ the p similarity values generated by the p different matching algorithms. A detailed description of the available matching algorithms is given in Section 7.2.

3. After the similarity matrix m_{sim} has been calculated, an aggregation algorithm is used to calculate the lifting $L_{S_i \to O}$ based on the similarity matrix m_{sim}. The aggregation algorithm again exploits the domain ontology as an additional information source. Details on how the aggregation of the similarity matrix is performed are given in Section 7.3.

The result of the proposed approach is a set of liftings $\{L_{S_1 \to O}, ..., L_{S_k \to O}\}$ from a schema S_i to the ontology O.

The composite matcher architecture was chosen for the OBM approach as in different integration scenarios different matching algorithms exploiting different schema and ontology features need to be combined to achieve high quality results. The reason is that in different integration scenarios usually different types of information are available for the automatic mapping creation. Depending on the available background knowledge (cf. Chapter 6) and the type of schema differ-

7.1 Overview

ent matching algorithms exploiting the available background knowledge and the available schema features need to be combined to automatically create the correct lifting. If, for example, no background knowledge regarding technical element names is available in the ontology, matching algorithms that exploit the similarly of schema element and ontology entity names might be used instead of algorithms that depend on the background knowledge regarding technical element names. Consequently, a composite matcher architecture was chosen for the lifting component based on the observations in the survey of Rahm and Bernstein [RB01]. Their analysis showed that *composite matchers* are the most flexible ones as they enable the flexible combination of different basic matching algorithms. While a basic matcher exploiting a certain schema feature, e.g. the schema element name, might perform well on one type of schema it might not perform well on other types of schemas. Therefore, composite matchers allow one to combine the results achieved by a set of independently executed, basic matching algorithms in order to calculate the final matching.[1]

However, even for a composite matcher it is important to select the appropriate matching algorithms for particular scenarios. While a set of different matching algorithms is presented in subsequent sections of this chapter, the evaluation in Chapter 10 provides a detailed analysis of which matchers perform well in the evaluation scenarios selected in this thesis.

Note that although the conceptual architecture of the lifting component is based on the COMA architecture introduced in [DR02] it differs significantly from the COMA architecture. The major differences between the presented architecture and the one of COMA is that the lifting component exploits the background knowledge modeled in the domain ontology during the aggregation step. In contrast to this, COMA does not exploit any background knowledge during the aggregation step. As it is shown later (cf. Section 7.3), background knowledge can be used during the aggregation step to enable more advanced aggregation strategies of similarity values in the similarity matrix m_{sim}. The goal of these advanced strategies is to eliminate wrong matches. Furthermore, the matching algorithms available in the OBM approach are specifically tailored towards exploiting the background knowledge in the ontology. In contrast to this, the matching algorithms in COMA only focus on the exploitation of schema information.

Example. Figure 7.2 shows an example for the lifting of the `BusinessParnter` schema to a small example ontology.[2] This example is used throughout the remainder of this chapter to explain the different algorithms. In Figure 7.2 the correct lifting from a schema entity to an ontology entity is represented by a

---
[1] Different approaches exist for the combination of the results of individual matching algorithms exist. See [Do06] and [Ehr06] for a discussions of different possible approaches.
[2] The schema as well as the ontology originate from the running example introduced earlier.

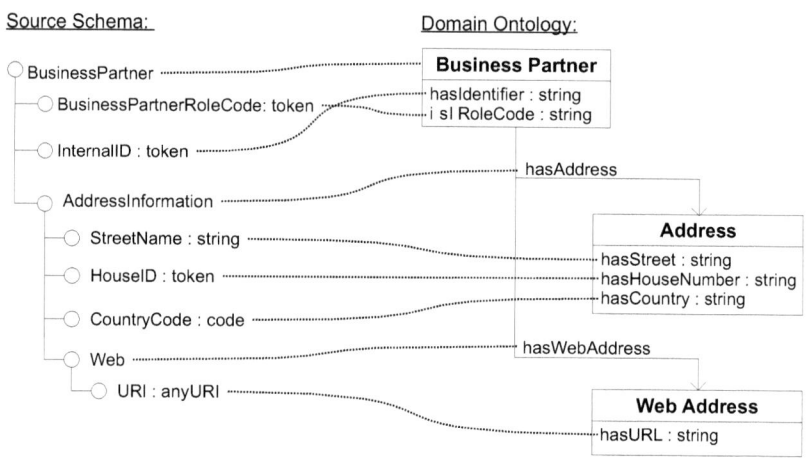

Figure 7.2: Example of a lifting from a source schema to an ontology.

dotted line. For example, the figure shows that the root element of the schema named `BusinessPartner` is lifted to the ontology concept `Business Partner`. In contrast to this the element named `BusinessPartnerRoleCode` is lifted to the attribute `hasRoleCode` and the element `Address` to the relation `hasAddress`.

This example already highlights some important features of a correct lifting. The root entity of the schema (i.e. the element named `BusinessPartner` in the example) is lifted onto a concept in the domain ontology. Other schema entities are lifted to relations and attributes that in the domain ontology are connected to the concept to which the root entity was initially lifted. Consider, for example, the schema entities `AddressInformation` or `Web`. They are lifted to the relation `hasAddress` and `hasWebAddress` respectively. The reason is that lifting a complex entity of a schema to a relation or attribute preserves some relationship information. As an example of this, consider a large B2B schema representing an order which contains numerous addresses, e.g. the shipping and the invoicing address, as complex sub-entities. If these sub-entities are lifted onto the `Address` concept of the ontology, it is impossible to distinguish between the shipping address entity and the invoicing address entity based on the lifting only. It is only possible to extract the information that each of them is an address and that they are related e.g. to the `Order` concept, but the information about which one is the shipping and which is the invoicing address is lost. If in contrast to that the schema entity representing the shipping address is lifted to a relation named `hasShippingAddress` and the entity representing the invoicing address to a relation named `hasInvoicingAddress`, the two can be differentiated. As a consequence of this observation the lifting approach needs to be able to lift schema entities to concepts, relations and attributes in order to capture this additional information.

7.2 Matching Algorithms

In this section the different methods available in the OBM approach for computing the similarity of schema and ontology entities are presented. First the available schema and ontology features for calculating the similarity of entities are discussed. Then the basic similarity metrics for calculating the similarity of strings, trees and sets of elements are presented. Based on these basic similarity metrics more advanced algorithms including algorithms especially tailored towards the exploitation of domain and integration knowledge modeled in the domain ontology are developed.

7.2.1 Exploitable Schema and Ontology Features

Before developing a set of similarity metrics for the lifting of schema entities to ontologies in the subsequent sections, this subsection identifies the different features available in schemas and ontologies that can be exploited during lifting. The analysis of the different available features is used to develop suitable similarity metrics exploiting these features.

Exploitable Schema Features

Table 7.1 provides an overview of the different schema features that can be exploited during lifting. These features are organized into four categories, namely *linguistic* features, *structural* features, features based on *constraints* and features based on *instance* data. In the following paragraphs each of these features is briefly introduced.

Entity Name. The entity name belongs to the category of linguistic features. It is an elementary feature exploited by most existing schema matching approaches (cf. the surveys in [RB01] and [ES07]). However, it is important to note that not the names of all schema entities can be exploited during lifting. Some schema languages, for example, provide constructs to create reusable building blocks. Depending on the schema language the names of these reusable building blocks might not be exploitable. As an example consider XML Schema. In this case only the name of the terminal symbols, i.e. the elements in the set T, are useful during lifting. In contrast to this, the non-terminal symbols in the set N are building blocks used together with the production rules in π to define the structure of the schema. Consequently, the non-terminal symbols N are not useful during lifting.

Table 7.1: The list of exploitable schema features together with a short explanation of each feature.

No.	Feature	Description
		Linguistic Features
1	Entity Name	The name of a schema entity.
2	Entity Documentation	The optional annotation containing a short documentation of the entity.
		Structural Features
3	Entity Path	The path to the current entity starting from the root.
4	Children	The children of a schema entity.
5	Parents	The parents of a schema entity.
6	Siblings	The siblings of a schema entity.
		Constraint-based Features
7	Data Type	The data type associated with a schema entity.
8	Cardinality	The optional cardinality constraints for a schema entity.
		Instance-based Features
9	Example Instance	A optional example instance provided for the schema.

Entity Documentation. The entity documentation is also a linguistic feature. Some schema languages offer the possibility to add optional short free text annotations to the schema entities. Especially when the schema entities use cryptic names this short documentation text can contain additional information that can beneficially be exploited during lifting. In contrast to the entity name the entity documentation is expressed in whole sentences or fragments of them. Consequently, simple string metrics are not suitable for exploiting this feature.

Entity Path. The path to the current entity belongs to the category of structural features. The path of an entity unambiguously identifies its location in a large schema. As an example, consider the schema entity `InternalID` in the running example introduced. The path that identifies this entity is `/BusinessPartner/InternalID`.[3] This feature is especially important in the case of large schemas where similar basic buildings blocks, e.g. an address, occur frequently in different positions of the same schema.

---

[3]This notation of the path of a schema element is based on the XPath [Wor99a] specification. The XPath notation is used in the remainder of this thesis to represent schema entity paths.

7.2 Matching Algorithms

Children, Parents & Siblings. Like the entity path these features belong to the category of structural features. The children, parents or siblings of a schema entity contain additional structural information that can be exploited during lifting. As an example of how the information regarding children of an entity can be exploited, consider the URI element in the running example. This entity is a leaf in the schema (i.e. it has no children entities). Consequently, a lifting to an attribute of a concept (e.g. the attribute hasURL in the example) should be preferred over a lifting to a concept or a relation. Of course these type of features are only available in hierarchically structured schema languages like e.g. XML Schema.

Data Type & Cardinality Constraints. The feature category of constraints consists of the data type and cardinality constraint information related to schema entities. While these features alone are not sufficient to calculate a lifting (cf. the schemas in the running example) they can provide valuable additional information.

Example Instance. In contrast to the previous features, example instances are not a pure schema feature. Instead, an example instance of a schema is used as additional information during lifting. For a discussion of how example data can be collected in Data Migration and B2B integration projects and how example data is related to the generic semi-automatic mapping process see Section 6.2.2.

Exploitable Ontology Features

Following the description of the schema features in the previous section this section focuses on the ontology features exploitable during schema lifting. Table 7.2 provides an overview of these ontology features. Ontologies also contain *linguistic*, *structural* and *constraint-based* features. In addition *integration-knowledge-based* features are included in the ontology as annotations (cf. Section 6.3.2) or, in the case of the example instance feature, as instances of concepts. As well, it is important to notice that not every type of integration knowledge listed in Table 7.2 is exploited in the lifting step of the OBM approach. Instead, some of the integration knowledge is only used to create the correct mapping between two schemas in the mapping extraction step. For a detailed description of the mapping extraction see Chapter 8. Nevertheless these features are listed in table 7.2 as they are exploitable features of the domain ontology. In the following paragraphs each ontology feature is briefly described.

Entity Name & Documentation. The entity name and optional entity documentation are the two linguistic ontology features that can be exploited. Similar to the schema case only the names of a subset of the entities will be used. The

Table 7.2: The list of exploitable ontology features.

No.	Feature	Description
	Linguistic Features	
1	Entity Name	The name of an ontology entity $e_i \in C \cup R \cup A$
2	Entity Documentation	An optional short text annotation containing a short textual description of the ontology entity $e_i \in C \cup R \cup A$.
	Structural Features	
3	Entity Hierarchy	The hierarchy information related to the concepts in the ontology, represented by leq_C.
4	Relations	The relations of a concept to other concepts, represented by R and σ_R
5	Attributes	The attributes of a concept entity in the ontology, represented by A and σ_A.
	Constraint-based Features	
6	Data Type	The data type associated with an attribute in the ontology, i.e. $sigma_A$.
	Integration-Knowledge-based Features	
7	Technical Names	The technical name annotation of an ontology entity (cf. Chapter 6).
8	Default Values	The annotation regarding possible default values for certain ontology entities (cf. Chapter 6).
9	Identifiers	The annotation regarding which entities in the ontology possibly represent internal or global identifiers (cf. Chapter 6).
10	Code Lists	Possible code lists used for a certain ontology attribute (cf. Chapter 6).
11	Example Instance Data	An example instance of the concepts, relations and attributes in the ontology (cf. Chapter 6).

entity names that will be exploited are the concept names, the relation names and the attribute names (i.e. the names of the entities e_i in the set $C \cup R \cup A$).[4] It is important to note that the entity documentation differs from the complex annotations introduced in Section 6.3.2. While these complex annotations are used to model integration knowledge simple short text annotations are often used in ontologies to provide a textual description of a certain concept, relation or attribute.

Entity Hierarchy. The entity hierarchy is one of the structural features in an ontology. Since concepts in an ontology are aligned in a hierarchy $<_C$, this information can be exploited during the lifting. As an example, consider the lifting example in Figure 7.2. In this ontology the concept Customer is a subconcept of the concept Business Partner. If a customer schema is now lifted, the knowledge that a Customer is also a Business Partner allows to also exploit the relations and attributes of the super-concept Business Partner during the lifting.

Relations & Attributes. The relations $r_i \in R$ are another type of structural information available in the ontology. The relations contain the information how different concepts in the ontology are related (represented by the signature of R, i.e. σ_R). In the example above, the relations hasAddress connects the concept Business Partner and Address. As the example shows, this feature also needs to be exploited in order to lift a schema otherwise a lifting of some sub-elements of the BusinessPartner schema would not be possible. The same is true for the attributes $a_i \in A$ in an ontology.

Furthermore, it is important to note that the entity hierarchy as well as the relation and attributes in the ontology have no directly corresponding schema features.

Data Type. Each attribute in the ontology is associated with a data type specifying the allowed data values for this attribute (represented by σ_a). In the lifting example, the data type of all attributes is string allowing any type of character string as a value for the attributes. The data types available for restricting the value range of attributes in the ontology depends on the ontology language. In the following discussions the data types supported by XML Schema [Wor04b] are also used in the ontology.

Technical Names. The first of the features belonging to the category of integration knowledge are the technical names. Section 6.3.2 describes how this type of knowledge is modeled in the ontology. The background knowledge regarding

---

[4]See Section 4.3 for the definition of these sets.

technical names is especially useful to lift schemas that use cryptical names for schema elements.

A detailed description how different types of integration knowledge are modeled in the ontology is given in Chapter 6.

Default Values & Identifiers. The integration knowledge regarding possible default values, internal and global identifiers is in the OBM approach only exploited during the mapping creation step. For details on how these features can be exploited see Chapter 8.

Code Lists. The integration knowledge regarding code lists relates ontology entities to the code lists used to represent certain information in a schema. This feature can be exploited together with example data in order to identify matchers between schema entities and certain entities in the ontology.

Example Instance Data. As in the case of the schema features example instances of the concepts in the ontology can be used as additional information during lifting. In contrast to the example schema instances that are created using the example data injection approach the example data in the ontology is not created manually in each integration project. Instead the example instance in the domain ontology only needs to be created once and can then be reused in numerous integration projects.

7.2.2 Similarity Metrics

In this subsection different basic similarity metrics are introduced. The similarity metrics presented were selected from the large number of existing similarity metrics (cf. e.g. [ES07]) because the matching algorithms available in the OBM approach are based on these metrics. The reasons for the usage of a particular similarity metric for the implementation of a certain matching algorithm is described together with the matching algorithms available Section 7.2.3.

Before investigating the different similarity metrics in more detail, it is important to first define the notion of a similarity metric that is used as a basis in the following discussion.

Definition 7.2.1 (Similarity Metric). *A similarity metric* sim *over a set A is a function*

$$sim : A \times A \to [0,1]$$

7.2 Matching Algorithms

that maps pairs of elements in a set A to a real number in the interval $[0,1]$ such that

$$\forall e, f \in A : \quad sim(e, f) \geq 0 \quad \text{(non-negative)}$$
$$\forall e, f \in A : \quad sim(e, f) = sim(f, e) \quad \text{(symmetric)}$$
$$\forall e, f, g \in A : \quad sim(e, g) \leq sim(e, f) + sim(f, g) \quad \text{(triangle inequality)}.$$

Furthermore, the similarity of identical elements in the set A is defined to be 1

$$\forall e \in A : \quad sim(e, e) = 1.$$

Using the generic definition of a similarity metric given above as a basis, different specific similarity metrics can now be introduced.

Equality

The simplest similarity metric that can be defined is the *equality similarity metric* which is based on the equality relation.

Definition 7.2.2 (Equality Similarity.). *The equality similarity metric is defined for any two objects $e, f \in A$ as*

$$sim_{equal}(e, f) := \begin{cases} 1 & : \text{ if } e = f \\ 0 & : \text{ otherwise} \end{cases}$$

It is obvious that the definition of the equality similarity metric satisfies the requirements of a similarity metric given above. To illustrate the equality similarity metric consider the two strings **Business Partner** and **BusinessPartner** from the lifting example. The similarity of these strings based on the equality similarity metric is $sim_{equal}(\text{BusinessPartner}, \text{Business Partner}) = 0$.

Lexical Similarity

In contrast to the equality metric that can be used to compare objects of any kind, the *lexical similarity metric* is a similarity metric for strings. It is based on the *Levenshtein distance* or *edit distance* originally proposed by Levenshtein in [Lev66]. The Levenshtein distance $ld(s_1, s_2)$ of two strings s_1 and s_2 is given by the minimal number of insertion, deletion or substitution operations necessary to transform s_1 into s_2. For calculating the Levenshtein distance each string operation is weighted equally. Staab and Maedche [MS02] propose the *lexical similarity metric* which is a normalized variant of the Levenshtein distance $ld(s_1, s_2)$ of two strings s_1 and s_2.

Definition 7.2.3 (Lexical Similarity.). *The lexical similarity metric for two strings is defined as*

$$sim_{lexical}(s_1, s_2) := max\left(0, \frac{min(|s_1|, |s_2|) - ld(s_1, s_2)}{min(|s_1|, |s_2|)}\right).$$

In the definition above $|s_i|$ denotes the length of a string s_i. To illustrate the lexical similarity metric consider the two strings `StreetName` and `hasStreet` from the lifting example presented above. The similarity of these strings based on the lexical similarity metric is $sim_{lexical}(\text{StreetName}, \text{hasStreet}) = max\left(0, \frac{9-7}{9}\right) \approx 0.22$.

Soft-TF-IDF

Like the lexical similarity metric the *Soft-TF-IDF* similarity metric is a metric for calculating the similarity of strings. It was developed by Cohen et al. [CRF03]. To calculate the $sim_{softtfidf}$, the input strings are first tokenized into two sets of tokens T_1 and T_2. In the next step the term frequency TF and the inverse document frequency IDF for each token in the two sets of tokens is calculated. The term frequency measures the occurrence of a certain term in a document whereas the inverse document frequency measures the importance of a term over a set of documents.

Definition 7.2.4 (Soft-TF-IDF Similarity.). *On the basis of TF and IDF the Soft-TF-IDF similarity metric $sim_{softtfidf}(s_1, s_2)$ is defined as:*

$$sim_{softtfidf}(s_1, s_2) := \sum_{\omega \in close(\theta, T_1, T_2)} V(\omega, T_1) \cdot V(\omega, T_2) \cdot D(\omega, T_2)$$

with:

$$V(\omega, T) := \frac{V'(\omega, T)}{\sqrt{\sum_{\omega'} V'(\omega', T)^2}}$$
$$V'(\omega, T) := log(TF_{\omega, T} + 1) log(IDF_\omega)$$
$$D(\omega, T) := max_{\nu \in T} (sim(\omega, \nu))$$

In the definition above $V(\omega, T)$ is the normalized TF-IDF weight of a token ω in a set of tokens T and $D(\omega, T)$ the maximal similarity $sim(\omega, \nu)$ of a token ω to all terms in a set T. The $sim(\omega, \nu)$ is calculated using a basic similarity metric for strings as e.g. the Lexical Similarity. As well, $close(\theta, T_1, T_2)$ is defined as the set of tokens where $\omega \in T_1$, $\nu \in T_2$ and $sim(\omega, \nu) \geq \theta$.

Note that the Soft-TF-IDF similarity of two strings can vary depending on the set of documents used to calculate the term frequency and the inverse document frequency. In order to apply the Soft-TF-IDF similarity to calculate similarities of schema and ontology entities, the set of all tokens of all schema entities names can, for example, be used as a basis to calculate the term frequency and the inverse document frequency of a token.

In order to illustrate the Soft-TF-IDF similarity the two strings `StreetName` and `hasStreet` from the lifting example are used. The first string consists of the

7.2 Matching Algorithms

tokens $T_1 = \{\text{street}, \text{name}\}$, the second one of the tokens $T_2 = \{\text{has}, \text{street}\}$. The term frequency and the inverse document frequency of these tokens are calculated using the set of tokens in the example ontology. The term frequencies for the different tokens in are: $has = 8$, $address = 4$, $web = 2$, $street = 1$, $number = 1$, $code = 1$, $country = 1$, $business = 1$, $role = 1$, $house = 1$, $partner = 1$, $URL = 1$, $identifier = 1$.

On the basis of these term frequencies the normalized TF-IDF weight $V(\omega, T)$ of the tokens in the example strings are:

$$V(\text{street}, T_1) = \frac{1,662}{2,350} \approx 0,707$$

$$V(\text{name}, T_1) = \frac{1,662}{2,350} \approx 0,707$$

$$V(\text{has}, T_2) = \frac{0,221}{1,677} \approx 0,131$$

$$V(\text{street}, T_2) = \frac{1,662}{1,677} \approx 0,991$$

Using the Lexical Similarity and a threshold $\theta = 0.6$ the set $close(\theta, T_1, T_2) = \{\text{street}\}$. Consequently, the Soft-TF-IDF similarity of the two strings StreetName and hasStreet is calculated as:

$$\begin{aligned} sim_{softtfidf}(\text{StreetName}, \text{hasStreet}) &= V(\text{street}, T_1) \cdot V(\text{street}, T_2) \cdot D(\text{street}, T_2) \\ &= 0,707 \cdot 0,991 \cdot 1 \\ &\approx 0,7 \end{aligned}$$

Dice Coefficient

In contrast to the previous two similarity metrics the *dice coefficient* is a similarity metric for calculating the similarity of sets. For two sets X and Y the dice coefficient is defined as

$$sim_{dice}(X, Y) := 2 \frac{|X \cap Y|}{|X| + |Y|}.$$

Relying on the definition of the dice coefficient different string distance metrics can be defined. These string distance metrics are based on the comparison of sets of N-Grams. As an example, consider the trigram (3-Gram) similarity metric. It is defined as

$$sim_{trigram}(s_1, s_2) := 2 \frac{n_{s_1 \cap s_2}}{n_{s_1} + n_{s_2}}$$

where $n_{s_1 \cap s_2}$ is the number of trigrams that occur in both strings and n_{s_1} and n_{s_2} the number of trigrams in the strings s_1 and s_2 respectively.

Again the strings `StreetName` and `hasStreet` will be used as an examples. The sets of trigrams that can be generated from the two strings are $\{str, tre, ree, eet, etn, tna, nam, ame\}$ and $\{has, ass, sst, str, tre, ree, eet\}$. Consequently, the similarity of the two strings using the trigram similarity metric is $sim_{trigram} = \frac{2 \cdot 4}{8+7} \approx 0.53$.

7.2.3 Matching Algorithm Details

Based on the basic similarity metrics introduced in the previous subsection different matching algorithms are developed in this section. These matching algorithms are used in the OBM approach to calculate the similarity of schema entities and ontology entities in the first step of the lifting (cf. Figure 7.1) resulting in the similarity matrix m_{sim}. The developed matching algorithms range from simple, string-similarity-based algorithms to more advanced ones exploiting integration knowledge.

String-Similarity-Based Algorithms

The first set of matching algorithms that are introduced are based on string similarity metrics. Using the string similarity metrics different features of the source schema and the domain ontology are compared in order to calculate the similarity of entities.

It is obvious from the discussion of the running example in Chapter 3 that matching algorithms exploiting only schema entity names are not suitable for use cases addressed in this thesis. Consequently, only one simple matching algorithm, the Name Matcher, is based solely on the comparison of schema and ontology entity names. This matcher was included to allow a comparison of the more advanced matching algorithms with a simple one commonly available in schema and ontology matching approaches (cf. [ES07]). The Documentation Matcher was included in the OBM approach to verify if the short documentation of schema entities can beneficially be exploited.

Name Matcher. The *Name Matcher* uses the lexical similarity metric, to calculate the similarity of schema and ontology entities. The schema as well as the ontology feature used for the similarity computation is the entity name. Using XML Schema as an example the Name Matcher implements the following similarity metric:

$$\forall e \in S, \forall o \in C \cup R \cup A \quad :$$
$$sim_{name}(e, o) := sim_{lexical}(name(e), name(o))$$

7.2 Matching Algorithms

where $name(e)$ is a function returning the name of a schema or ontology entity respectively.[5]

Documentation Matcher. In contrast to the Name Matcher, the *Documentation Matcher* uses the short documentation of entities optionally available in some schema languages as the schema feature. Documentation matchers are also quite common in existing schema matching approaches. Depending on the configuration this feature is either matched against the documentation of an ontology entity or its name. The similarity metric applied in this matcher is the Soft-TF-IDF metric. the Soft-TF-IDF metric was chosen for the implementation of the Documentation Matcher as this similarity metric has achieved promising results in the comparison of short texts [CRF03]. The similarity metric implemented by the Documentation Matcher is:

$$\forall e \in S, \forall o \in C \cup R \cup A :$$
$$sim_{documentation}(e, o) := sim_{Soft-TF-IDF}(doc(e), (doc(o)))$$

Additionally, *doc* is defined as a function returning the optional documentation of an entity.

Structural Algorithms

The next two matching algorithms that are introduced exploit structural information. Both use different strategies to exploit the structural information. While *Node-Path Matcher* compares path information, the *Related Entities Matcher* computes the similarity of elements based on the similarity of their children.

Node-Path Matcher. The node-path matcher uses the node-path of an entity in a schema or an ontology to calculate the similarity of entities, an approach commonly used in different schema and ontology matching approaches. In a schema the node-path to an entity is simply defined as the concatenation of all names of a node's parent entities. In the running example the node-path of the CountryCode entity is /BusinessPartner/AddressInformation/CountryCode. In the ontology the node-path is defined as the path from the given entity in the ontology to the one to which the root entity of the schema is mapped. Consequently, the node path of the attribute hasCountry in the running example is /Business Partner/hasAddress/Address/hasCountryCode.

The similarity of the node-paths of a schema and an ontology entity is calculated using any of the string based mapping algorithms presented above. The string based mapping algorithm used to calculate the similarity of node-paths is

---

[5] Note that the Name Matcher, as well as all other matching algorithms described in subsequent sections, is executed for each schema element $e_i \in S$ in the source schema and each ontology entity $o_j \in C \cup R \cup A$ of the domain ontology (cf. Section 7.1).

in the following referred to as a *constituent matcher*. According to the classification presented by Rahm and Bernstein in [RB01] the node-path matcher is a hybrid matcher. The similarity metric implemented by the node-path matcher is:

$$\forall e \in S, \forall o \in C \cup R \cup A :$$
$$sim_{node-path}(e, o) := sim_{con}(nodePath(e), nodePath(o))$$

where $nodePath(e)$ is a function retuning the node-path of a schema or an ontology entity and sim_{con} is the similarity metric implemented by the constituent matcher. If the node-path matcher, for example, uses the lexical similarity metric as the constituent matcher, $sim_{con}(nodePath(e), nodePath(o)) := sim_{lexical}(nodePath(e), nodePath(o))$.

Related Entities Matcher. The related entities matcher is also a hybrid matching algorithm that calculates the similarity of two entities based on the similarity of their children. Therefore, it first calculates the similarities of leaf entities in the schema tree and ontology entities. This is done using a constituent matcher. The constituent matcher can again be any of the other matching algorithms. After that the similarity of non-leaf entities in the schema and ontology entities is calculated. Since each non-leaf schema entity has a set of children as well as each non-leaf ontology entity has a set of related ontology entities, the similarity of these entities is calculated using an extension of the dice coefficient. Consequently, the related entities matcher implements the following similarity metric:

$$\forall e \in S, \forall o \in C \cup R \cup A :$$
$$sim_{related}(e, o) := \begin{cases} sim_{con}(e, o) & \text{iff } e \text{ is a leaf} \\ 2\frac{matching(\theta, e, o)}{|c(e)| + |c(o)|} & \text{otherwise} \end{cases}$$

In the previous formula $sim_{con}(e_1, o)$ is the similarity of two entities as derived by the constituent matcher. Furthermore, $c(e)$ is defined as the set of direct children of a schema entity e, $c(o)$ as the set of directly related ontology entities (i.e. relations and attributes) of an ontology entity o and the function $matching(\theta, e_1, e_2)$ as the number of entities with a similarity above a certain threshold $(sim_{related}(e_1, e_2) \geq \theta)$.[6] The Related Entities Matcher is an extension of the Children Matcher introduced in COMA++ [DR02].

---

[6] The relation between the dice coefficient and the equation $2\frac{matching(\theta, e, o)}{|c(e)| + |c(o)|}$ becomes obvious if $matching(\theta, e, o)$ is interpreted as $|X \cap Y|$, $c(e)$ as $|X|$ and $c(o)$ as $|Y|$.

Integration-Knowledge-Based Algorithms

After the introduction of matching algorithms capable of exploiting the linguistic and structural features of schemas and ontologies this subsection now focuses on matchers exploiting the background knowledge modeled in the domain ontology. Three novel matchers, namely i) the *Technical Names Matcher*, ii) the *Instance Equality Matcher*, and iii) the *Instance Split/Concat Matcher* are introduced. These matchers are specially tailored towards exploiting the background knowledge modeled according to the approach presented in Section 6.

Technical Names Matcher. The *Technical Names Matcher* exploits the integration knowledge regarding technical names (cf. Section 6.3.2) that is modeled in the domain ontology to calculate the similarity of schema and ontology entities. Depending on the configuration the Technical Names Matcher either uses the equality similarity metric or the lexical similarity metric to calculate the similarity of a schema element and an ontology entity. Consequently, the similarity returned by the technical names matcher is either

$$\forall e \in S, \forall o \in C \cup R \cup A :$$
$$sim_{tech-name}(e, o) := sim_{equal}(e, techName(o))$$

where $techName(o)$ is a function returning the possible technical name for a given ontology entity $o \in C \cup R \cup A$, or

$$sim_{tech-name}(e, o) := sim_{lexical}(e, techName(o)).$$

Note that in the description of $sim_{tech-name}$ the notion of context in which a technical name is valid was omitted for readability reasons.

The Technical Names Matcher allows for two configurations due to the different usage of the integration knowledge regarding technical names. If the matcher is used in a context for which integration knowledge is available in the domain ontology it is assumed that this integration knowledge is correct. Consequently, the equality similarity metric is used as a basis for the Technical Names Matcher. As an example for that assumption consider the `HouseID` element in Figure 7.2. If the background knowledge contains the information that the `hasHouseNumber` attribute of the ontology is in this particular context represented by the technical name `HouseID`, this information is trusted. If an element in the schema is named differently, it is not a possible match according to the Technical Names Matcher. However, the Technical Names Matcher can also be used in situations where integration knowledge is reused to, for example, create a mapping for a new version of a schema or to create a mapping for similar schemas. In this situation the lexical similarity measure is used as basis for the Technical Names Matcher.

Instance Equality Matcher. The *Instance Equality Matcher* exploits the example instances available for the schema and the ontology to calculate a lifting. It is based on the equality metric. Using the equality similarity metric the instance equality matcher compares an example instance provided for a schema with the example instance modeled in the ontology. Consequently, the matcher implements the following similarity metric:

$$\forall e \in S, \forall o \in C \cup R \cup A:$$
$$sim_{inst-equal}(e, o) := sim_{equal}(inst(e), inst(o))$$

where $inst(o)$ and $inst(e)$ are functions that return the example instance for a given ontology entity o or a schema element e respectively.

Instance Split/Concat Matcher. The *Instance Split/Concat Matcher* also exploits available example data. Compared to the instance equality matcher it checks example instance data for splitting or concatenation relationships. The similarity calculated by this matcher is

$$sim_{inst-split-concat}(e, o) := \begin{cases} 1: & \text{iff } substring(inst(e), inst(o))) = 1 \\ 0: & \text{otherwise} \end{cases}$$

where $substring(x, y)$ is a function that returns 1 if either x is a substring of y or vice versa.

Note that the Instance Split/Concat Matcher only checks if the example instance of a schema element is a substring of the example instance of an ontology entity and vice versa. The Instance Split/Concat Matcher does not identify how example instances need to split or concatenated (i.e. the mapping expression). The mapping expression is identified in the mapping extraction step which is described in Chapter 8.

The Instance Equality Matcher as well as the Instance Split/Concat Matcher where first introduced in the QuickMig system [DSDR07].

7.3 Aggregation

The third step in the proposed lifting approach is the aggregation of the results of the individual matching algorithms in order to create the final lifting. The aggregation of the results of the individual matching algorithms is performed in two steps as depicted in Figure 7.3. First the individual similarity scores of each matcher are combined into one overall similarity score during the *similarity matrix aggregation* step. The result of this aggregation is the two-dimensional similarity matrix m'_{sim}. After that the resulting similarity matrix m'_{sim} is used

7.3 Aggregation

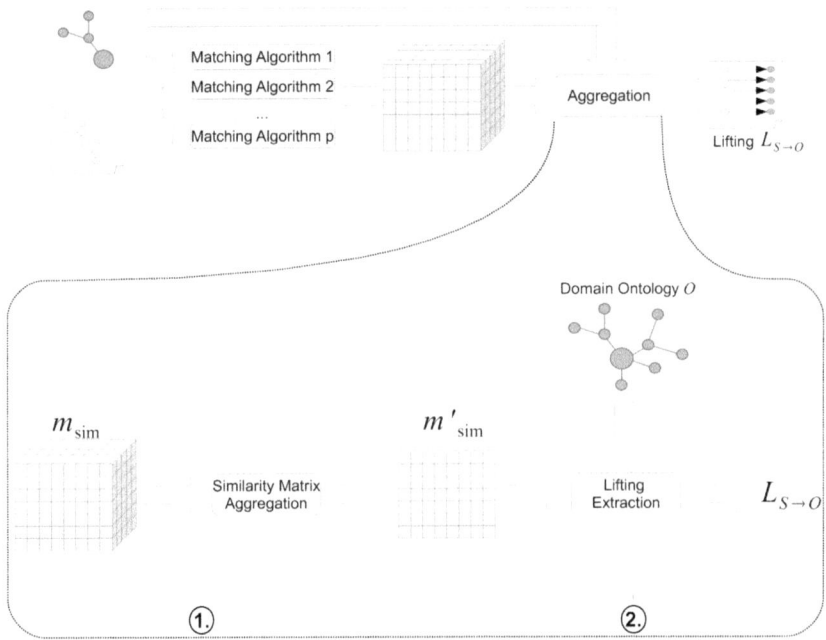

Figure 7.3: The aggregation of the matcher results.

in the *lifting extraction* step together with the domain ontology to calculate the resulting lifting.

In the following subsections each of the two steps of the similarity aggregation is described in more detail.

7.3.1 Similarity Matrix Aggregation

The similarity matrix aggregation is a step necessary in all schema matching approaches based on the execution of individual matching algorithms. Both Do [Do06] and Ehrig [Ehr06] suggested different possible aggregation approaches including a pessimistic aggregation using the minimum of all similarity values, an optimistic aggregation using the maximum similarity value and also the calculation of a weighted average similarity. According to the presentation in [Ehr06] a weighted average similarity is calculated as follows:

$$sim_{i,j} = \frac{\sum_p w_p \cdot adj\left(sim_{i,j,p}\right)}{\sum_p w_p}$$

In the above formula p is the number of matching algorithms executed to calculate m_{sim}, w_p is a weight assigned to each of the p matching algorithms and $adj : [0,1] \rightarrow [0,1]$ is an adjustment function.

If $w_k = 1$ is chosen as a weighting for the matching algorithms and $adj(x) = id(x)$[7] as an adjustment function, the aggregated similarity values are simply the average of the individual similarity values. A more advanced adjustment function also suggested by Ehrig in [Ehr06] is the sigmoid adjustment function

$$adj_{sig}(x) = \frac{1}{\left(1 + e^{\kappa(-x+0.5)}\right)}$$

with κ defining the slope of the function. The rational behind using a sigmoid adjustment function is that low similarity values are further decreased whereas high similarity values are further emphasized [ES04].

In the OBM approach a sigmoid adjustment function together with an equivalent weighting of each of the involved matching algorithms is used to calculate the two-dimensional similarity matrix m'_{sim}.

7.3.2 Lifting Extraction

In the next step, the lifting extraction step, the resulting lifting is calculated based on m'_{sim} and the domain ontology. The goal behind exploiting the domain ontology during the lifting extraction step is to avoid errors in the resulting lifting. Instead of simply selecting the pair of entities with the highest similarity as lifting candidates as performed by most existing matching algorithms, the search space for possible lifting elements is restricted to entities in the ontology that are related to previously matched ones. This is especially valuable when lifting large schemas to complex ontologies. In these cases, usually similar names for different schema and ontology entities exist. Selecting matching entities based on the domain ontology therefore helps to remove false lifting candidates. Figure 7.4 depicts the idea underlying the lifting extraction.

Figure 7.4 shows on the left hand side an excerpt of a customer schema containing two schema elements named `CountryCode`. One belongs to the sub-schema describing the address information and one to the sub-schema describing the telephone number of a customer. On the right hand side the corresponding ontology excerpt is shown. This ontology contains two attributes named `hasCountry`. One of them belongs to the concept `Address` and one to the concept `Telephone`. If, for example, just the linguistic similarity metric is used to calculate the similarity of these elements and attributes, the resulting similarity would be the same for all four possible combinations (the resulting similarity is 0.8 in the example). Based solely on the similarity information it is not possible

---
[7]Where $id(x)$ is the identity function.

7.3 Aggregation

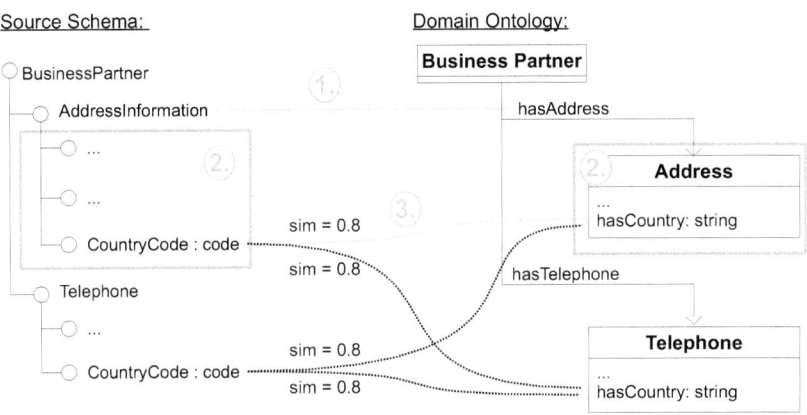

Figure 7.4: Example showing the idea underlying the domain-ontology-based lifting extraction.

to determine the correct lifting.[8] By using the domain ontology, ambiguities of the similarity values can easily be solved as depicted in the figure. The example is based on the assumption that in a previous step the aggregation algorithm determined that the schema element AddressInformation is lifted to the concept Address (depicted by the step number 1 in the figure). In the next aggregation step only schema elements and ontology entities in the neighborhood of the lifted schema entity and the target ontology entity are taken into account (step number 2 in the figure). By applying this restriction of the search space for possible lifting elements, the correct lifting can be identified by the algorithm in step 3.

A detailed specification of the lifting extraction algorithm is given in Algorithm 1.

The aggregation algorithm performs the aggregation starting from the root entities of a schema. For each root entity $r \in Ro$[9] the aggregation algorithm is initialized by first adding the root schema entity r and the most similar ontology concept o_j to a map M between ontology entities and schema entities. Additionally the lifting element (r, o_j) is added to the resulting lifting $L_{S \rightarrow O}$ and the ontology entity o_j to the list Q of currently processed ontology entities. After this initialization, the aggregation is performed by iterating over the list Q of current ontology entities and performing the following steps:

1. The set of ontology entities El in the neighborhood of the current ontology entity is calculated. The neighborhood is defined as all entities in the

---
[8]Note, that in this simplified example the problem could also be solved by using, for example, the node-path matcher to calculate the similarity of the elements and attributes.
[9]For a definition of the set Ro see the definition of XML Schema given in Section 4.2.

Algorithm 1: The ontology-based lifting extraction algorithm.

Input: The similarity matrix m'_{sim}, the domain ontology O, the schema S, maximum search depths θ_O and θ_S, cut off threshold τ

Output: The resulting lifting $L_{S \to O}$

1 **forall** $r \in Ro$ **do**
2　　$M = \{(r, o_j) \mid \max_{o_i \in C} (m'_{sim}(r, o_i))\}$
3　　$L_{S \to O} = M$
4　　$Q = \{o_j \mid (r, o_j) \in M\}$
5　　**while** $Q \neq \emptyset$ **do**
6　　　　$e = \text{first}(Q)$
7　　　　$El = $ set of entities $x \in O$ connected to e with distance smaller θ_O
8　　　　$n = \pi_1(x) : x \in M \land \pi_2(x) = e$
9　　　　$Nl = $ set of all children of n in range θ_S
10　　　　**forall** $n \in Nl$ **do**
11　　　　　　$o = x \in El : m'_{sim}(n, x) = \max_{y \in El}(m'_{sim}(n, y))$
12　　　　　　**if** $m'_{sim}(n, o) \geq \tau$ **then**
13　　　　　　　　$L_{S \to O} = L_{S \to O} \cup \{(n, o)\}$
14　　　　　　　　$Q = Q \cup \{o\}$
15　　　　　　　　$M = M \cup \{(e, n)\}$

16 **return** $L_{S \to O}$

  ontology that have a distance $\leq \theta_O$ to the current ontology entity (lines 6 and 7 of Algorithm 1).

2. The set of children nodes Nl of the current node is calculated (lines 8 and 9 in Algorithm 1). Again a parameter θ_S is used to define the maximum search depth.

3. For each element in the set of ontology entities El, the most similar node in the set of child nodes Nl is identified (lines 10-11 of Algorithm 1).

4. If the similarity of n and o is $\geq \tau$, n and o are added to the lifting and added to the respective lists (lines 12-15 of Algorithm 1).

The algorithm terminates as soon as the list of currently processed ontology entities Q does not contain any further elements. This happens as soon as no further lifting elements are found in the neighborhood of recently processed ontology entities.

  The lifting extraction algorithms presented above was developed with the goal to reduce the possibility of wrong matches when creating a lifting from aggregated matcher results. It is based on the assumption that the domain ontology dominates the schema with respect to its information capacity (cf. Section 5.3). Under this assumption it is obvious why the aggregation step is driven from the domain ontology. First, all possible lifting elements can be identified. Since in the approach presented the ontology dominates the schema with respect to its information capacity (cf. Section 5.3.2), the situation that no matching ontology entity exists for a schema entity does not occur. Second, this approach effectively enables the reduction of possible wrong matches as shown in the example. Since the domain ontology models the domain, all important concepts in this domain, as well as their relations and attributes are available. Restricting the search for matching entities to the neighborhood of previous matches significantly reduces the search space and consequently the possibility of wrong matches.

7.4 Summary

The chapter provided as description how the lifting from schemas to a domain ontology, the first and second step in the OBM approach, is performed. First an overview of the different steps comprising the lifting approach was given. Next, based on an analysis which features in a schema and which features in an ontology can be exploited for a similarity calculation, different matching algorithms where developed. These matching algorithms are based on general similarity metrics and exploit different features of schemas and ontology in order to calculate the similarity of entities. Finally, an aggregation algorithm exploiting the domain ontology in order remove wrong matching candidates was introduced.

Chapter 8

Mapping Extraction

This chapter focusses on how a mapping between two schemas is extracted on the basis of two liftings.

First, this chapter provides an overview of how the mapping extraction is performed (Section 8.1). Then, the concept of mapping categories, which is fundamental to the presented approach for mapping extraction, is introduced (Section 8.2) before the algorithm used to calculate a mapping based on two liftings is presented (Section 8.3).

8.1 Overview

The conceptual approach to the mapping extraction as well as how it relates to the overall OBM approach is depicted in Figure 8.1. The figure shows that the mapping extraction takes two liftings $L_{S_1 \to O}$, between the source schema S_1 and the domain ontology O, and $L_{S_2 \to O}$, between the target schema S_2 and the domain ontology O, as well as the domain ontology O as input. Based on these inputs the mapping extraction calculates the resulting mapping $M_{S_1 \to S_2}$ between the source to the target schema. The calculation of the resulting mapping $M_{S_1 \to S_2}$ is performed in two steps:

1. In the first step, the *matching extraction* step, a set $Mat_{S_1 \to S_2}$ of matches between the source and the target schema is calculated based on the two liftings $L_{S_1 \to O}$ and $L_{S_2 \to O}$. The algorithm for calculating the set $Mat_{S_1 \to S_2}$ on the basis two liftings is described in Section 8.3.1.

2. In the second step, the *mapping category identification* step, a *mapping category* for each match $mat_i \in Mat_{S_1 \to S_2}$ is identified. The resulting mapping element $m_j = (e_{S_1,m}, \ldots, e_{S_1,n}, e_{S_2,k}, cat)$ consisting of the identified mapping category cat and the source and target schema entities is added to the resulting mapping $M_{S_1 \to S_2}$. The concept of mapping categories is

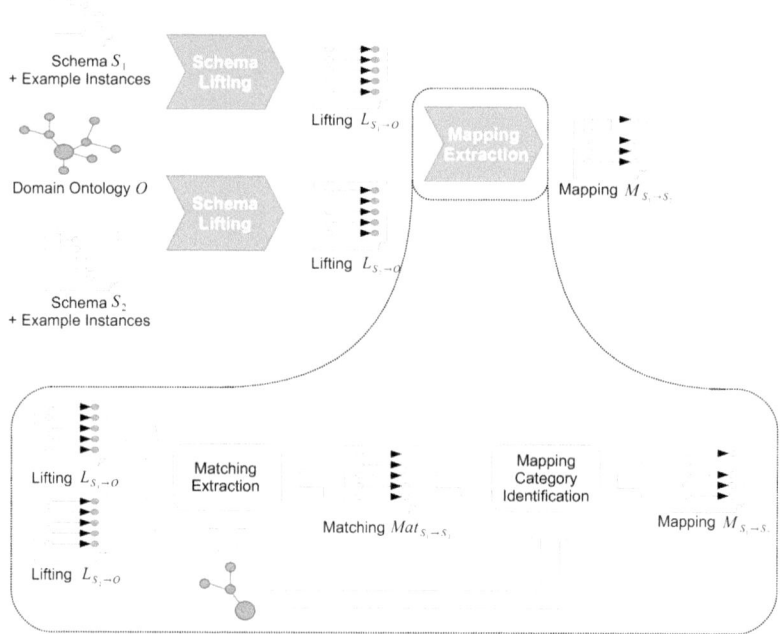

Figure 8.1: Overview of the mapping extraction approach.

introduced in Section 8.2 while a detailed discussion of how the different mapping categories can be identified is given in Section 8.3.2.

It is important to note that the mapping extraction step identifies a *mapping category* for each match instead of a concrete mapping expression like e.g. a copy expression in the XSLT language [Wor99b].[1] The introduction of the concept of mapping categories is based on the observation (see [DSDR07]) that in the general case not all mapping expressions required to translate between two schemas can be created automatically. In the most general case a complex program is required to perform the actual mapping. The idea underlying the mapping categories is to abstract from the details of a particular mapping expression and group similar mapping expressions into one mapping category. This abstraction enables the identification of the correct mapping category even in cases where the correct mapping expression could not be created automatically. On the basis of the identified mapping categories, a user can be supported during the map-

---

[1] A copy expression in the XSLT language copies the content of a source XML element to a target XML element.

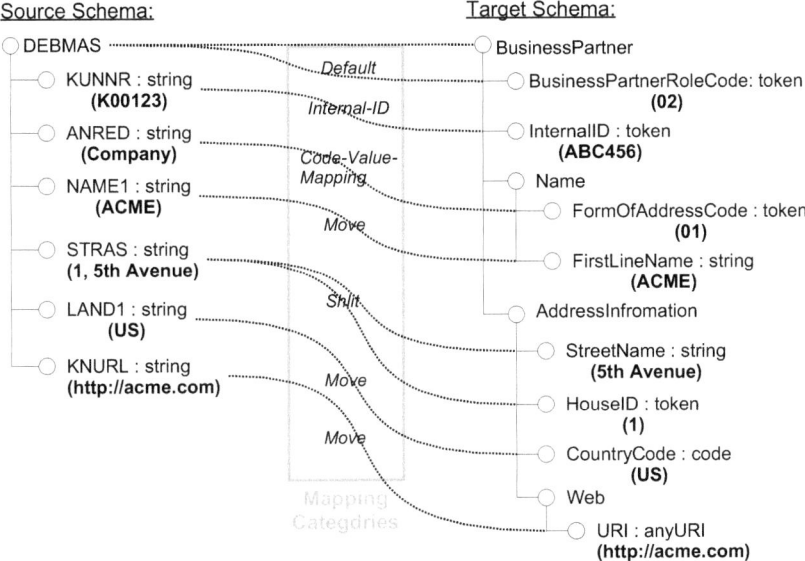

Figure 8.2: The running example including the mapping categories associated to the correspondences.

ping completion in the review, correction and testing step. In the next section a detailed description of the concept of mapping categories is provided.

8.2 Mapping Categories

The mapping extraction step not only identifies corresponding schema elements but also a mapping category associated to them. In Figure 8.2 the two schemas comprising the running example as well as the matches between the schema entities are depicted. For each match between the entities of the DEBMAS schema and the entities of the BusinessPartner schema the associated mapping category is shown.

Move: The simplest mapping category used in the example is *Move*. It is the mapping category assigned to the correspondence between the source schema entity NAME1 and the target schema entity FirstLineName. The interpretation of this mapping category is that the content of the source schema entity needs to be copied into the target schema entity without modification.

Split: The mapping category *Split* is assigned to the correspondence between the source schema entity STRAS and the target schema entities StreetName and HouseID. The meaning of the category *Split* is that the content of the element STRAS needs to be split and distributed across the target schema elements StreetName and HouseID.

Default: *Default* is the mapping category assigned to the correspondence between DEBMAS and BusinessPartnerRoleCode. The interpretation of this category is that a default value exists for the target schema entity and that this default value should be used.

As mentioned in the overview at the beginning of this chapter, the main reason for introducing the mapping categories is that automatically creating the complex mapping expressions necessary in the area of data migration or B2B integration is not possible in the general case. Even though one goal of this thesis (cf. the requirements in Section 1.1) is to create complex mapping expressions automatically the examination of existing mappings originating from B2B integration and Data Migration projects conducted by SAP showed that this goal can only be partially achieved. Most examined mappings contained at least some very complex mapping elements relating n source to m target elements by complex mapping expressions involving loops or advanced mathematical computations. One example of such a complex mapping expression is the calculation of the total amount of a purchase order based on the individual amounts of the items in this purchase order. Creating these mapping expressions automatically is not possible. However, the majority of mapping elements is much simpler (cf. occurrence frequency of different mapping categories given in Table 8.2). Even when multiple schema elements are mapped by a mapping element simple mapping expressions like e.g. string splitting or concatenation are used frequently.

The idea underlying the mapping categories is to abstract from the complex details of particular mapping expressions. This results in two simplifications: First, similar mapping expression can be grouped into one mapping category. As an example of such a simplification, consider the *Split* category in the running example. It abstracts from the particular delimiter (the character "," in the example) at which the input string is split. This abstraction enables the mapping extraction algorithm to identify the correct mapping category even in situations where the correct mapping expression could not be determined. Second, the mapping category eases the development of the correct mapping expression by a user. In the case of some of the simple mapping categories it is even possible to generate the mapping expressions required by a certain execution environment automatically. In the case of the more complex ones at least templates of mapping expressions can be created automatically. These templates need to be completed by the user afterwards. In these cases the mapping category at least provides the user with additional information regarding the needed mapping expression consequently simplifying the development task of the user.

8.2 Mapping Categories

Next, the mapping categories available in the OBM approach are introduced. In order to define a comprehensive set of mapping categories existing mappings in the areas of data migration and B2B integration have been studied. These mappings were created by experts through a manual development process in real integration projects. Based on these existing mappings, ten mapping categories have been identified. These mapping categories are capable of covering all mapping expression in the studied mappings. Table 8.1 lists each of the identified mapping categories together with a short explanation and an indicator of their occurrence in the B2B integration and Data Migration scenario.

8.2.1 Mapping Category Details

In the following paragraphs each mapping category listed in Table 8.1 is described in more detail. For each mapping category a short example is provided. After the introduction of the mapping categories a detailed discussion on how executable mapping code can be generated based on these mapping categories is presented.

Move: *Move* is the simplest of all identified mapping categories. As already explained in the example in the beginning of this section, it is used to directly relate one source schema entity to one target schema entity. If two entities are connected using *Move* the content of the source schema entity is copied without modification to the target schema entity. An example of the usage of the mapping category *Move* is given in the running example in Figure 8.2. In the examined schema mappings (cf. Chapter 10) *Move* was by far the most frequently occurring mapping category. It is obvious that executable mapping code for this category can easily be generated automatically.

Split: The mapping category *Split* is used whenever the content of one source schema entity needs to be split and distributed across several target schema entities. For example, the mapping category *Split* is assigned to the correspondences between source schema entity **STRAS** and the target schema entities **StreetName** and **HouseID**. In this case, the content of the source schema element needs to be split at the "," character. The first of the two resulting strings is then used as the content of the **HouseID** schema entity, whereas the second is used as the content of the **StreetName** schema entity.

Note that the mapping category *Split* does not imply any specific split algorithm. Details on how the content of source schema entities is split (e.g. at specific separating characters or at a particular index) are not part of the mapping category. Instead, the details of how the content of schema elements needs to be split in the context of a particular mapping is independent of the mapping category and needs to be identified separately.

Table 8.1: Overview of the identified mapping categories together with a short explanation.

Category Name	Short Description	DM	B2B
Move	Move the content of the source schema entity to the target entity.	✓	✓
Split	Split the source schema entity content into multiple target schema entities based on a specific split algorithm.	✓	✓
Concatenate	Concatenate multiple source schema entities into one target schema entity based on a specific concatenation algorithm.	✓	✓
Code-Value-Mapping	Either the source schema entity, the target schema entity or both contain a code according to a specific code list. Therefore a value mapping between the code value and the textual representation according to the code list or between different code lists is necessary.	✓	✓
Key-Value-Mapping	The source schema entity and target schema entity contain the identifiers of an instance. A mapping of this identifier is required.	✓	✗
Internal-ID	The target schema entity contains the internal identifier of an instance.	✓	✗
Default-Value	The target schema entity is defaulted with a special value.	✓	✓
Create-Instance	In Data Migration this category states that a new entry in the target system needs to be created for every entry in the source instance or whenever the source element contains a particular value. In the context of B2B integration this category identifies the creation of complex sub-structures.	✓	✓
Query	The target schema entity contains an internal identifier of a related object and multiple source schema entities are used to find the correct identifier.	✓	✗
Complex	A complex mapping expression is required.	✓	✓

8.2 Mapping Categories

Concatenate: The mapping category *Concatenate* is the inverse category to the mapping category Split. In the case of *Concatenate* the contents of several source schema entities is concatenated and used as the content of one target schema entity. As an example, consider the running example but with the `BusinessPartner` schema as the source and the `DEBMAS` as the target schema. In this case *Concatenate* would be the mapping category associated to the correspondence between the entities `StreetName`, `HouseID` and `STRAS`.

Again, as in the case of Split, the mapping category *Concatenate* does not imply a specific concatenation algorithm like e.g. used delimiter and concatenation order.

Code-Value-Mapping: A *Code-Value-Mapping* is required whenever either the source schema entity, the target schema entity or both represent data according to a specific code list. In this case a mapping of the source entity content (either a code value according to a code list or a text value) to the appropriate value of the target schema entity (also either a code value according to a code list or a text value) is required. Note that *Code-Value-Mappings* not only occur when a standardized code list (e.g. ISO 3166-1 for representing country names [Inta]) is used for the code values of the schema entities. Instead a code value mapping is also required when proprietary code lists are used. As an example of a *Code-Value-Mapping* consider the elements `ANRED` and `FormOfAddressCode` in the running example. In the source schema the form of address is represented by the plain text value "Company" whereas the target system uses the value "01" to represent this information. Consequently a mapping between these values is required.

Key-Value-Mapping: A mapping of type *Key-Value-Mapping* occurs when the content of the source schema entity as well as the content of the target schema entity are identifiers of instances of other objects. As an example consider the migration of customer data. For each customer its banking details are also migrated. However, bank specific information like the name of the bank or its address are usually stored independently from the customer. Each customer record simply contains a reference to the correct bank information.[2] In this case it is very likely that the source system uses a different identifier to identify a particular bank. Consequently a mapping of the different key values is required.

The *Key-Value-Mapping* mapping category is common in data migration. However, in contrast to the previous mapping categories, it is not present in B2B integration. The reason is that B2B messages are tailored towards

---
[2]This reference could, for example, be implemented using a foreign key relation in a relational data base system.

supporting interoperability between different companies. Consequently internal identifiers are not part of B2B messages, since the receiver would usually not be able to interpret them correctly. Instead, the internal reference is removed in B2B messages. This can be done by either including the complete referenced instance in the message if it is required by the business partner or omitting it otherwise.

Internal-ID: The mapping category *Internal-ID* is similar to the previous one as it also only occurs in the data migration context. A mapping of this category is required whenever the target schema entity contains a system internal identifier used to identify a particular instance. An example of this category is given in the running example. The source schema entity KUNNR as well as the target schema entity InternalID contain an internal identifier of a certain customer. However, the internal identifiers for one particular instance are usually different across systems. In the example the internal identifier in the source schema consists of a letter followed by a five digit number whereas in the target schema the identifier consists of three letters followed by three numbers. Consequently a mapping of these identifiers is necessary.

The reason that mappings of the type *Internal-ID* are not present in the B2B case is, as in the case of *Key-Value-Mappings*, that internal information is usually not part of B2B messages.

Default-Value: Mappings of the type *Default-Value* assign a special, predefined value to a target schema entity. The assignment of a default value becomes necessary when either this specific information is not available in the source schema or is modeled differently in the source and the target schema (cf. semantic heterogeneities in Section 3.3.2). In the running example a default value is assigned to the target schema entity BusinessPartnerRoleCode. In this case the correct default value depends the source schema. The target schema can be used to represent different types of business partners like customers and suppliers while a different source schema exists for each type of business partner. Consequently, whenever the source schema is the DEBMAS schema the BusinessPartnerRoleCode has to be set to "02" as this is the value necessary to represent customers in the target schema.

Mappings of type *Default-Value* also occur in the context of B2B integration.

Create-Instance: The mapping category *Create-Instance* is used whenever a complex substructure or an instance needs to be created based on an element in the source schema. While the former case usually occurs in mappings in the context of B2B integration, the later only occurs in the context of data migration. Note that creating a complex substructure in a B2B

8.2 Mapping Categories

context is essentially the same as creating an instance in a system in the context of Data Migration. A B2B message needs to contain all information required by the target system to interpret the message correctly. Therefore, a complex substructure can correspond to an independent instance in the target system. As an example of a mapping of type *Create-Instance* in the context of Data Migration consider again the migration of customer data. Consider a source system that stores banking information together with the other customer information and a target system that stores it independently in a different object. When migrating customer objects containing banking information new objects for storing banking information need to be created in the target system depending on the information in the source system.

Query: A mapping of type *Query* is necessary when the information of one or several source schema elements needs to be used to find the correct internal identifier of a related object in the target system. The type of queries represented by the mapping category Query are queries that select information in the target system based on certain parameters. As an example, again consider banking information. In the source system the information to which branch of a bank an account belongs is stored together with the account information, while in the target system the branch information is stored separately in a bank directory. In order to find the correct identifier for the branch of a bank the elements of the source system describing the branch must be used to query the bank directory. In B2B messages such a separation of the necessary information never occurs. B2B messages always contain the information required by the receiving party to perform the requested operation. Consequently, *Query* is again a mapping category that only occurs in the context of data migration.

Complex: All other possible mapping expressions that are not part of any of the previously presented categories, belong to the mapping category *Complex* In addition to complex mapping expressions not captured by any of the presented mapping categories, this mapping category also contains mappings resulting from a combination of the previous categories. As an example consider the combination of a *Concatenation* and *Split*. If the content of some source schema entities is first concatenated and then split across several target schema entities the associated mapping category would be *Complex*.

Using the data sets from the data migration scenario described in Chapter 10 the occurrence frequencies of the different mapping categories were evaluated (cf. [DSDR07]). Table 8.2 summarizes the results of this analysis. In the analyzed data migration scenario the mapping category *Move* is the most frequently occurring one. It is used as the mapping category for about 36% of the matches. The second and third most frequently used mapping categories where *Complex*

Table 8.2: Absolute number of occurrences and occurrence frequency of the different mapping categories in the evaluation scenarios (cf. Section 10.2.1).

Category Name	Number of Occurrences	Occurrence Frequency (in %)
Move	365	$\sim 36,1$
Complex	150	$\sim 14,9$
Code-Value-Mapping	146	$\sim 14,4$
Query	134	$\sim 13,2$
Split	75	$\sim 7,4$
Create-Instance	69	$\sim 6,8$
Internal-ID	24	$\sim 2,4$
Key-Value-Mapping	23	$\sim 2,3$
Default-Value	20	$\sim 2,0$
Concatenate	4	$\sim 0,4$

which occurred in approximately 15% of the matches and *Code-Value-Mapping* which occurred in approximately 14%. The occurrence frequencies for the different mapping categories in the context of B2B integration are similar to the ones presented in the table.

8.2.2 Generation of Mapping Code

This subsection now describes for which mapping categories this automatic generation of the mapping expression is possible and which information is required to perform the generation correctly. Again, it is important to note that this discussion is not limited to a specific mapping language like e.g. XSLT but rather describes the generation of mapping expressions on an abstract level.

Table 8.3 provides an overview how the mapping expressions for a certain mapping category can be generated. The table shows for each mapping category if the mapping expressions for this category can be generated automatically or semi-automatically or needs to be developed manually. The subsequent paragraphs describe in detail how the generation of the mapping expressions can be performed.

Move. As mentioned earlier in this section, mapping expressions for the mapping category *Move* can be created automatically. In order to create the correct mapping expression only the path of the source and target schema entities is required.

Split. Using example data as additional information, the mapping expression for the mapping category *Split* also can be generated automatically. As an

8.2 Mapping Categories

Table 8.3: Generation of mapping expressions for the different mapping categories.

Category Name	Mapping Code Generation
Move	automatic
Split	automatic
Concatenate	automatic
Default-Value	automatic
Code-Value-Mapping	semi-automatic
Key-Value-Mapping	semi-automatic
Internal-ID	semi-automatic
Create-Instance	semi-automatic
Query	semi-automatic
Complex	manual

example, consider the example data associated to the schema entities `STARS`, `StreetName` and `HouseID`. By analyzing the example data, it is obvious that the string "1, 5th Avenue" needs to be split at the comma into the two parts "1" and "5th Avenue". Using the example instance, it is also easy to identify that the first part of the split result needs to be copied into the schema entity named `HouseID` and the second part into the schema entity named `StreetName`.

It is important to note that the automatic creation of the mapping expression for the mapping category *Split* split is based only on the example instance. No machine learning over a set of instances needs to be performed. Instead the automatic creation of the mapping expression is based on splitting strings at fixed positions or certain characters (e.g. the character "," in the above example).[3]

Concatenate. As in the case of *Split* the mapping expressions for the category *Concatenate* can also be generated automatically using example data. Based on the analysis of the example data, even the delimiter that needs to be added when concatenating the contents of different schema entities can be identified. As an example simply reverse the one presented above. Using the two example data values "1", "5th Avenue" and "1, 5th Avenue" it is easy to identify the required delimiter, namely a comma followed by a space in this case.

Code-Value-Mapping. In the case of *Code-Value-Mappings* the possibility for creating the mapping expressions depends on the availability of information regarding code lists. If standardized code lists are used to represent the values of

---

[3]Note that the automatic splitting of strings based on a certain delimiter only works if the delimiter is used consistently throughout the data.

certain entities and the integration knowledge regarding these code lists is available, the mapping expressions can automatically be created. However, especially in the context of Data Migration, it is common that legacy systems use proprietary, undocumented code lists to represent data. In this case only a template for a mapping expression can be created. The actual mapping between certain code values and their textual representation has to be added afterwards to this template by the user.

Default-Value. The mapping expression for this category can be created automatically. Based on the integration knowledge regarding possible default values, the default value valid in this particular context simply needs to be used as the target entity value.

Key-Value-Mapping. The mapping expressions for the mapping category *Key-Value-Mapping* cannot be generated automatically. The reason is that a suitable method for translating between the key values of different systems can not be deducted from the available information. In this case only a mapping expression template, which needs to be completed by a user, can be generated automatically. While the details of the mapping expression template depend on the language used, the mapping expression template needs to consist of two parts. First, the source system needs to be queried for details of the object represented by the particular source key value. The resulting information then needs to be used to query the target system for the correct key value. The details how the querying of the source and the target system is performed needs to be specified by the user.

Internal-ID. Similar to the previous mapping category, the mapping expression for the category *Internal-ID* also cannot be generated automatically. The reason is again, that the necessary information is not available. Nevertheless it is still possible to generate a template that a user needs to complete afterwards. This generated mapping expression template needs to support 2 strategies for the translation of internal identifiers. Depending on the target system an internal identifier originating from the source system can either be translated using an algorithm that needs to be specified by the user, or drawn from a particular number range. The idea behind the second approach is, that sometimes auto-generated internal identifiers are used. As an example consider the target schema in the example in Figure 8.2. Now assume that business partners are in the system that use the target schema identified by a key consisting of the letters "ABC" followed by a running number. In this case the correct mapping expression for the mapping category *Internal-ID* simply needs to insert the next unused key from the range of valid numbers (e.g. "ABC456" in the example).

Create-Instance. The mapping expression of the *Create-Instance* category can not be created automatically. In this case only a template for the mapping expression which a user needs to complete can be created. The reason is that the information regarding the necessary function that needs to be invoked in order to create an instance in the target system is not available. This information has to be provided by the user.

Query. The mapping expressions for the mapping category *Query* cannot be created automatically. Again, only a template of the mapping expression which needs to be completed by the user can be created. The reason is that the information regarding the specific functionality in the target system that should be used for querying the appropriate identifier is not known. Consequently, this part of the mapping expression needs to be completed by the user.

Complex. As mentioned earlier, the mapping expression for the mapping category *Complex* can only be created manually. The reason is that this mapping category subsumes all complex mapping expressions that are not part of any of the other categories. Since in the case of the mapping category *Complex* no information regarding the functionality achieved by the needed mapping expression is available, no automatic support like the creation of a template can be provided.

8.3 Mapping Extraction Algorithm

This section describes the mapping extraction algorithm in detail. As mentioned in the overview section at the beginning of this chapter, the *mapping extraction* algorithm consists of two steps, the identification of matching schema entities and, based on that, the identification of the appropriate mapping category.

8.3.1 Inferring Matching Schema Entities

Identifying matches between the source and target schema is the first step to create the final schema mapping. Recall that the input to the mapping extraction step are the two liftings $L_{S_1 \rightarrow O}$ between the source schema S_1 and the domain ontology O and $L_{S_2 \rightarrow O}$ between the target schema and the domain ontology as well as the domain ontology O. In order to identify all matches between S_1 and S_2, the lifting $L_{S_2 \rightarrow O}$ is used as a start. Each lifting element $l_k = (e_1, \ldots, e_j, o) \in L_{S_2 \rightarrow O}$ consists of a set of target schema entities $\{e_1, \ldots, e_j\}$ and one ontology entity o. Algorithm 2 calculates for each lifting element l_k the set of related source schema lifting elements, creates a match on the basis of this lifting elements and adds it to the resulting matching $Mat_{S_1 \rightarrow S_2}$.

The algorithm to infer matching source and target schema entities performs three basic steps for all lifting elements $l_{S_2} = (e_1, \ldots, e_j, o) \in L_{S_2 \rightarrow O}$:

Algorithm 2: The algorithm to infer matching source and target schema entities.

Input: The source schema lifting $L_{S_1 \to O}$, the target schema lifting $L_{S_2 \to O}$, the domain ontology O

Output: $Mat_{S_1 \to S_2}$

1. $Mat_{S_1, S_2} = \emptyset$
2. **foreach** $(e_1, \ldots, e_j, o) \in L_{S_2 \to O}$ **do**
3. $OE = \emptyset$
4. $Q = \{(t_1, \ldots, t_k, p) \in L_{S_1 \to O} \mid p = o\}$
5.   **if** $Q \neq \emptyset$ **then**
6. $SE = \{t_i \mid (t_1, \ldots, t_i, \ldots, t_k, p) \in Q\}$
7.   **else**
8. $SE = \emptyset$
9.   **if** $o \in C$ **then**
10. $OE = OE \cup \{e \in C \mid e \leq_C o\}$
11. $OE = OE \cup \{e \in C \mid o \leq_C e\}$
12.   **foreach** $\bar{o} \in OE$ **do**
13. $P = \{(x_1, \ldots, x_l, y) \in L_{S_1 \to O} \mid y = \bar{o}\}$
14. $SE = SE \cup \{x_i \mid (x_1, \ldots, x_i, \ldots, x_l, y) \in P\}$
15.   **else if** $o \in R$ **or** $o \in A$ **then**
16. $OE = OE \cup similar(o)$
17.   **if** $OE = \emptyset$ **then**
18. $OE = OE \cup neighbour(o)$
19.   **foreach** $e \in OE$ **do**
20. $P = \{(x_1, \ldots, x_l, y) \in L_{S_1 \to O} \mid y = \bar{o}\}$
21. $SE = SE \cup \{x_i \mid (x_1, \ldots, x_i, \ldots, x_l, y) \in P\}$
22.   **if** $SE \neq \emptyset$ **then**
23. $Mat_{S_1 \to S_2} = Mat_{S_1 \to S_2} \cup \{(SE, e_1, \ldots, e_j)\}$
24.   **else**
25. $Mat_{S_1 \to S_2} = Mat_{S_1 \to S_2} \cup \{(\epsilon, e_1, \ldots, e_j)\}$
26. **return** $Mat_{S \to T}$

8.3 Mapping Extraction Algorithm

1. Identify directly related source schema entities.

2. Search entities in reach if no directly related source schema entities can be found.

3. Add related schema entities to the resulting matching $Mat_{S_1 \rightarrow S_2}$.

A detailed description of each step of the matching extraction algorithm is provided in the following paragraphs.

In order to infer the resulting matching $Mat_{S_1 \rightarrow S_2}$ the algorithm starts by iterating through all lifting elements $l_{S_2} = (e_1, \ldots, e_j, o) \in L_{S_2 \rightarrow O}$. First, the algorithm checks if the source lifting $L_{S_1 \rightarrow O}$ contains a directly related lifting, i.e. a lifting to the ontology entity o (line 4). If this is the case, the schema entities of the respective lifting element are added to the set of source schema entities SE (line 5 and 6). Based on the identified sets of source schema entities SE, a new match is added to the result matching $Mat_{S_1 \rightarrow S_2}$ at the end of each iteration (line 21-24). Note that when a new match is added to the result matching $Mat_{S_1 \rightarrow S_2}$ a check is performed if the set SE actually contains any elements. If this is not the case, a match consisting only of target schema entities is added to the result (line 24). These "empty" matches allow to identify certain types of mapping categories, like e.g. *Default Value* (cf. Section 8.3.2), in the mapping category identification step that could not be identified otherwise.

If no directly related lifting is found, ontology entities in the reach of the ontology entity o are checked for related liftings. In this case, the further execution of the algorithm depends on the type of the ontology entity o. If o is a concept in the ontology ($o \in C$) then all sub- and super-concepts of o in the ontology O are checked for related liftings. This check is performed in lines 8-13 of the listing. If o, in contrast to the previous case, is either an attribute or a relation ($o \in A \cup R$) the algorithm uses two steps to find related liftings (lines 14-20). First, it searches in the concept hierarchy for liftings to similar attributes or relations (line 15). If no related liftings are found in the first step the neighborhood of the ontology entity o is searched in the second step (line 17).

In this algorithm, similar attributes or relations are defined as attributes or relations that have the same name and for which the domain is a sub- or superclass of the domain of the entity o. More precisely the set $similar(o)$ of attributes or relations similar to o is defined as:

$$similar(o) := \{u_i\}$$
$$u_i : \begin{cases} u_i \in R & iff \quad o \in R \\ u_i \in A & iff \quad o \in A \\ name(o) = name(u_i) \\ dom(o) \leq_C dom(u_i) \end{cases}$$

As an example consider the small excerpt of a domain ontology depicted in Figure 8.3. The attribute `hasIdentifier` of the concept `Customer` is according to

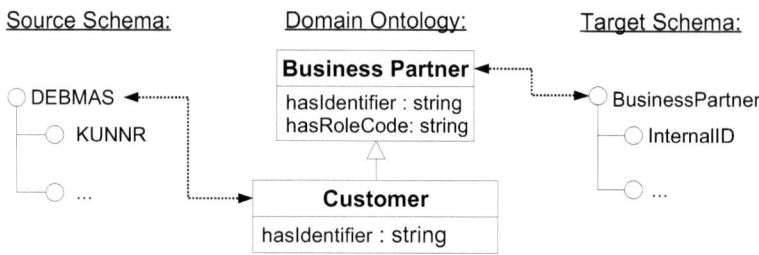

Figure 8.3: Example of liftings related through a sub-class relation.

this definition similar to the attribute hasIdentifier of the concept Business Partner as, i) both are attributes, ii) the name of both attributes is identical and iii) Business Partner is a superclass of Customer (Customer $\leq_C$ Business Partner)

The neighborhood of an ontology entity o is the set of relations and attributes that either have the domain of o as their range or their domain. More precisely the set $neighbour(o)$ contains all relations and attributes n_i with:

$$neighbour(o) := \{n_i\}$$
$$n_i : \begin{cases} n_i \in R \cup A \\ dom(o) = dom(n_i) \vee range(o) = range(n_i) \end{cases}$$

According to this definition, for example, the attributes hasRoleCode and hasIdentifier are elements of the neighborhood the of the concept Business Partner (cf. Figure 8.3).

The rational underlying the algorithm and definitions presented above is the following: Whenever entities of the source and the target schema are lifted to the same ontology entities, a match between those entities should be identified. If no lifting to the same ontology entity can be identified, the cases where a schema entity is lifted to a concept in the ontology or to a relation or attribute need to be treated differently. If the ontology entity to which the target schema entities are lifted is a concept, the algorithm searches in the concept hierarchy for a related lifting. As an example consider the situation depicted in Figure 8.3. In addition to the two schemas the figure shows a domain ontology containing the concept Business Partner and its sub-concept Customer. The correct lifting elements for the two top level elements of the two examples schemas are (DEBMAS, Customer) and (BusinessPartner, Business Partner). In this case no direct related lifting can be found by the presented algorithm. Therefore, the algorithm checks the sub- and super-classes for related liftings and would, therefore, be able to identify (DEBMAS, Customer) as a related lifting. Consequently, the match (DEBMAS, BusinessPartner) would be added to the result.

8.3 Mapping Extraction Algorithm

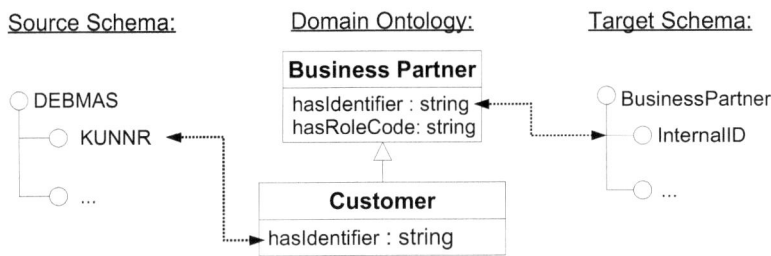

Figure 8.4: Example of liftings related through inheritance.

In the cases, where the target schema entity is lifted to a relation or an attribute, the situation is a little bit more complex. First, similar relations or attributes in the concept hierarchy are checked for related liftings. The rational is that first inherited relations and attributes should be checked for related liftings. An example of this situation is depicted in Figure 8.4. In this example, the source schema entity KUNNR is lifted to the attribute hasIdentifier of the concept Customer and the target schema entity InternalID is lifted to the attribute hasIdentifier of the concept Business Partner. Again, no directly related lifting can be identified for the target schema lifting. Therefore, the algorithm checks the attributes similar to the attribute hasIdentifier of the concept Business Partner. In this case, the set $similar(hasIdentifier)$ only consists of the attribute hasIdentifier of the concept Customer. Based on this attribute, the correct match (KUNNR, InternalID) can be identified.

The neighborhood of an entity is only checked for related liftings if the previous steps could not identify any related liftings.

Example Execution. In order to illustrate the execution of the Algorithm 2, the examples depicted in Figure 8.3 and 8.4 are used. Based on this example, the algorithm is executed using the following input:

- $L_{S_1 \to O} = \{(\text{DEBMAS}, \text{Customer}), (\text{KUNNR}, \text{hasIdentifier})\}$

- $L_{S_2 \to O} = \{(\text{BusinessPartner}, \text{Business Partner}), (\text{InternalID}, \text{hasIdentifier})\}$

- The domain ontology O.

Based on these inputs, the following two iterations of the main foreach loop of the Algorithm 2 are performed:

1. Iteration:

    (a) The target lifting element (BusinessPartner, Business Partner) is selected. Consequently $e_1 = $ BusinessPartner and $o = $ Business Partner.

(b) No directly related lifting element is found. $Q = \emptyset$ after line 4.

(c) As $o \in C$ all sub- and super-classes of o are added to the set $OE = \{\text{Business Partner}, \text{Customer}\}$ in lines 10 and 11.

(d) Source schema lifting elements related to the ontology entities in OE are (DEBMAS, Customer). Consequently $SE = \{\text{DEBMAS}\}$ after line 14.

(e) As SE is not empty $Mat_{S_1 \to S_2}$ is set to $Mat_{S_1 \to S_2} = \{(\text{DEBMAS}, \text{BusinessPartner})\}$ in line 23.

2. Iteration:

   (a) The target lifting element (InternalID, hasIdentifier) is selected. Consequently $e_1 = $ InternalID and $o = $ hasIdentifier.

   (b) No directly related lifting element is found. $Q = \emptyset$ after line 4.

   (c) As $o \in R$ similar relations are identified and added to $OE = \{\text{hasIdentifier}\}$ in line 16.

   (d) As OE in not empty line 18 is not executed.

   (e) Source schema lifting elements related to the ontology entities in OE are (KUNNR, hasIdentifier). Consequently $SE = \{\text{KUNNR}\}$ after line 21.

   (f) As SE is not empty $Mat_{S_1 \to S_2}$ is set to $Mat_{S_1 \to S_2} = \{(\text{DEBMAS}, \text{BusinessPartner}), (\text{KUNNR}, \text{InternalID})\}$ in line 23.

After the second iteration, the execution of the algorithm ends since all target schema lifting elements have been visited in the main `foreach` loop. Consequently, the result of the execution of Algorithm 2 using the example input is the matching $Mat_{S_1 \to S_2} = \{(\text{DEBMAS}, \text{BusinessPartner}), (\text{KUNNR}, \text{InternalID})\}$.

8.3.2 Identification of Mapping Categories

After matching schema entities have been identified in the matching extraction step, the next step is to identify the appropriate mapping category for each of the matches. In order to identify the correct mapping category for a given match, different types of background knowledge are required. Table 8.4 provides an overview of the types of knowledge required to identify the mapping category of a match. The table indicates if the identification of a particular mapping category requires example data or integration knowledge modeled in the ontology. In the subsequent paragraphs for each category the rules used in the OBM approach to identify them based on the available background knowledge are explained.

8.3 Mapping Extraction Algorithm

Table 8.4: Required background knowledge for the identification of the different mapping categories. The required type of knowledge is indicated by a ✓ in the table, not required knowledge by a ✗.

Category Name	Example Data	Integration Knowledge
Move	✗	✗
Split	✓	✗
Concatenate	✓	✗
Code-Value-Mapping	✓	✓
Key-Value-Mapping	✗	✓
Internal-ID	✗	✓
Default-Value	✗	✓
Create-Instance	✗	✓
Query	✗	✓
Complex	✗	✗

Move. Move is the default mapping category assigned to a matching between one source schema and one target schema entity if no background knowledge is available. Consequently, no background knowledge is necessary to identify this mapping category. However, example data can be beneficial to check if the mapping category Move is correct. Only if the example instance for the source and the target schema entity are equal, Move is the correct mapping category.

Complex. Complex is the default mapping category assigned to any $m : n$ matches between the source and the target schema whenever no background information is available. This mapping category is assigned also whenever none of the other mapping categories is applicable for a given match.

Split. The mapping category Split indicates that the contents of the source schema entity needs to be split and distributed across several target schema entities. Therefore, Split can only occur in the case of a $1 : m$ match. In order to identify the mapping category Split example data is necessary. The category Split is assigned to a $1 : m$ match $mat_i = (e_1, e_2, \ldots, e_j)$ if the example data associated to each of the target schema entities $e_2, \ldots, e_j \in S_2$ is a sub-string of the example data associated to the source schema entity $e_1 \in S_1$. If this is not the case the mapping category Complex is assigned to the match.

Concatenate. As Concatenate is the opposite mapping category to Split, it consequently only occurs in the case of $n : 1$ matches. The identification of the mapping category Concatenate is also based on example data. If for a given match $mat_i = (e_1, \ldots, e_j, e_k)$ the example data for each source schema entity $e_1, \ldots, e_j \in S_1$ is a sub-string of the example data associated to $e_k \in S_2$ the mapping category of this match is Concatenate, otherwise Complex is the mapping category used for this match.

Code-Value-Mapping. In order to identify the mapping category Code-Value-Mapping example data as well as integration knowledge is required. If in the case of a 1 : 1 match the mapping category Move is not applicable as the example data of the schema entities differs, the integration knowledge is checked. If for either the source or the target schema entity or for both information regarding used code lists is available in the integration knowledge, then the mapping category Code-Value-Mapping is assigned to this match.

Furthermore, the example data can then be used to check if this mapping category is correct. The example data associated to the source schema entity is translated using the available code lists information. If the result of this transformation is the example data associated with the target schema entity the mapping category Code-Value-Mapping is most likely correct.

Key-Value-Mapping. The mappings category Key-Value-Mapping is identified based on integration knowledge. In this case, example data is not useful as the key values used in different system to identify instances of objects is certainly different. In the OBM approach the mapping category Key-Value-Mapping is assigned to a 1 : 1 match if the target entity of the match is a global identifier of an instance (cf. Section 6.3.2).

Internal-ID. The mapping category Internal-ID can only be identified based on integration knowledge. As the internal identifiers used in different systems certainly differ, example data is not useful to identify this mapping category. The category Internal-ID is assigned to a 1 : 1 match if the integration knowledge contains the information that the target entity of the match is used as an internal identifier.

Default-Value. The identification of the mapping category Default-Value depends solely on integration knowledge. If for a match $mat_i = (\epsilon, e_1)$ only consists of a target schema entity $e_1 \in S_2$ the integration knowledge is checked if a default value exists for this target schema entity. If this is the case, the mapping category Default-Value is assigned to the match. Otherwise no mapping category is assigned.

Create-Instance. Similar to the previous two mapping categories, the mapping category Create-Instance is identified based on integration knowledge. It is assigned to 1 : 1 matches if the target schema entity is a complex entity, i.e. an entity consisting of a complex sub-structure that has been lifted to a concept in the domain ontology. Only in this case the complex schema entity represents an independent object that needs to be created in the target system.

Query. The mapping category Query can easily be identified based on the integration knowledge. If the target schema entity $e_k \in S_2$ of a $n : 1$ match $mat_i = (e_1, \ldots, e_j, e_k)$ is, according to the integration knowledge, an internal identifier, the mapping category Query is assigned to this match.

Using the different rules described above, the mapping categories for each match $mat_i \in Mat_{S_1 \to S_2}$ is identified in the Mapping Category Identification step. After this step, the resulting mapping $M_{S_1 \to S_2}$ is available and can be presented to the user for review, completion and testing (Step 5 in the semi-automatic mapping process introduced in Section 5.2).

8.4 Summary

This chapter introduced an approach for the extraction of schema mappings on the basis of two liftings. First, an overview of the proposed mapping extraction approach was given. After that the concept of mapping categories was introduced. These mapping categories abstract from the details of particular mapping expressions and group similar mapping expressions into one mapping category. The advantage of this abstraction is that the correct mapping category associated to a match can be identified even in cases where the correct mapping expression cannot be created. Furthermore, the mapping categories simplify the finalization of the proposed mapping by a user. After this Section 8.3.1 presented an algorithm for identifying matching schema entities on the basis of two liftings. The chapter closed by introducing a set of rules that can be used to identify the correct mapping expression for each match between two schemas by exploiting the background knowledge in the ontology.

Part III

Implementation and Evaluation

Chapter 9

Implementation

In Part II of this thesis the Ontology-Based Schema Mapping (OBM) approach was introduced. In order to evaluate the OBM approach and compare it to the main requirements identified for semi-automatic mapping approaches in industrial environments presented in Chapter 1 it is necessary to apply the OBM approach to real integration problems. Consequently, a prototypical implementation of the OBM approach has been developed. This chapter describes this prototypical implementation and highlights its main features (Section 9.1). Furthermore, a set of tools that were developed to simplify the evaluation of the approach are described in this chapter (Section 9.2).

9.1 The OBM Framework

The *OBM Framework* is the prototypical implementation of the OBM approach. Figure 9.1 shows the high-level architecture of the OBM approach in *Fundamental Modeling Concepts (FMC)* notation [KGT06]. The OBM Framework mainly consists of the three components *Lifting* together with the *Matcher Repository*, the *Mapping Extraction*, and the *Repository Adapter*. The functionality offered by the OBM Framework is solely available through an API (for details see Appendix B). For example, the Evaluation Toolkit Evanto, which is described in the following section, uses this API to execute evaluation scripts.

The Lifting component mainly consist of two parts, the *Matching* component and the *Aggregation* component. Both are using the interface of the Repository Adapter component to read schemas and the domain ontology from the *Input Data Repository* into the internal representation. The current prototypical implementation of the OBM Framework supports XML Schema as the schema language and OWL-DL as the ontology language. The Lifting component accesses the *Matcher Repository* in order to instantiate particular matchers. The results of the individual matchers are aggregated by the Aggregation component

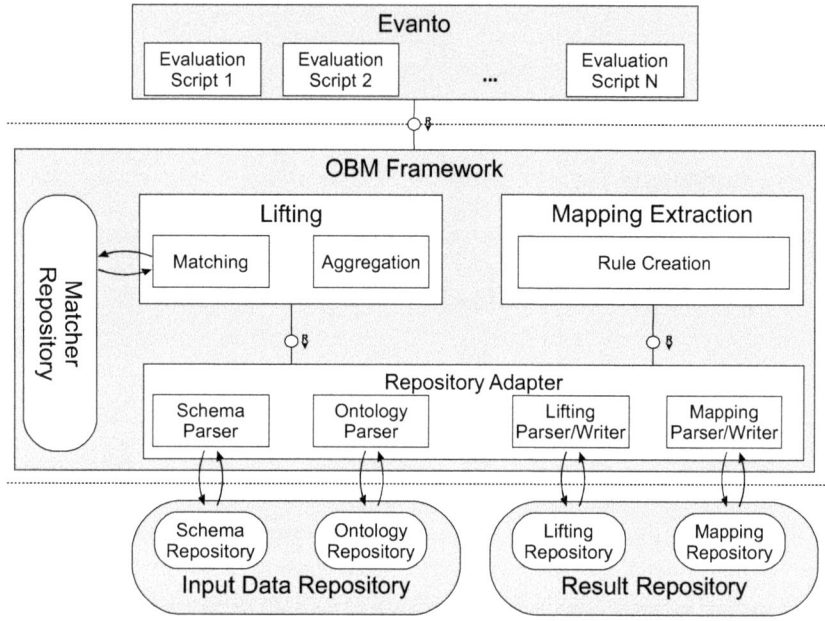

Figure 9.1: Architecture of the OBM Framework.

using the algorithm introduced in Section 7.2.3. The resulting lifting is stored to the *Lifting Repository* using the interface offered by the Repository Adapter.

The Mapping Extraction accesses the schemas, the domain ontology and the corresponding liftings using again the interface of the Repository Adapter. Based on two previously created liftings, the *Rule Creation* extracts the resulting mapping between the two schemas and stores it to the *Mapping Repository*. Again the interface of the Repository Adapter is used to store the results. The current implementation of the OBM Framework only supports the file system for storing schemas, ontologies, liftings and mappings. Nevertheless, the described architecture would allow to use different storage systems like e.g. a relational database.

In the following subsections the in-memory representation as well as the serialization formats for schemas, ontologies, liftings and mappings used in the OBM Framework are described. Furthermore, necessary optimizations performed in the implementation of the OBM Framework are discussed.

9.1.1 Schema and Ontology Representation

In the file system based repository implementation XML Schemas as well as OWL Ontologies are simply stored as files.

However, the memory representations of both are optimized to support optimized access to the information frequently required by the matching algorithms. In the case of XML Schema, the matching algorithms frequently require access to different facets of the schema entities like e.g. name or associated XML Schema data types as well as to the parent and child entities. Consequently XML Schemas are represented in memory as node labelled trees. Each node in this tree has attributes like name, minimum and maximum cardinality, associated XML Schema data as well as a list of children elements. Furthermore, each node (except the root node of a schema) also has a link to its parent node.

The ontology is represented in memory as sets of objects that contain the concepts, relations and attributes comprising the ontology.

9.1.2 Lifting Representation

Liftings are in the OBM Framework represented as a set of `LiftingElements`. Each `LiftingElement` relates an entity path in the source schema to a concept, relation or attribute in the ontology. Furthermore, each lifting contains a reference to the schema and the ontology the particular lifting has been created for. Figure 9.2 shows a small excerpt of the XML-based serialization format used by the OBM Framework to store liftings in the file system.

The figure shows that for each lifting the path to the source schema and the ontology are stored (marked by the `<sourceSchema>` and `<targetOnto>` elements respectively). The figure shows that in this example the `/DEBMAS06/IDOC/E1KNA1M/STRAS` schema entity is lifted to the relation `hasHouseNumber` that relates the concepts `PostalAddress` and `HouseID` as well as to the relation `hasStreetName` that relates the concepts `PostalAddress` and `StreetName`. Furthermore, for each lifting element the aggregated similarity value that was calculated in the lifting step of the OBM approach is stored.

9.1.3 Mapping Representation

Mappings are represented in the OBM Framework as a list of `MappingRules`. Each such `MappingRule` consists of the path of a source schema entity, the path of the target schema entity and the associated mapping category. An excerpt of the XML-based serialization format used by the OBM Framework to store mappings in the file system is shown in Figure 9.3. The figure shows an excerpt of the mapping between the SAP R/3 `DEBMAS` and the SAP

```
<Lifting>
    <sourceSchema> *.xsd </sourceSchema>
    <targetOnto> *.owl </targetOnto>
    <liftingList>
        ...
        <element>
            <schemaEntity> /DEBMAS06/IDOC/E1KNA1M/STRAS </...>
            <relation>
                <domain> *.owl#PostalAddress </domain>
                <property> *.owl#hasHouseNumber </property>
                <range> *.owl#HouseID </range>
            </relation>
            <plausibility> 0.8 </plausibility>
        </element>
        <element>
            <schemaEntity> /DEBMAS06/IDOC/E1KNA1M/STRAS </...>
            <relation>
                <domain> *.owl#PostalAddress </domain>
                <property> *.owl#hasStreetName </property>
                <range> *.owl#StreetName </range>
            </relation>
            <plausibility> 0.9 </plausibility>
        </element>
        ...
    </liftingList>
</Lifting>
```

Figure 9.2: Excerpt of the serialization format used to store liftings.

Business ByDesign `BusinessPartner` schema (cf. evaluation scenarios in Chapter 10). The excerpt contains for example the mapping rule that the source schema entity `/DEBMAS06/E1KNA1M/PFACH` is mapped to the target schema entity (`/BusinessPartner/AddressInformation/PostalAddress/Elements/POBoxID`) using the mapping category *Move*.

9.1.4 Implementation Considerations & Optimizations

An important decision taken during the implementation of the OBM Framework is the representation of the three-dimensional similarity matrix m_{sim} which is created during the lifting step of the OBM approach (cf. Chapter 7) due to the possibly high memory consumption of this matrix. In the OBM Framework the similarity matrix m_{sim} is simply represented as a three-dimensional array of floating point numbers. The following simple example shows that no optimization

9.1 The OBM Framework

```
<Mapping >
  <sourceSchema  xmlns = "" > ../source/*.xsd </sourceSchema>
  <targetSchema  xmlns = "" > ../target/*.xsd </targetSchema>
...
  <rule>
    <sourceSchemaEntity> /DEBMAS06/IDOC/E1KNA1M/STRAS </...>
    <targetSchemaEntity> /../PostalAddress/Elements/HouseID </...>
    <operation> SPLIT </...>
  </rule>
  <rule>
    <sourceSchemaEntity> /DEBMAS06/IDOC/E1KNA1M/PFACH </...>
    <targetSchemaEntity> /../PostalAddress/Elements/POBoxID </...>
    <operation> MOVE </...>
  </rule>
  <rule>
    <sourceSchemaEntity> /DEBMAS06/IDOC/E1KNA1M/ORT01 </...>
    <targetSchemaEntity> /../PostalAddress/Elements/CityName </...>
    <operation> MOVE </...>
  </rule>
  <rule>
    <sourceSchemaEntity> /DEBMAS06/IDOC/E1KNA1M/REGIO </...>
    <targetSchemaEntity> /../PostalAddress/Elements/RegionCode
    </...>
    <operation> CODE_VALUE_MAPPING </...>
  </rule>
  <rule>
...
</Mapping>
```

Figure 9.3: Excerpt of the serialization format used to store mappings.

of the memory representation of the similarity matrix m_{sim} is necessary. In order to store the similarity matrix calculated using 5 different mapping algorithms for a schema consisting of 1000 entities and an ontology consisting of 5000 entities, the three-dimensional array requires roughly 95 MB of main memory which can easily be handled by current desktop computers.[1]

The only optimization performed during the implementation of the OBM Framework was the caching of intermediate results of the matching algorithms. This caching ensures that e.g. the lexical similarity of two identical strings is only calculated once. The calculation of identical similarity values occurs quite often due to the reuse of complex elements like an address in different parts of

---
[1]The calculation above assumes that a floating point number is stored using 4 bytes which e.g. is true for the data type `float` in the Java language.

large schemas. Consequently, the caching of the similarity values improved the overall performance of the OBM Framework significantly.

The implementation details of the OBM Framework are not further discussed in this chapter as they do not add to the understanding of the OBM approach.[2] The following section introduces the evaluation toolkit *Evanto* which was developed to facilitate the evaluation of the OBM Framework in real world scenarios.

9.2 The Evaluation Toolkit *Evanto*

The evaluation toolkit *Evanto* was developed in order to enable the evaluation of the OBM Framework. While the implementation of the OBM Framework facilitates the integration of the OBM Framework into existing applications, it makes the evaluation of the OBM approach underlying the OBM Framework rather complex. The reason is that functionality necessary for the evaluation of an automatic schema mapping approach such as, for example, automatic comparison of generated mappings with manually created ones or the calculation of certain quality metrics, is usually not available in existing applications.

The goal of Evanto is to enable a highly automated evaluation of the OBM approach. This requires the execution of a series of tests using different combinations of matchers and different schemas and ontologies as input. Furthermore, a set of quality metrics needs to be calculated for each test in order to enable the comparison of the OBM approach with previous test results and other existing approaches.

Evanto achieves this goal by enabling a user to easily specify test scripts that can later be executed automatically. Figure 9.4 shows a simple example of an Evanto script. This test script consist of one test case (lines 21 − 35) including the calculation of the test results (lines 33 − 34). For a detailed explanation of this example script cf. Appendix C.

In addition to the possibility to define and execute evaluation scripts the Evanto toolkit offers additional tools for analyzing the mappings created by the evaluation scripts. The analysis tools enable e.g. the automatic creation of HTML based reports describing the quality of the automatically created mappings using different metrics.[3] The generated reports ease the analysis of the OBM approach as they e.g. allow to quickly compare the mapping quality achieved by different matchers or across different schemas.

Agile Development. Besides enabling a highly automated evaluation of the OBM approach, Evanto also enables the agile development of novel matching and

---

[2] The interested reader may refer to Appendix B were additional implementation details are provided.

[3] A detailed description of the metrics used for analyzing the quality of automatically created mappings is given in the following chapter.

9.2 The Evaluation Toolkit *Evanto*

```
1  setup do
2    # Set some variables that are used later
3    set :result_target_dir, "./results/"
4    set :domain_onto, "./IntegrationOnto.owl"
5    # instanziate OBM Framework
6    @source_fw = OBMFramework.new(File.new("./OCRD.xsd"), File.
7                     new("./OCRD.xml"), File.new(domain_onto), nil,
8                     true)
9    @target_fw = OBMFramework.new(File.new("./d_CUSTOMER.xsd"),
10                    File.new("./d_CUSTOMER.xml" ),File.new(
11                    domain_onto), nil, true)
12   # read master mapping from file
13   @mastermapping = Mapping.deserializeFromXMLString(File.
14                    read(master_mapping))
15   # initialize the matchers and the aggregation algorithm
16   @matcher = []
17   @matcher << SampleInstanceMatcher.new()
18   @aggregator = OntoBasedAggregator.new(0.5)
19 end
20
21 run :OCRD_to_CUSTOMER_Mapping do
22   # lift the source schema and target schema
23   @source_lifting = @source_fw.doLifting(@matcher,
24                      @aggregator)
25   @target_lifting = @target_fw.doLifting(@matcher,
26                      @aggregator)
27   # extract the mapping from the two liftings
28   # and store it for later analysis
29   mapping_extraction = MappingExtraction.new(@source_lifting,
30                      @target_lifting, @source_fw,
31                      @target_fw)
32   mapping = mapping_extraction.extract_mapping()
33   result(:mapping, :list => mapping , :master => ".
34       /OCRD_CUSTOMER.xml")
35 end
```

Figure 9.4: Example of an Evanto script.

mapping extraction algorithms as well as the improvement of existing ones. One of the practices used in agile software development [Bec00] is called test driven development [Bec02]. The idea underlying test driven development is to implement automatic tests programs in the first step of the development cycle. These automatic test programs are usually called unit tests. Once the unit tests are available, the implementation of the actual functionality is frequently tested during development. Using this approach, errors in the program code can be detected early during the development phase of new functionality and therefore easily be fixed. Agile development methods have proven very successful in improving code quality.

Evanto builds upon these ideas and enables their usage in the context of automatic schema mapping. Evanto scripts can be used to develop unit tests for schema matching and mapping extraction algorithms. Once an Evanto script as well as the required master mappings are available, this script can be executed whenever the implementation of a schema matching or mapping extraction algorithms is modified. On the basis of the automatically created HTML reports, the results of the performed changes can immediately be identified. Consequently, the test scripts allow to easily identify problems or bugs and therefore help to improve the quality of schema matching and mapping extraction algorithms.

9.3 Summary

This chapter provided a brief overview of the OBM Framework, the prototypically implementation of the OBM approach, as well as the Evanto toolkit. The OBM Framework was implemented as a Java package which is accessible using a simple API. This enables an easy integration of the OBM Framework into existing applications. Consequently the OBM Framework offers no user interface to analyze automatically created mappings. Therefore, the Evanto toolkit was developed to facilitate the evaluation of the OBM approach as well as the analysis of automatically created mappings. In the following chapter the detailed evaluation of the OBM approach that was performed using the OBM Framework together with the Evanto toolkit is presented.

Chapter 10

Evaluation

This chapter focuses on the evaluation of Ontology-Based Mapping (OBM). First, industrial state of the art tools together with their functionality supporting the creation of schema mappings are described (Section 10.1). Next, the general evaluation approach and the scenarios used in the evaluation are introduced (Section 10.2). A detailed description of the conducted experiments and their results is given (Section 10.3). The conducted experiments consist of three parts. First, experiments aiming at the evaluation of the two approaches for collecting background knowledge, namely the schema reduction and the example data injection, are conducted in Section 10.3.1 and Section 10.3.2 respectively. Following this, several different experiments are conducted to evaluate the OBM approach itself. For each of the conducted experiments a detailed analysis and explanation of the experimental results is given. The chapter closes by analyzing how well the OBM approach achieves the requirements stated in Chapter 1.

10.1 Industrial State of the Art

As the integration scenarios described in chapter 2 are well known problems, a large number of tools from different vendors exist to support these integration scenarios. In order to put this evaluation of the OBM approach into perspective, this section reviews the functionality offered by the different industrial tools to support the creation of schema mappings.

10.1.1 Tools supporting B2B Integration

Depending on the focus two main types of tools exist, namely i) stand-alone schema mapping tools and ii) fully fledged B2B integration middleware consisting of design-time and runtime components.

Stand-alone Schema Mapping Tools

Examples of stand-alone schema mapping tools are Altova Mapforce[1] and Stylus Studio[2]. Although these tools are developed by different vendors, the functionality offered is quite similar. They support the manual creation of schema mappings using graphical editors as well as standardized data transformation and querying languages, e.g. XSLT [Wor99b] and XQuery [Wor07]. The resulting mappings can usually be exported using two technologies:

1. They are exported using the standardized data transformation languages (e.g. XSLT [Wor99b]). These mappings can be executed on any integration server supporting these standards.

2. The mappings are used to generate executable code in a programming language, e.g. Java, which can then be used to integrate the mapping into existing applications.

The stand-alone schema mapping tools usually offer none or only very limited support for the automatic creation of schema mappings. The only functionality that is generally available is the automatic generation of mappings for identical schemas or identical parts of them.

Furthermore, the stand-alone tools often support the data extraction from different data sources like e.g. data bases, XML files or spreadsheets. Consequently these tools could also be used to support the Data Migration of legacy data. However, as important functionality (like test functionality integrated with the target system; cf. Section 10.1.2) required to support legacy Data Migration is missing in these tools they are usually not used for this purpose.

B2B Integration Solutions

Today B2B integration is usually implemented using an integration middleware [Ber96], e.g. SAP Exchange Infrastructure [SO05], IBM WebSphere Message Broker[3] or Microsoft BizTalk Server.[4] Such an integration middleware typically consists of a repository, a runtime component and a design time tool. The repository stores all integration information and design time artifacts like the service descriptions and endpoint addresses, the message schemas and corresponding schema mappings and also additional configuration information. The runtime component is responsible for invoking the integration services and for executing the message mappings, whereas the design time tool is used for developing

---

[1] http://www.altova.com/products/mapforce/data_mapping.html

[2] http://www.stylusstudio.com/xml_mapper.html

[3] Additional information available online at http://www-306.ibm.com/software/integration/wbimessagebroker/.

[4] Additional information available online at http://www.microsoft.com/biztalk/default.mspx

10.1 Industrial State of the Art

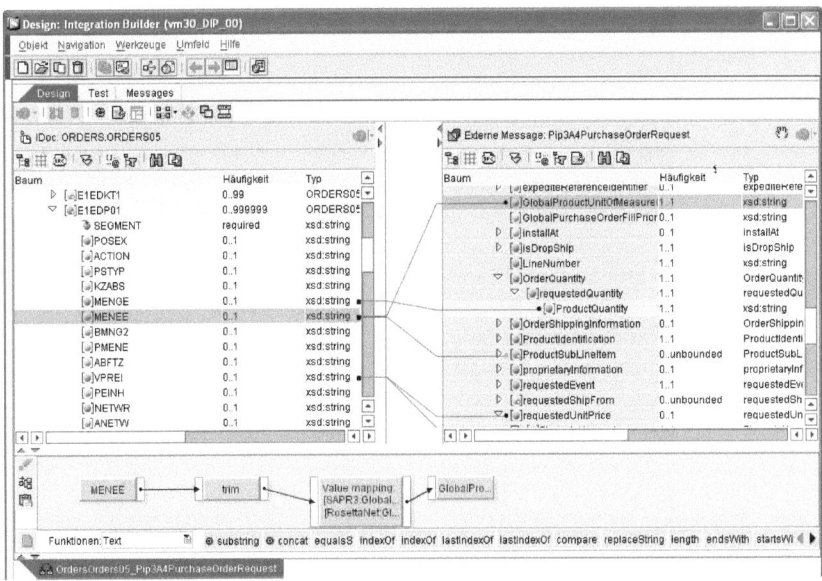

Figure 10.1: The design time tool of the SAP Exchange Infrastructure showing two messages.

and testing the necessary mappings and configuring the runtime. Some vendors of B2B integration solutions already offer mappings between a number of well known industry standards (e.g. Seeburger and SAP) together with their solutions.

The commercially available design time tools support the graphical development of the necessary message mappings. An example of such a graphical tool for the manual development of message mappings is shown by the screen shot in Figure 10.1. It shows the design time tool of the SAP Exchange Infrastructure. On the left hand side of the picture the structure of the source schema is shown, while the right hand side shows the structure of the target schema. The lines connecting entities of the two schemas represent matching schema entities while the lower part of the figure shows the complex mapping rule associated to the match between two schema entities.

Users of these tools create mappings between any elements of the source and the target schema by connection them visually through drag and drop operations. Complex mapping expressions can be created by associating predefined mapping functions to the matches (lower part of the user interface). More advanced tools even offer some kind of integrated development environment for mappings. Using these tools a user can either create mappings by connecting nodes in the tree representation of the schemas or by writing mapping scripts using a specialized programming language. The tool takes care of synchronizing both representations of the mapping.

Besides a graphical modelling of message mappings most integration middleware also allows the development of message mappings using general purpose programming languages like e.g. C and Java or specialized scripting languages like XSLT [Wor99b].

In commercial B2B integration solutions only very basic functionality for the semi-automatic creation of schema mappings is available. These tools usually only offer functionality to automatically create mappings for identical schemas or sub-schemas. Furthermore, only limited support for the reuse of previous mapping results is available. The approaches for reuse mostly rely on some kind or reusable mapping template that can be created by a user.

10.1.2 Data Migration Tools

State of the art Data Migration tools are often tightly integrated with the target system for which they support the Data Migration. Consequently it is difficult to get information about those tools, as they are usually not sold separately. As a result of this situation only the SAP Migration Workbench is reviewed in this section as one example of current Data Migration tools. However, other Data Migration tools are likely to offer similar functionality to the one provided by the SAP Migration Workbench.

Similar to general purpose B2B integration tools the SAP Migration Workbench consists of design-time tools, a repository and a runtime engine. While the design-time tools are used to develop the necessary transformations, the runtime is responsible for executing them to perform the actual migration of the legacy data.

The functionality offered by the design-time tools of the SAP Migration Workbench to support the mapping development is very similar to the one offered by the B2B integration tools presented above. Figure 10.2 shows a screen shot of the SAP Migration Workbench tool for developing schema mappings. The central part of the screen shows the source schema on the left hand side and the target schema on the right hand side. Furthermore, different types of meta information like e.g. the version of the mapping and who changed it is shown on the screen. However, the SAP Migration Workbench currently offers no support for the automatic creation of schema mappings.

One important additional feature of the SAP Migration Workbench is its ability to perform correctness checks of the created mappings automatically using example data. As it is tailored to support the migration of legacy data to specific SAP solutions, the SAP Migration Workbench can be tightly integrated with the specific target systems. This integration enables the SAP Migration Workbench to invoke the interfaces offered by the target system to support the migration of legacy data in a so called *test mode*. In this test mode the interface is invoked

10.1 Industrial State of the Art

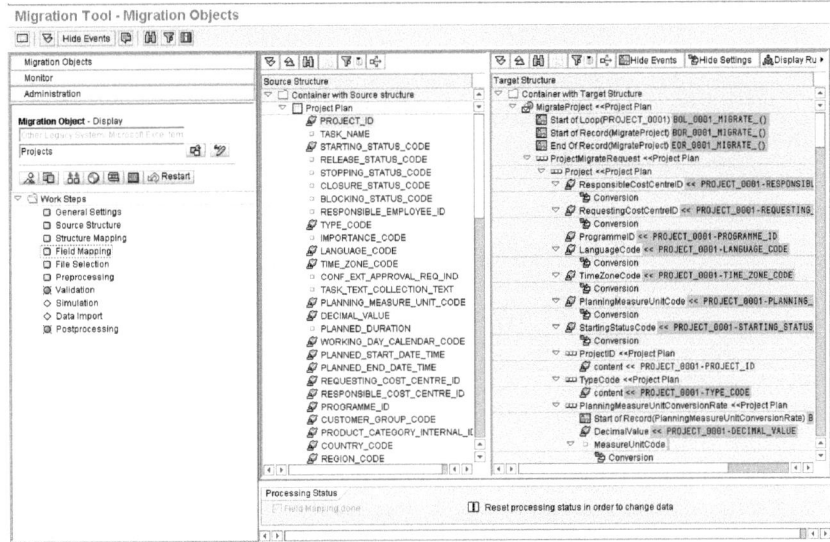

Figure 10.2: Creation of schema mappings in the SAP Migration Workbench.

with test data but no actual data migration to the target system is performed. However, a result of this invocation is that possible errors in the current mapping can be identified. If e.g. the current mapping transforms a given test data string into a code according to a custom code list but the result of this transformation is not valid in the target system, an error is raised. The errors returned by the data migration interface can then be used to present the developer of the mapping with a list of possible errors existing in the current mapping. Such a list of possible errors created by the invocation of the migration interface in test mode is shown in Figure 10.3.

Although different tools are used for creating the mappings in the Data Migration scenario they suffer from the same limitations as the tools used for B2B integration. The creation of the necessary mapping is a purely manual process and only rudimentary automatic support is provided to the developer during the creation of the mappings. Reuse is also only supported through the usage of templates.

10.1.3 Documentation Tools

Besides the set of specific B2B integration and Data Migration tools mentioned in the previous sections, there are also tools available enabling the development

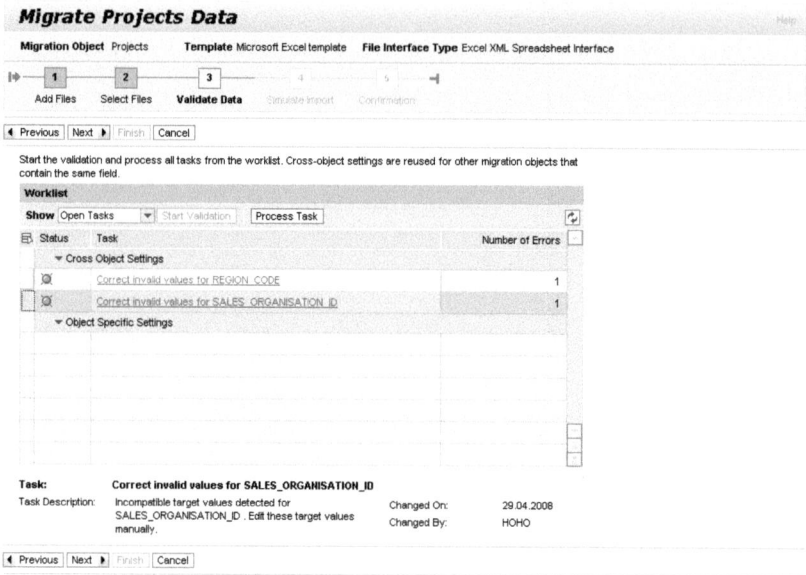

Figure 10.3: A list of possible errors in a schema mapping generated by the invocation of a migration interface in test mode.

of integration guidelines. Examples of these tools are GEFEG.FX[5] and Contivo Vocabulary Management System[6]. Both tools allow the documentation of existing data formats using meta data and the creation of documents for guiding integration projects on the basis of this annotation.

While these tools allow the documentation of schemas and the creation of integration guidelines it is not possible to exploit this information to (semi-) automatically generate schema mappings. As a result, the necessary documentation is in industrial integration projects in most cases not captured in such tools. Instead the necessary mappings are developed without a previous documentation of the required integration knowledge. Consequently, this knowledge is not available for reuse in future integration projects.

10.2 Evaluation Approach

In order to evaluate the OBM approach different real world scenarios in the area of data migration are used. In each of the scenarios a set of schemas together with

---

[5] http://www.gefeg.com
[6] http://www.contivo.com/

10.2 Evaluation Approach

the correct mappings between them are used as a basis for the evaluation. The correct mappings between the schemas were developed by experts in the context of real integration projects prior to the experiments. By comparing the mappings automatically generated by the OBM approach with the correct mappings and also with the mappings proposed by other existing automatic schema mapping approaches, the absolute mapping quality as well as the relative quality compared to existing approaches is evaluated. The evaluation of the OBM approach focuses on scenarios in the area of Data Migration as the mappings required there tend to be more complex compared to B2B integration scenarios. The reason is, for example, that more different mapping categories exist in the Data Migration case. Consequently, an approach achieving good results in Data Migration scenarios will also be capable of achieving good results in B2B integration scenarios.

Prior to the experiments focussing on evaluating the quality of the mappings proposed by the OBM approach two, more experiments are conducted. These experiments aim at evaluating the two approaches for the collection of domain knowledge proposed in Section 6.2.

Before describing the experiments the following subsections describe the scenarios used throughout the evaluation in more detail.

10.2.1 Evaluation Scenarios

The scenarios used throughout the evaluation originate from the area of *Data Migration from legacy systems to SAP Business ByDesign*.[7] As the name already suggests, the scenario originates from the area of data migration. Using SAP Business ByDesign, a novel SAP solution for small and medium enterprises, as a target system, the creation of schema mappings required for the migration of master data from various source system is evaluated.

Schemas

The schemas used in the data migration scenario introduced above are the schemas describing customer and supplier master data in different SAP systems. In particular the following schemas are used during the evaluation:

Source schemas:

- The DEBMAS and CREMAS schemas used to represent customers and suppliers in SAP R/3 release 4.0
- The DEBMAS, CREMAS and ADRMAS schemas used to represent customers, suppliers and address data in SAP ERP
- The OCRD schema used to represent business partners in SAP Business One (B1).

---
[7] http://www.sap.com/solutions/sme/businessbydesign/index.epx

Table 10.1: The four evaluation scenarios.

Scenario	Source	Target
Scenario 1	R/3 Customer (SAP R/3 DEBMAS schema)	ByD Business Partner (BusinessPartner schema)
Scenario 2	B1 Customer (SAP Business One OCRD)	ByD Business Partner
Scenario 3	R/3 Vendor (SAP R/3 CREMAS)	ByD Business Partner
Scenario 4	B1 Vendor (SAP Business One OCRD)	ByD Business Partner

Target Schema:

- BusinessPartner schema originating from SAP Business ByDesign (ByD).

In the cases where two or more schemas are mentioned in the list above, the information regarding customers and suppliers is split across several schemas. Consequently, all of these schemas need to be matched against the BusinessPartner schema of the target system.

Scenarios

Based on the schemas introduced above the four evaluation scenarios listed in Table 10.1 were defined. In the case of SAP Business One the suitable moulding of the OCRD schema for representing either a vendor or a customer was chosen in the respective scenarios.

Note that even though all schemas used in the evaluation originate from different SAP solutions they differ largely with respect to size, structure and used naming conventions. The reason is that the solutions from which the different schemas originate have been developed independently. For example, SAP Business One originates from the acquisition of a smaller software company by SAP. Consequently these schemas exhibit most of the characteristics expected in complex migration projects. The naming of the elements ranges from cryptic eight letter names in the DEBMAS and CREMAS schemas to very verbose naming in the case of the BusinessPartner schema. The structure of the schemas ranges from rather flat structures in the case of the DEBMAS and CREMAS schemas to deeply nested structures in the case of the target schema. In addition, each schema groups the information differently. As an example of the differences of the evaluation schemas consider Figure 10.4 and Figure 10.5. The figures show a graphical representation of a small excerpt from the BusinessPartner and the DEBMAS schema.

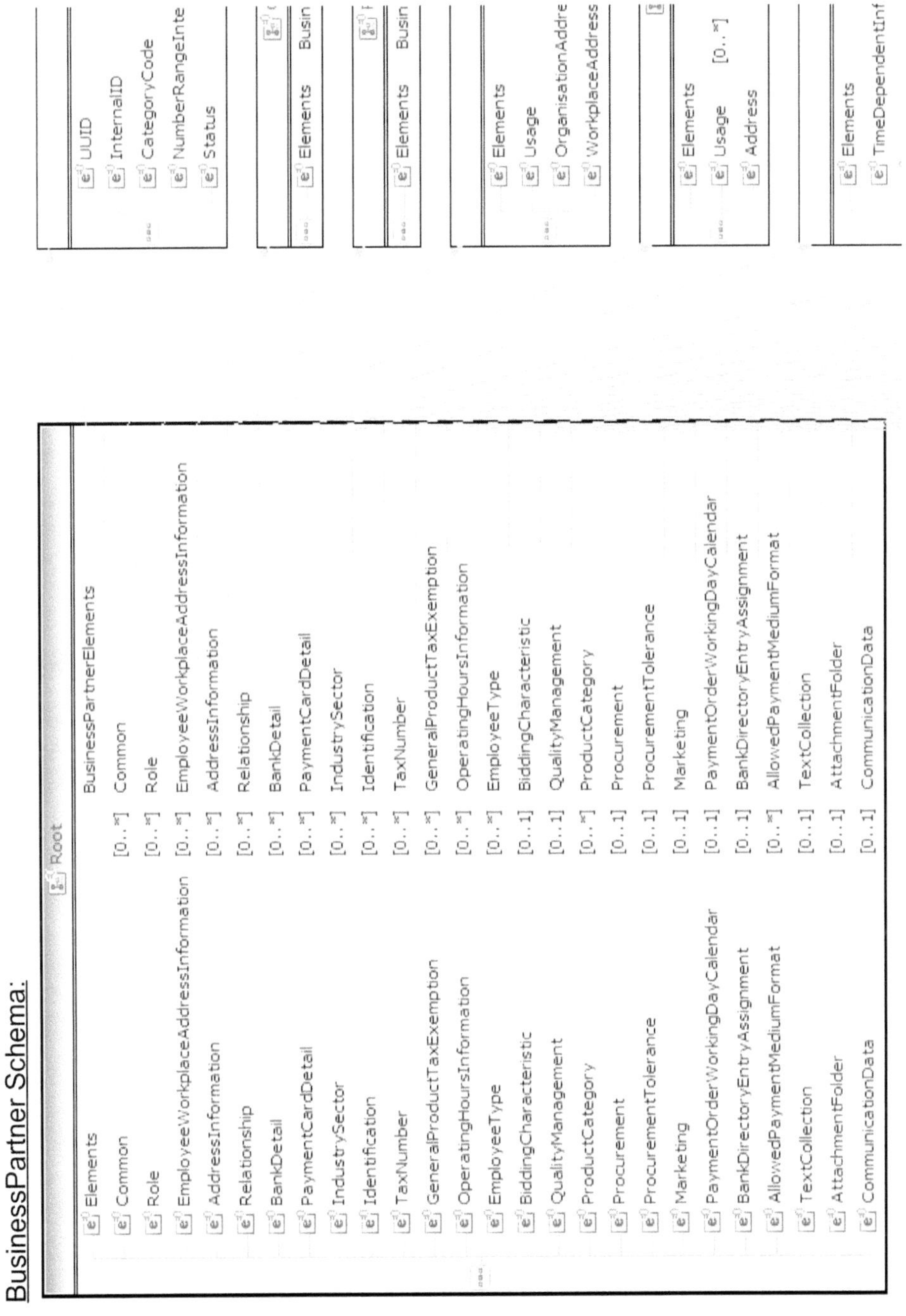

10.2 Evaluation Approach

BusinessPartner Schema:

- Root
  - Elements
    - BusinessPartnerElements
      - Common [0..*]
      - Role [0..*]
      - EmployeeWorkplaceAddressInformation [0..*]
      - AddressInformation [0..*]
      - Relationship [0..*]
      - BankDetail [0..*]
      - PaymentCardDetail [0..*]
      - IndustrySector [0..*]
      - Identification [0..*]
      - TaxNumber [0..*]
      - GeneralProductTaxExemption [0..*]
      - OperatingHoursInformation [0..*]
      - EmployeeType [0..*]
      - BiddingCharacteristic [0..1]
      - QualityManagement [0..1]
      - ProductCategory [0..*]
      - Procurement [0..1]
      - ProcurementTolerance [0..1]
      - Marketing [0..1]
      - PaymentOrderWorkingDayCalendar [0..1]
      - BankDirectoryEntryAssignment [0..1]
      - AllowedPaymentMediumFormat [0..*]
      - TextCollection [0..1]
      - AttachmentFolder [0..1]
      - CommunicationData [0..1]

- UUID
- InternalID
- CategoryCode
- NumberRangeInte
- Status

- Elements
  - Busin...

- Elements
  - Busin...

- Elements
  - Usage
  - OrganisationAddre
  - WorkplaceAddress

- Elements
  - Usage [0..*]
  - Address

- Elements
  - TimeDependentInf

Figure 10.4: Partial graphical representation of the structure and naming of the BusinessPartner schema.

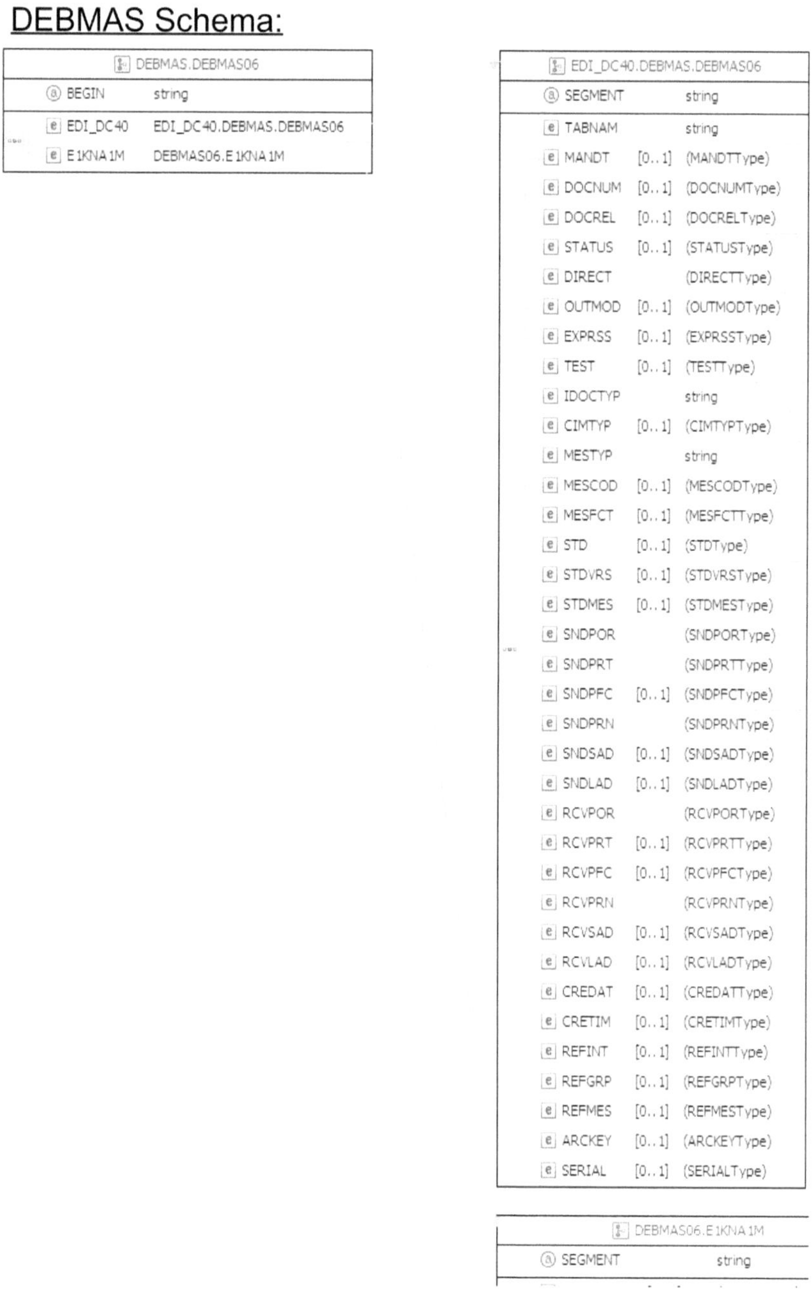

DEBMAS Schema:

DEBMAS.DEBMAS06	
ⓐ BEGIN	string
e EDI_DC40	EDI_DC40.DEBMAS.DEBMAS06
e E1KNA1M	DEBMAS06.E1KNA1M

EDI_DC40.DEBMAS.DEBMAS06		
ⓐ SEGMENT		string
e TABNAM		string
e MANDT	[0..1]	(MANDTType)
e DOCNUM	[0..1]	(DOCNUMType)
e DOCREL	[0..1]	(DOCRELType)
e STATUS	[0..1]	(STATUSType)
e DIRECT		(DIRECTType)
e OUTMOD	[0..1]	(OUTMODType)
e EXPRSS	[0..1]	(EXPRSSType)
e TEST	[0..1]	(TESTType)
e IDOCTYP		string
e CIMTYP	[0..1]	(CIMTYPType)
e MESTYP		string
e MESCOD	[0..1]	(MESCODType)
e MESFCT	[0..1]	(MESFCTType)
e STD	[0..1]	(STDType)
e STDVRS	[0..1]	(STDVRSType)
e STDMES	[0..1]	(STDMESType)
e SNDPOR		(SNDPORType)
e SNDPRT		(SNDPRTType)
e SNDPFC	[0..1]	(SNDPFCType)
e SNDPRN		(SNDPRNType)
e SNDSAD	[0..1]	(SNDSADType)
e SNDLAD	[0..1]	(SNDLADType)
e RCVPOR		(RCVPORType)
e RCVPRT	[0..1]	(RCVPRTType)
e RCVPFC	[0..1]	(RCVPFCType)
e RCVPRN		(RCVPRNType)
e RCVSAD	[0..1]	(RCVSADType)
e RCVLAD	[0..1]	(RCVLADType)
e CREDAT	[0..1]	(CREDATType)
e CRETIM	[0..1]	(CRETIMType)
e REFINT	[0..1]	(REFINTType)
e REFGRP	[0..1]	(REFGRPType)
e REFMES	[0..1]	(REFMESType)
e ARCKEY	[0..1]	(ARCKEYType)
e SERIAL	[0..1]	(SERIALType)

DEBMAS06.E1KNA1M	
ⓐ SEGMENT	string

Figure 10.5: Partial graphical representation of the structure and naming of the **DEBMAS** schema.

10.2 Evaluation Approach

Table 10.2: Complexity of the schemas used for evaluation in the data migration scenario.

Schema	Number of elements
SAP Business ByDesign (Target Schema)	4639
SAP R/3 4.0	953
SAP ERP	2150
SAP Business One	480

As mentioned earlier, schemas encountered in B2B and Data Migration scenarios are usually very complex. The complexity of the schemas that comprise the evaluation scenarios are shown in Table 10.2. For each set of schemas the complexity in terms of schema elements comprising the schemas is listed in the table.

In order to conduct the experiments the correct mappings, the so-called *master mappings*, as well as the domain ontology need to be created for each of the four scenarios. The following subsections describe in detail how the master mappings as well as the domain ontology where created.

10.2.2 Master Mappings

As mentioned above, the master mappings used for the evaluation of the OBM approach originate from real integration projects. The only preprocessing of the existing mappings that was performed was the substitution of the concrete mapping expressions. Each concrete mapping expression was substituted with the corresponding mapping category. Therefore, information contained in the master mappings used in the experiments only consisted of the matches between the source and the target schema and the mapping category associated to each of the matches.[8]

Furthermore, Table 10.3 shows the size of the master mappings with respect to the number of mapping expressions comprising a master mapping for the different evaluation scenarios. Note that the size of the master mappings is significantly smaller then the size of the involved schemas. Based on this observation it is obvious that in each of the evaluation scenarios only a subset of the schema entities needs to be mapped in order to create a correct mapping.

10.2.3 Evaluation Ontology

The evaluation ontology was created independently of any of the schemas used in the evaluation scenarios. Instead the domain ontology was modeled based on the conceptual description of an internal data model for the concept business partner.

---

[8] An excerpt of one of the mappings used in the evaluation is shown in Figure 9.2.

Table 10.3: The size of the master mappings in the different evaluation scenarios.

Scenario	Number of Mapping Expressions
Scenario 1	164
Scenario 2	49
Scenario 3	108
Scenario 4	40

On the basis of this documentation, the domain ontology could be created by a domain expert within one to two weeks.

The evaluation ontology consists of two parts:

Business Partner Ontology: The *Business Partner Ontology* is an ontology describing the domain of the evaluation scenarios, namely the domain of business partners.

Integration Knowledge Ontology: The *Integration Knowledge Ontology* builds upon the Business Partner Ontology and contains the integration knowledge associated to different concepts, relations and attributes in the Business Partner Ontology.

Note that in order to enable different types of experiments, the Integration Knowledge Ontology only contains integration knowledge, i.e. annotations regarding technical names, default values, internal and global identifiers and code lists, related to the SAP R/3 DEBMAS schema and the parts of the ORCD schema related to customers. Details on the conducted experiments are given in the following section.

The evaluation ontology was developed using OWL-DL as the ontology language [Wor04a] and is quite complex. The Business Partner Ontology itself consists of about 490 concepts, about 440 object properties and about 10 datatype properties. In total, the Business Partner Ontology consists of approximately 1950 axioms. On the basis of this domain ontology the Integration Knowledge Ontology was developed. It contains only the few additional concepts, object and datatype properties that are necessary to model the integration knowledge as presented in Section 6.3.2. In order to model the integration knowledge necessary for the DEBMAS and the ORCD schema, nearly 790 individuals where created in the Integration Knowledge Ontology. These individuals consists of about 330 individuals representing technical names of schema entities. The largest fraction of the remaining individuals, namely approximately 350 individuals, are used to model the example data while the others are used to model the rest of the integration knowledge.

Note that the number of individuals is directly related to the modeled integration knowledge and the complexity of the integrated schemas. For example, modeling one technical name in the ontology requires one instance (cf. Chapter 6). Consequently, the 330 individual s representing technical names model the technical names of 330 schema elements. The number of individuals necessary to represent the technical names of a particular schema only depends on the size of this schema. This is true for all different types of integration knowledge modeled in the ontology.

10.2.4 Quality Metrics

To quantify the quality of the automatically obtained mappings the standard quality metrics Precision, Recall and F-Measure [DMR02] are used. Below these three quality metrics are defined on the basis of a master mapping $\overline{M_{S \to T}}$ from a source schema S to a target schema T and an automatically created mapping $M_{S \to T}$. Note that the definitions given below are based on the ones presented by Ehrig in [Ehr06].

Definition 10.2.1 (Precision). *The Precision of a mapping $M_{S \to T}$ with respect to a master mapping $\overline{M_{S \to T}}$ is defined as:*

$$Precision\left(M_{S \to T}, \overline{M_{S \to T}}\right) = \frac{\left|M_{S \to T} \cap \overline{M_{S \to T}}\right|}{|M_{S \to T}|}$$

Definition 10.2.2 (Recall). *The Recall of a mapping $M_{S \to T}$ with respect to a master mapping $\overline{M_{S \to T}}$ is defined as:*

$$Recall\left(M_{S \to T}, \overline{M_{S \to T}}\right) = \frac{\left|M_{S \to T} \cap \overline{M_{S \to T}}\right|}{|\overline{M_{S \to T}}|}$$

As it is obvious that a schema matching approach can easily be optimized to achieve a high Precision at the cost of a low Recall and vice versa, therefore the F-Measure combines Precision and Recall into one result.

Definition 10.2.3 (F-Measure). *For a given Precision and Recall and a weighting factor α F-Measure is defined as:*

$$F-Measure(\alpha) = \frac{Precision * Recall}{(1-\alpha) * Precision + \alpha * Recall}.$$

As F-Measure is most commonly used with a weighting factor $\alpha = 0.5$ (cf. [DMR02, Ehr06]), i.e. Precision and Recall are equally weighted, this thesis also uses this weighting factor. The resulting formula for calculating the F-Measure is $F-Measure = 2 * \frac{Precision * Recall}{Precision + Recall}$.

10.3 Experiments

This section describes the different experiments conducted in order to evaluate different aspects of the OBM approach in detail. First, the described approaches for schema reduction as well as the example data injection are evaluated before Section 10.3.3 focuses in detail on the experiments evaluating the quality of the automatically created schema mappings.

10.3.1 Schema Reduction

As described in Section 5.2 the first step in the automatic schema mapping process is the Knowledge Collection step. The collection of the usage characteristics of a particular schema by answering an electronic questionnaire as proposed in Section 6.2.1 is part of this step. The answers to the questionnaire are then exploited in the Preprocessing step to reduce the complexity of the mapping problem.

In order to evaluate the usability of this approach a questionnaire covering the capabilities of the `BusinessPartner` schema of the target system was developed.[9] In the next step, the questionnaire was answered according to the capabilities of the different source schemas. Based on these answers the `BusinessPartner` schema was reduced to the capabilities of the source schemas. Note that this reduction was performed manually as the automatic schema reduction based on an electronic questionnaire has not yet been implemented as part of the OBM framework (cf. Chapter 9), yet.

The time necessary to answer the questionnaire mainly depends on how detailed the person answering the questionnaire knows the involved systems. In the conducted experiments, the user that was answering the questionnaire had very detailed knowledge of the source and the target system and was therefore able to answer the questionnaire in about 15 minutes. The general assumption is that answering the questions of the questionnaire should not take longer than 1 hour even for inexperienced users. However, since the knowledge required to answer the questionnaire is essential to create the schema mappings, the time necessary to answer the questionnaire is not lost.

The results of the schema reduction experiments are listed in Table 10.4. It shows the complexity of the reduced target schema based on the different source system capabilities. Generally speaking, the proposed schema reduction approach is capable of reducing the target schema to about 10-15% of its original size in the evaluated cased. Furthermore many of the complex sub-structures can be removed or largely simplified using this approach.

It is not possible to state exactly what elements of the target schema were removed as this largely depends on the source schema capabilities. However, a

---

[9]The complete questionnaire is available in Appendix A

10.3 Experiments

Table 10.4: Complexity of the target schema after the reduction

Scenario	Number of Schema Entities
BYD Business Partner Schema	4639
reduced to capabilities of R/3 4.0	645
reduced to capabilities of SAP ERP	612
reduced to capabilities of SAP B1	639

typical example from the experiments is that the target schema supports storing multiple, time dependent addresses per business partner. Some of the source systems in the experiments do not support address information on this level of detail. Consequently the complexity of the parts of the target schema responsible for storing time dependent address information could significantly be reduced.

As the original target schema contains about 4600 elements which turned out to be difficult to handle for the developed prototype, the following experiments were only conducted with the reduced schemas. Therefore, it can only be pointed out that the complexity of the target structure can be reduced significantly with the proposed schema reduction approach. However, no absolute numbers on the increase of the mapping quality compared to the unreduced schemas are available.

Nevertheless, one important benefit of the schema reduction approach is available even if the schema reduction would not improve the mapping quality. Due to the fact that the reduced schemas are significantly less complex than the original ones, the schema reduction obviously simplifies the manual review of the resulting mappings. Fewer mapping elements need to be reviewed and the individual mapping expressions tend to be simplified. This advantage alone already justifies the usage of the schema reduction approach.

10.3.2 Example Data Injection

In order to test the viability of the example data injection, an example instance of a customer and a vendor according to the information contained in the `BusinessPartner` schema were created in a human understandable format. A small excerpt of the human understandable representation of the customer example data used in the experiments is shown in Table 10.5. The Table contains one example data value for each attribute of a customer. Using this human understandable representation of the data as a basis, the user interfaces of the different systems (i.e. SAP R/3, SAP ERP and SAP B1) were used to manually create the example data in the respective systems.

These experiments resulted in a number of important observations. First, the experiments showed that the creation of example data using the user interface of a system is indeed easily possible. Since the well-known user interfaces are used

Table 10.5: Excerpt of the example data for a customer.

Attribute	Example Data Value
Identifier	LMASCHMIXU
Role	Customer
Role valid from	2003-03-03
Role valid to	2004-04-04
Form of Address	Company
Name	Maschmi Maximum AG
Verbal Communication Language	English
Search Term	SEARCH
Search Term2	TERM2
Salutation Text	Hello
Foundation Date	2001-01-01
Liquidation Date	2002-02-02
Street	Street Name
ZIP Code	76131
City	Karlsruhe
Country	Germany

to create example data instances, very little effort is required for the creation of example data. In the evaluation scenarios described, the creation of one example instance (i.e. a customer or a supplier) took around 10 minutes. However, it is obvious that the time necessary for creating an example instance depends heavily on the involved systems and can therefore not be quantified in detail. Second, it became obvious that providing example data does not make sense for all possible attributes of a business object, e.g. customer or vendor. The reason is that the example data needs to be easily understandable by a business user, who has to create the data in the source system. Consequently, the example data should e.g. not include code values, which are usually not understandable by a business user and also no system specific attributes. Finally, the schema mapping experiments conducted later showed that the attributes of the example data should not contain equal values as this reduces the accuracy of the example data based matching algorithms. For this reason the example data shown in Table 10.5 does not contain any identical date values.

10.3.3 Automatic Schema Mapping

In order to asses the quality of the schema mapping generated by the OBM Framework, a number of experiments were performed using the scenarios introduced above. The experiments can be grouped into three sets. In the first set of experiments the OBM Framework was executed using string-similarity and structure-based lifting algorithms. These experiments aimed at assessing the effectiveness of string-similarity and structure-based algorithms in the evaluation scenarios. In the next set of experiments the OBM Framework was executed using the integration-knowledge-based lifting algorithms. The goal of these experiments was to assess how well the integration knowledge modeled in the integration ontology can be exploited by the OBM approach. Finally, the third set of experiments investigated how well the integrated reuse of the OBM approach performs.

Exploitation of Entity Names and Structure

In the first experiment the OBM Framework was executed using only string-similarity based lifting algorithms. In particular, the Name Matcher and the Documentation Matcher where used in these experiment. In addition COMA++ [DR02] was executed on the same schemas using its standard configuration.[10]

In the experiments using only string-based lifting algorithms, the OBM approach is not capable of creating any mappings between the different schemas. Consequently the achieved Precision and the achieved Recall was 0. COMA++ in contrast is able to achieve a average Precision of ~ 0.23 and an average Recall of ~ 0.07, resulting in an average F-Measure of 0.1.

In the second experiment the OBM Framework was executed using only structural lifting algorithms. In particular the Node Path Matcher in combination with the Related Entities Matcher was used in this experiment. The Related Entities Matcher was configured to use the Name Matcher as its constituent matcher. Again, the OBM approach was not capable of creating any mappings between the different schemas. COMA++ was used in the same configuration as in the previous experiment. Consequently, it achieved equal results.

Analysis. The results of the first two experiments indicate that neither the usage of string-similarity-based nor the usage of structural lifting algorithms alone is sufficient for creating mappings in the evaluation scenarios. Even COMA++ using a combination of several more advanced string-based matching algorithms, including e.g. dictionary-based ones, is only capable of achieving poor matching results. An important fact of the results achieved by COMA++ is not visible in the average values for COMA++ shown in the figures above. On the schemas using only cryptical entity names in a flat structure (i.e. the schemas originating from SAP R/3) COMA++ was also not able to create any correct matches between the source and the target schema. Only in the schemas using more verbose entity names COMA++ was able to identify some matches. Furthermore, it is

---

[10]This configuration uses a number of different string-based and structure-based matching algorithms.

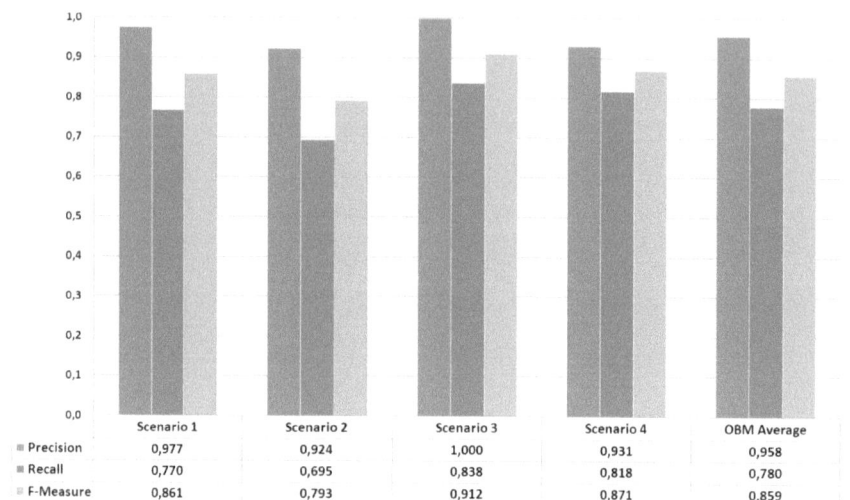

Figure 10.6: The results achieved by the OBM Framework using the Technical Names matcher.

important to note that in contrast to COMA++ the OBM Approach identifies mappings between the schemas and not only matches: a much more complex task.

The main conclusion of the previous experiments is that automatic schema matching approaches relying solely on schema information (cf. Section 7.2.1) are not able to achieve high quality results in the used evaluation scenarios. Therefore, the next set of experiments aimed at assessing the possibility of exploiting the different types of integration knowledge introduced in Section 6.1.

Exploitation of Integration Knowledge

In the first experiment aiming at assessing the exploitation of integration knowledge the OBM Framework was executed using only the Technical Names Matcher. The results of this experiment are depicted in Figure 10.6. Using only the technical names matcher the OBM approach achieved, depending on the evaluation scenario, a Precision between ~ 0.92 and 1, a Recall between ~ 0.69 and ~ 0.83 and consequently a F-Measure between ~ 0.79 and ~ 0.91. Note that the ontology used in these experiments only contained the technical names annotations for some of the used schemas (cf. Section 10.2.3). A detailed analysis on how well the OBM approach can reuse existing annotations in novel scenarios is performed in Section 10.3.3.

In the next experiment the OBM approach was executed using only the Instance Equality and the Instance Split/Concat Matcher. To do so, a predefined

10.3 Experiments

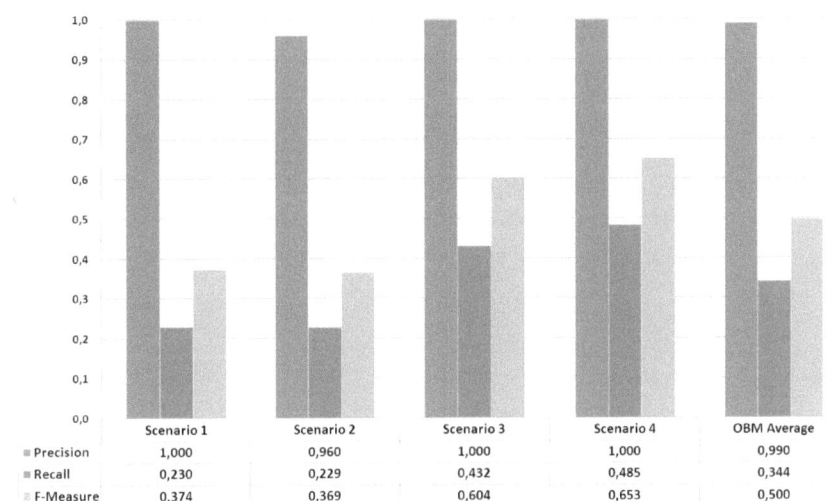

Figure 10.7: The results achieved by the OBM Framework using the combination of the Instance Equality and the Instance Split/Concat matcher.

example instance was generated in the source and the target system using the example data injection approach. The results achieved by the OBM approach using these two matchers is depicted in Figure 10.7. Using the example data based matchers as well as the generated example instances the OBM approach achieved, depending on the scenario, a Precision between ~ 0.96 and 1, a Recall between ~ 0.23 and ~ 0.48 and consequently a F-Measure between ~ 0.37 and ~ 0.65. The rather low Recall in this experiments originates from the fact that example data does not exist for all schema entities. The result is that these elements are not lifted to the ontology and consequently no mapping is created for them. An explanation why example data is only created for a subset of the entities of a schema is given in the previous section.

In the last experiment the OBM approach was executed using a combination of the Technical Names, the Instance Equality and the Instance Split/Concat Matchers. Using this combination of matchers the OBM approach achieved the results depicted in Figure 10.8. The Precision achieved in this experiments ranges from ~ 0.95 to 1, the Recall from ~ 0.66 to ~ 0.86. Consequently the F-Measure achieved ranges from ~ 0.78 to ~ 0.93. In addition to the results achieved by the OBM Framework, Figure 10.8 also contains the average results achieved by QuickMig [DSDR07] and COMA++ on in these scenarios. It is obvious that using a combination of the Technical Names Matcher and the example-data-based matchers, the OBM approach is capable of creating significantly better mappings then COMA++. Furthermore, the results show that while the OBM Framework

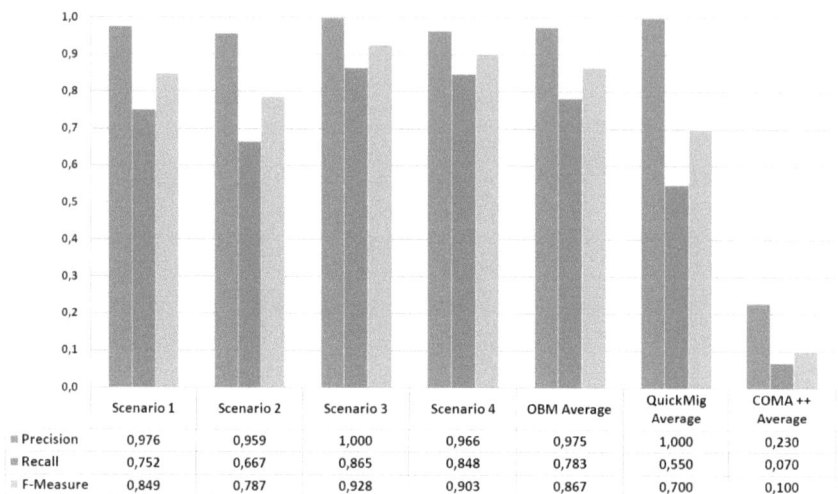

Figure 10.8: The results achieved by the OBM Framework using the combination of Technical Names and example data based matchers.

achieves in comparison to QuickMig a slightly worse Precision, the average Recall is significantly higher. This results in a significant improvement of the F-Measure in comparison to QuickMig.

Analysis. An analysis of the three experiments above leads to two main observations:

1. The exploitation of integration knowledge enables the creation of high quality mappings.

2. The mapping quality is significantly improved in comparison to the Quick-Mig approach.

In the following section, each of these two observations is discussed in more detail.

All three experiments conducted indicate that the OBM approach is capable of creating high quality mappings. In particular, the third experiment shows that the best results are achieved by the combination of different algorithms. The reason for this improvement is that the combination of different matching algorithms enables the exclusion of false positives. This feature becomes obvious in the situation where integration knowledge of similar scenarios is reused (i.e. the evaluation scenarios 2 and 4). In these cases, the Technical Names Matcher for example proposes some false liftings on the basis of the existing integration knowledge. The combination of different algorithms by aggregating the similarity values calculated by the individual matchers as presented in Section 7.3.1 helps to remove these false proposals and thereby improve the overall quality.

The improvement of the results achieved by the OBM approach over Quick-Mig are twofold. First, the OBM approach has more integration knowledge available. As QuickMig mainly exploits example data it is only capable of identifying mappings of the categories Move, Split and Concatenate. Using the additional integration knowledge available, OBM is capable of identifying matches of all available categories. Consequently, the Recall achieved by OBM is much higher. However, as in the OBM approach matches between schemas are not only identified based on example data but also on other integration knowledge, the possibility for proposing wrong mapping elements is higher, resulting in a slightly lower Precision compared to the QuickMig approach.

Integrate Reuse

In order to evaluate the reuse of existing integration knowledge Figure 10.9 compares the result achieved by the OBM approach by reusing existing integration knowledge to QuickMig. The figure show the results achieved by the OBM approach in evaluation scenarios 2 and 4. In these two scenarios existing integration knowledge from the evaluation scenarios 1 and 3 was reused. Furthermore, the figure shows the average results achieved by OBM in the evaluation scenarios 2 and 4 as well as the average results achieved by QuickMig and COMA++ across all evaluation scenarios. In the case of QuickMig the average results where already achieved by reusing existing mappings. The reuse approach used by QuickMig is based on the assumption of the transitivity of mappings introduced in [DR02] as well as on a predefined reuse path (cf. [DSDR07] for details). This means that in the QuickMig approach, the systems knows in advance which existing schema mapping can be reused in a particular case. This approach significantly simplifies the reuse of existing mappings.

Analysis. The results depicted in Figure 10.9 show that by reusing existing annotations, OBM achieves results comparable to the QuickMig approach. While QuickMig retains an average Precision of 1, the OBM approach achieves higher Recall values resulting in an improvement of the average F-Measure from 0.70 to ~ 0.84. The results, however, are solely based on the reuse of existing integration knowledge. QuickMig achieves an average Precision of 1 as it only reuses matches and the corresponding mapping expressions that can be verified with the available example instance. Consequently, not all possibly reusable matches and mappings expressions can be identified leading to the lower Recall values. The OBM approach reuses all available integration knowledge and is therefore capable of achieving significantly higher F-Measure values.

These results show that indeed integration knowledge gained in previous projects can be exploited to create high quality mappings. Furthermore, adding

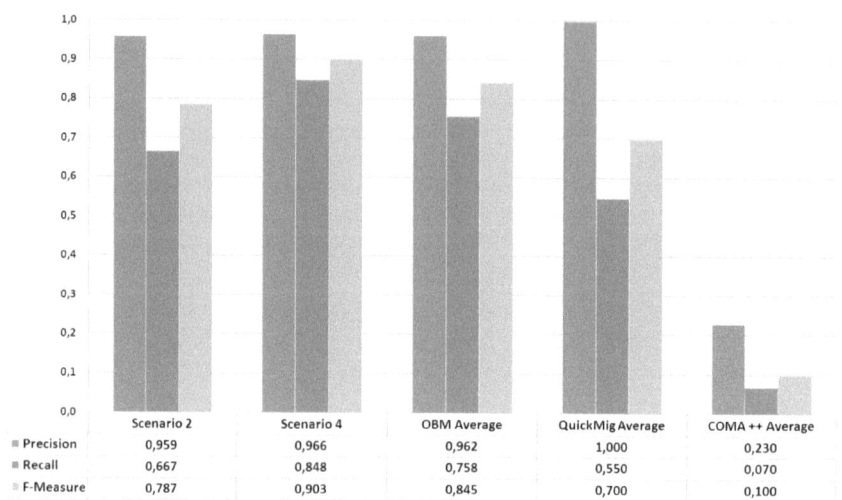

Figure 10.9: The results achieved by the OBM Framework by reusing integration knowledge from related integration scenarios.

contextual information to the integration knowledge as proposed in Section 6.3 simplifies the selection of the integration knowledge for reuse. While COMA++ requires a manual selection of possible reuse paths through a number of existing mappings and QuickMig used predefined reuse paths, the integrated reuse approach of the OBM approach is much more flexible. It only relies on a definition of similar contexts, which can easily be given in industrial scenarios.

Analysis Summary

In summary, the results achieved by the OBM approach show that by exploiting domain and integration knowledge about 80% of the manual effort can be automated. As the overall approach requires an initial schema reduction and the maintenance and extension of the domain ontology and integration knowledge, this effort also has to be taken into account. However, as this knowledge can be reused across different projects, the initial effort for creating the domain ontology as well as the maintenance of the integration knowledge can quickly be amortized.

10.3.4 Requirements Revisited

In this subsection the requirements introduced in Chapter 1 are revisited. For each of the requirements this section will check to which degree it is achieved by the OBM approach and indicate possibilities for future enhancements.

R1 (Quality). As stated in Chapter 1, the quality of the created mappings is the most important requirement for the application of an automatic mapping approach in industrial settings. As indicated by the results achieved in the evaluation scenarios the OBM approach is capable of creating schema mappings with very high quality. Especially the property of the OBM approach to generate mappings with a very high Precision is important in an industrial setting. Only if mappings are generated with a Precision close to 1 is a reduction of the development effort achieved. If the Precision is too low, the identification and the correction of the wrong mapping elements requires more effort than developing the mapping from scratch. In addition, the achieved Recall of ~ 0.78 on average shows that most mapping expression can be identified correctly by the OBM approach. A user only needs to manually create the remaining mapping expressions.

In summary, it is obvious that the OBM approach provides a significant improvement over existing approaches regarding the quality of automatically generated schema mappings.

R2 (Mappings) and R3 (Complex Mapping Expressions). As mentioned in Section 8 the OBM approach identifies mapping expressions for each match between two schemas. The correct mapping expression is identified with a very high accuracy even for the more complex mapping categories. In fact, matches between two schemas with the wrong mapping category assigned to it have been counted as false positives in the experiments above. However, creating an executable mapping expression from the mapping categories can only be partially automated as described in Section 8.2.2.

In summary it can be stated that the OBM approach is a significant step towards the semi-automatic creation of schema mappings instead of schema matchings. Given the possible complexity of mapping expressions in industrial integration scenarios identifying the correct mapping category for over 75% of the mapping expressions is a very good result. The possibility to at least create mapping expression templates for all mapping categories except the category Complex show that the OBM approach fully meets the requirement R2.

R4 (Capture and Reuse Integration Knowledge). In the OBM approach, integration knowledge is captured by augmenting a domain ontology and exploited during the automatic mapping creation. This is one part of the requirement R4. Furthermore, R4 states that the chosen representation of the integration knowledge should enable a developer to easily query the available integration knowledge. While this part of the requirement has not been investigated in this thesis the choice of an ontology as the representation formalism enables the usage of the integration knowledge by humans. The reason is that representing the concepts in a domain in a human interpretable way is one of the design goals underlying the development of ontologies (cf. Section 3.5). While current ontology languages require significant training to enable a human user to understand the represented knowledge it is possible to support a user by tools to simplify the querying of the available integration knowledge. In addition the availability of example instances for the concepts in the ontology should further facilitate the human understanding of the integration knowledge.

R5 (Flexible Mapping Execution). All mappings generated by the OBM approach are represented using the mapping categories introduced in Section 8.2. These mapping categories provide an abstract representation of a mapping which can semi-automatically be translated into the representation required by a particular execution environment. Consequently the OBM approach achieves the requirement R5 based on the design underlying the approach.

R6 (Performance). The requirement for the performance of the OBM approach was to be executable in the area of minutes on typical mapping problems. In the experiments conducted during the evaluation, the OBM Framework took between 30 and 120 seconds for the automatic calculation of a schema mapping. The execution time of the OBM Framework was mainly influenced by the complexity of the source and the target schema. This execution time is inside the time frame required by requirement R6. However, the current implementation of the OBM Framework has not been optimized regarding performance. Consequently, it might be possible to significantly improve execution time by an optimization of the implementation.

10.4 Summary

This section focused on the evaluation of the OBM approach. After describing industrial state of the art tools the general evaluation approach was introduced. Next, a number of experiments aiming at the assessment of the feasibility of different parts of the OBM approach were described. These experiments showed that the proposed schema reduction as well as the proposed example data injection approach are both viable solutions for the collection of integration knowledge. The next set of experiments focused on assessing the quality of the mapping generated by the OBM approach. The results of these experiments indicated that the OBM approach is capable of automatically creating schema mappings of high quality. Furthermore a comparison with existing tools showed that the OBM approach achieved significantly better results as compared to state-of-the-art research prototypes. Finally, the requirements listed in the introduction were revisited. The analysis showed that indeed the OBM approach is capable of archiving the requirements stated in Chapter 1.

Part IV

Summary and Outlook

Chapter 11
Summary & Future Work

In this chapter a summary of the presented work as well as an outlook on possible future extensions is presented. After an outlook on possible future work (Section 11.1) the possible application of the OBM approach to bootstrap semantic Web services is presented. This chapter closes by presenting possible industrial applications of the OBM approach within SAP (Section 11.3).

11.1 Future Work

This section details possible future extensions and improvements to the work presented in this thesis. For the discussion of possible future work related to the OBM approach, the generic ontology-based mapping process introduced in Section 5.2 is taken as a guideline. For each of the process steps which are highlighted in Figure 11.1 possible directions for future work are discussed.

11.1.1 Knowledge Collection

The Knowledge Collection step is the first step in the ontology-based mapping process. In this thesis two possible approaches for knowledge collection were presented. The following paragraphs list future research directions for the knowledge collection prior to the semi-automatic creation of schema mappings.

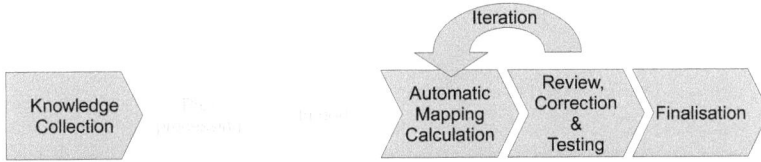

Figure 11.1: Steps of the ontology mapping process discussed in the future work.

Exploitable Types of Knowledge. The collection and exploitation of usage characteristics and example data proved very successful in the presented scenarios. However, other types of background knowledge are not yet exploited. Other types of knowledge that could possibly be exploited are, for example, knowledge regarding extensions and customizations of a system or messaging standard or knowledge regarding known usage characteristics (cf. Section 6.1.2).

Although the relevant integration knowledge presented in Section 6.1.2 is quite general, other types of integration knowledge could be more relevant in scenarios that were not investigated in this thesis. Therefore future work on the topic of Knowledge Collection should investigate wether the integration knowledge relevant in B2B integration and Data Migration is also important in other scenarios requiring the development of schema mappings or if other types of integration knowledge need to be taken into account.

Knowledge Collection Approaches. The knowledge collection approaches presented in Section 6.2 focus specifically on the collection of usage characteristics and implementation details. These approaches to knowledge collection can be improved and extended into different directions.

First, the existing approaches, namely example data injection and collection of usage characteristics, should be integrated into a real tool. In contrast to this thesis where the two knowledge collection approaches were implemented and evaluated independently of the implementation of the OBM approach, an integrated tool would allow to study the user interaction with a mapping tool. Based on observations resulting from this interaction, the processes used for the knowledge collection approaches could be further refined and optimized.

Second, new approaches for the collection of different types of integration knowledge should be investigated. As any additional knowledge improves not only the quality achieved by an automatic schema mapping system but also helps in the documentation of a system, the collection of additional knowledge is definitely beneficial. However, when developing new knowledge collection approaches, a strong focus needs to be put on enabling the non-intrusive collection of knowledge. Approaches that require users to learn complex tools or to invest significant effort in the knowledge collection step will most likely not be used in industrial scenarios.

Third, the knowledge collection step should not only take the process of generating schema mappings into account. Instead, approaches to collect integration knowledge already during the development of systems should also be investigated. Collecting the required integration knowledge already throughout system development, e.g. through the annotation of source code or configuration files, would significantly simplify the future creation of schema mappings.

Integration of Knowledge Collection and Context. Another promising option is the integration of knowledge collection approaches and contextual information. As an example, consider the collection of usage characteristics. By presenting users only with the questionnaires related to the current migration task, this knowledge collection approach already takes the current context into account.

However, contextual information can potentially be exploited in much more detail and can also be beneficially combined with any knowledge collection approach. As an example consider the example data injection. In its current version, a user receives a textual description of the example data and enters this data in the system at hand. However, some of this example data is not applicable in certain scenarios as e.g. particular data is not supported by the involved system. Consequently, the example data injection could be simplified if only applicable example data is presented to the users.

11.1.2 Automatic Mapping Calculation

The general future work related to the overall OBM approach is its application and evaluation in different scenarios. The evaluation performed in this thesis was focused on the two scenarios B2B integration and Data Migration and used different SAP schemas for the evaluation. While these schemas contained all types of integration challenges presented in Chapter 3, an evaluation of the OBM approach with additional schemas originating from different integration scenarios would nevertheless be interesting. In addition to this, the OBM approach should be evaluated in different scenarios, e.g. Master Data Management,[1] that require mappings between schemas.

Specific future work focussing on the Automatic Mapping Calculation step in the OBM approach is related to two parts, namely the lifting and the mapping extraction. In both areas different improvements, especially regarding the selection of mapping algorithms and the parameterization of the algorithms, are possible.

Domain-specific Parametrisation. Most semi-automatic schema mapping tools require a user to set certain parameters i.e. setting threshold values for matching or cut off values for the search depth in the ontology, manually. This is also true for the OBM approach. As in different scenarios different parameters are necessary to achieve high quality mappings,

---

[1] See http://en.wikipedia.org/wiki/Master_Data_Management for a short description of the term Master Data Management.

correctly setting the required parameters is difficult. One approach to improve the usability of mapping tools is to automatically adjust the required parameters to the current domain.

Different approaches for this automatic adjustment of parameters is possible. Either a set of parameters that perform well in certain domains could be defined. Using contextual information that can e.g. be collected in the Knowledge collection step, the appropriate set of parameters could be selected. Another possible approach would be through a user interaction during the Review and Iteration steps. In this case, the system would have to monitor which mapping elements of a proposed mapping are accepted and which rejected or changed. Based on this information the system could try to adjust the parameter of a mapping tool. However, this approach to setting the parameters of a mapping approach would require a very iterative approach to schema mapping (cf. Section 11.1.4).

Selection and Weighting of Matching Algorithms. Instead of preselecting a set of matching algorithms that are executed in order to lift a given schema, the domain ontology also allows a dynamic selection and weighting of matching algorithms. For example, instead of using a general purpose instance-based matcher to match date and code-list instances either specific matchers could be selected or the weighting of the matchers could be adjusted based on concepts in the domain ontology and the associated integration knowledge. If, for example, a concept in the ontology is a sub-concept of a date, a specialized date-instance matcher could be given a higher weight during the aggregation of the matcher results (cf. Section 7.3).

Semi-Automatic Extension of the Domain Ontology. One important assumption that was made during the development of the OBM approach is that the domain ontology dominates the schemas regarding the information capacity (see Section 5.3 and [MIR93]). However, while this feature of the domain ontology can be guaranteed in the case of Data Migration scenarios[2] it can not be guaranteed in the case of B2B integration projects. Therefore, an application of the OBM approach in industrial scenarios also requires functionality to extend and version the domain ontology if the domain ontology does not dominate the schemas with respect to its information capacity. One possible approach for the domain-specific extension of a domain ontology used for B2B integration is given in [Stu07]. However, the extension of the domain ontology needs to be further investigated and also integrated with approaches for ontology modeling.

---

[2]In this case the domain ontology only needs to dominate the target schema as information that cannot be represented by the target schema cannot be migrated.

11.1.3 Review, Correction & Testing

Despite the fact that the Review, Correction & Testing step was not the focus of this thesis, it plays an important role in productive scenarios. Only if automatically created mappings can easily and quickly be reviewed, possibly corrected and tested, will automatic schema mapping approaches be used in industrial scenarios. Regarding the testing of mappings, the industrial tools for Data Migration already provide powerful solutions (see Section 10.1.2). However, especially the review and correction of automatically created mappings needs to be improved.

User Interface for Large Schemas. The user interfaces to support the schema mapping task of both, research prototypes and industrial solutions, are quite similar. Usually these tools present the source and target schema or schemas as trees and mappings as lines connecting elements in these trees. This kind of user interface is not very useful when creating mappings for large schemas, as it quickly becomes cluttered and difficult to use. This problem is even more important when large, automatically-generated mappings need to be reviewed and corrected by a user. In order to enable an efficient review and correction for mappings novel user interface paradigms for schema mappings need to be explored. User interfaces should focus on the user's current task, easily allowing one to hide currently unnecessary information and thereby supporting a user much better than current tools.

One possibility for different user interfaces could be the use of *confidence markers* for mapping elements. Current user interfaces of automatic schema mapping tools like COMA often display a similarity value for identified mapping elements. The idea is that a higher similarity represents a higher confidence, that a mapping is correct. However, this is not sufficient especially when handling large schemas. A user needs to be able to quickly identify which mapping elements need to be checked, which are certainly correct or where additional work for completing the expression is needed. That could, for example, be achieved by visual markers for mapping elements. Furthermore, a user should have the possibility to filter for certain types of mappings, e.g. ones already accepted by him or ones mainly generated on the basis of example data. This would allow a user to more easily identify relevant mapping expressions for review and correction.

Automatic Testing of Mappings. Testing functionality similar to the one already available in Data Migration tools is also required in the case of B2B integration tools. Testing automatically generated mappings using example data allows to quickly identify possible problems in the mapping. Highlighting possibly wrong mapping elements enable a user to quickly fix the errors leading to the wrong mapping.

11.1.4 Iteration & Finalization

The Iteration step is an important part of the ontology-based mapping process that has not been discussed in this thesis. Developing a schema mapping using the support of automatic mapping approaches will in real projects always result in an iterative development process. For example, a user might create a first mapping using the automatic mapping functionality, after that the user corrects some mappings and also uses the automatic functionality to create a mapping for a small sub-part of the schemas. In order to develop the OBM approach into a complete solution, this Iteration step consequently has to be taken into account. The following paragraphs highlight possible extensions of the OBM approach that can be integrated into the iteration step.

Iterative Mapping Creation. The idea of an iterative mapping creation is to support the creation of schema mappings in a highly interactive fashion. While the user corrects an initial proposal created by the automatic schema mapping approach, an updated proposal is calculated in the background. In order to support this kind of interactive mapping creation user feedback from the Review, Correction & Testing step needs to be used immediately to update the automatically created mapping. Therefore, the execution time of the performance of the matching algorithms needs to be significantly improved. In addition, selection and weighting of the matching algorithms based on user feedback is also required.

Integrating Knowledge into the Ontology. During the Review, Correction & Testing step additional integration knowledge is generated. This additional integration knowledge should be integrated into the integration knowledge ontology in order to enable its exploitation in the future. This integration could, for example, be performed in the finalization step. However, several problem exist for this integration. First, the correct ontology entity for associating the new integration knowledge with needs to be identified. Second, approaches for ontology versioning and conflict resolution have to be taken into account. Finally, the integration of new integration knowledge should happen non-intrusively and should only require minimal user interaction

11.2 Application of the OBM Approach to semantic Web services

A recent development in research are semantic Web services [MSZ01]. The rational behind the development of semantic Web services is the automation of certain tasks during the life cycle of a Web service. Typical tasks that semantic

11.2 Application of the OBM Approach to semantic Web services

Web services aim to automate are the discovery of suitable services or the composition of different services in order to perform some complex task. In order to achieve this, semantic Web services extend Web service descriptions with a formal description of the Web service functionality, its inputs and outputs, and its behavioral requirements. The formal description of semantic Web services includes an annotation which is expressed by using an ontology. Currently, there exist two competing frameworks for the expression of semantic Web services: OWL-S[The04] and WSMO[Dig04]. The METEOR-S project[Lar05] aims at the same target, but is restricted to the adaptation of existing languages, like WSDL-S[AFM+05]. OWL-S and WSMO were developed completely from scratch to fully support the whole potential of semantic technologies.

The goal of all semantic Web service frameworks is to create semantic Web services based on existing Web services in order to reuse existing development. To achieve this, all frameworks require the annotation of existing Web services using ontologies. Take a B2B service that accepts purchase orders in the message format depicted in Figure 2.2 as an example. Creating a semantic Web service based on this Web service would, besides other tasks, require the annotation of each element of the schema with entities of an ontology. In the context of a B2B service performing this annotation requires significant effort due to the size of the involved message schemas. Therefore, in order to bootstrap the usage of semantic Web services in industry, an automation of the initial annotation of existing Web services is required [HK03]. The following discussion focuses on the annotation of the input and output messages of existing Web services.

Automating this annotation requires the creation of a mapping between the schema elements of the input and output messages and the entities of the ontology used for annotating the Web service. The mappings necessary for annotating semantic Web services differ from the ones required in the areas of B2B integration and Data Migration as they map between different representation formalisms. In the B2B integration or Data Migration scenarios both, the source and the target, are schemas while when annotating Web services the sources of the mapping are schemas and the target are ontologies. In the following paragraphs, the special mappings necessary for annotating Web services are referred to as *schema liftings*. A formal definition of the term is given in Section 4.5. For now it is sufficient to understand that a schema lifting is a mapping between a schema and a given ontology. The task of creating such a schema lifting is required whenever a existing Web service needs to be annotated with an existing ontology.

Schema lifting involves two steps:

1. Identifying correspondences between the source schema and the target ontology
2. Creating the mapping rules for the identified correspondences.

However, the second step is optional in the schema lifting use case.

It is important to note that an annotation of an existing schema can only be performed with good quality if the ontology used for annotation is sufficiently detailed. If this is not the case, it is only possible to create the annotation for a limited number of schema elements.

11.3 Industrial Applications

In order to show the applicability of the OBM approach in industrial applications, this paragraph highlights three possible SAP applications or prototypes where semi-automatic mapping functionality on the basis of the OBM approach could be applied beneficially. It is important to understand that this list does not contain applications into which the OBM approach will be integrated in the near future, but rather a list of possible candidates for an integration. Nevertheless, first prototypes exist for some applications (e.g. a prototype related to the SAP Migration Workbench) in which at least parts of the OBM approach have already been integrated. Furthermore, the list of possible applications presented below is not extensive, but rather represents a selection of applications where first work regarding semi-automatic schema matching was performed. The OBM approach could also be applied to other SAP applications like SAP NetWeaver Master Data Management or the SAP Exchange Infrastructure. The SAP applications for which an extension with the OBM approach is discussed below are i) the SAP NetWeaver Composition Environment, ii) the SAP Migration Workbench and iii) the SAP CCTS Modeller Wrap 10.

11.3.1 The SAP NetWeaver Composition Environment

The SAP NetWeaver Composition Environment is part of SAPs NetWeaver offering. It enables users to develop so-called composite applications. These composite applications compose functionalities of legacy systems as well as SAP systems into new applications. In a recent press release SAP announced a future extension of the SAP NetWeaver Composition Environment called *Galaxy* [Nie08]. Galaxy consists of a runtime and a design-time component and enables the modeling, execution, management and monitoring of business processes.

Figure 11.2 shows a screen shot of the design-time component of Galaxy, the Galaxy Workbench. The central part of the screen shows a complex business process modeled within the tool. Each of the independent, automated process steps, like e.g. the process step "Sales Order", is implemented using a Web service. As different steps in the process are implemented using independently developed Web services, a mapping between the input and output messages of the Web services and the global data representation of the whole process is required. These mappings are developed using the mapping editor which is shown in the lower part of the screen.

11.3 Industrial Applications

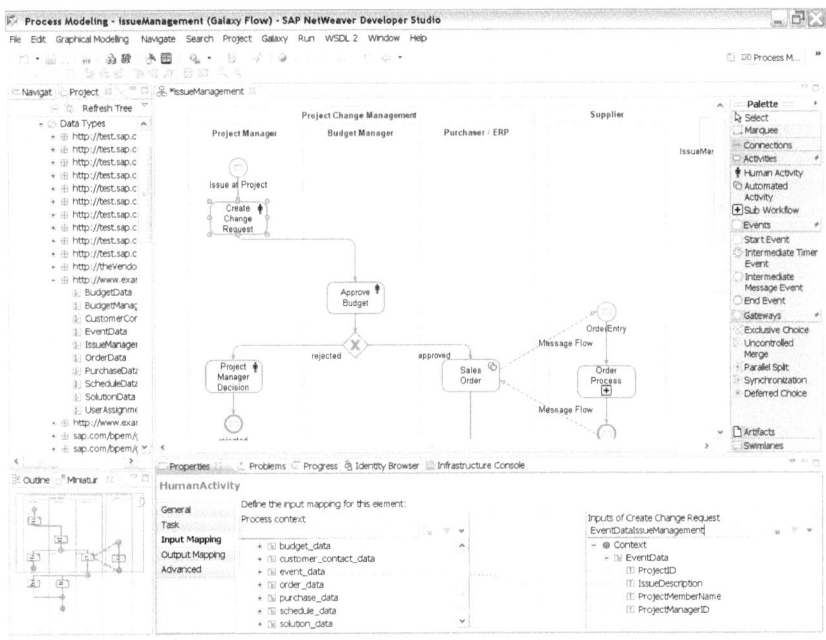

Figure 11.2: The Galaxy Workbench showing a simple process and a schema mapping.

As the input and output messages of Web services in industrial scenarios are usually quite complex, the mapping editor of the Galaxy Workbench is a natural candidate for an extension with the automatic mapping functionality provided by the OBM approach. Currently only basic mapping functionality based on simple name matching algorithms is available in the Galaxy Workbench.

11.3.2 The SAP Migration Workbench

The SAP Migration Workbench is a tool developed by SAP to support the migration of legacy data to SAP solutions. Its functionality has already been described in Section 10.1.2. The SAP Migration Workbench is targeted specifically on migration experts supporting customers in the migration of their legacy data.

The OBM approach can be used to extend the SAP Migration Workbench into two directions. First, the OBM approach could be integrated directly into the SAP Migration Workbench in order to support consultants during the creation of mappings in Data Migration projects. Second, the OBM approach could be used to extend the target user group of the SAP Migration Workbench into the direction of non-expert users. As the first option is very similar to the one discussed in the context of the Galaxy Workbench, the following paragraphs focus on the second one.

The main idea underlying an extension of the SAP Migration Workbench in the direction of non-expert users is to allow inexperienced users to create an initial mapping between their legacy system and the SAP solution. This initial mapping could be taken in a second step and completed by a migration expert in order to complete the mapping. The OBM approach would be a suitable fit to enable such a solution. Using the example data and the schema reduction approach, valuable integration information could be gathered even by inexperienced users. The OBM approach could then be used to create a first mapping. A first sanity check of this mapping would be performed again by the user. As the mapping is expressed using the mapping categories, this sanity check does not require any expert knowledge. In the subsequent step a migration expert would take the initial mapping and complete it before performing the actual Data Migration.

This approach separates the rather complex task of creating an executable mapping and testing it from the much simpler task of injecting example data, answering a questionnaire and performing a first sanity check of a mapping. Consequently, this extension of the SAP Migration Workbench would allow inexperienced users to perform some parts of the tasks that currently need to be performed by migration experts.

11.3.3 SAP CCTS Modeller Warp 10

SAP CCTS Modeller Warp 10 [Stu07, SC07] is a recent prototype developed by SAP aiming at solving three difficult problems. The first goal of the CCTS Modeller Warp 10 is to enable the easy adaptation of existing B2B messaging standards to the specific needs in a certain domain. Based on this, the second goal of the CCTS Modeller Warp 10 is to enable a harmonization of extensions and modifications made to a B2B messaging standard. Third, CCTS Modeller Warp 10 aims at automating the creation of mappings between different messaging standards.

The CCTS Modeller Warp 10 tries to achieve these ambitious goals by mapping existing B2B messaging standards to a central ontology which is based on the UN/CEFACT Core Component Technical Specification [WSC$^+$07]. Extensions and modifications to B2B messages are then not performed at the level of the message schemas, but rather at the ontology level. The required schemas are later on automatically extracted from the central ontology.

Figure 11.3 shows the high-level architecture of the CCTS Modeller Warp 10. One of the central parts of this architecture is the *context-driven semi-automatic mapping* of B2B standards. The OBM approach would be an ideal fit for implementing the functionality required by this component. The reason is that the CCTS Modeller Warp 10 is already based on the idea of a central ontology. Consequently, the primary requirement of the OBM approach is already fulfilled.

11.3 Industrial Applications

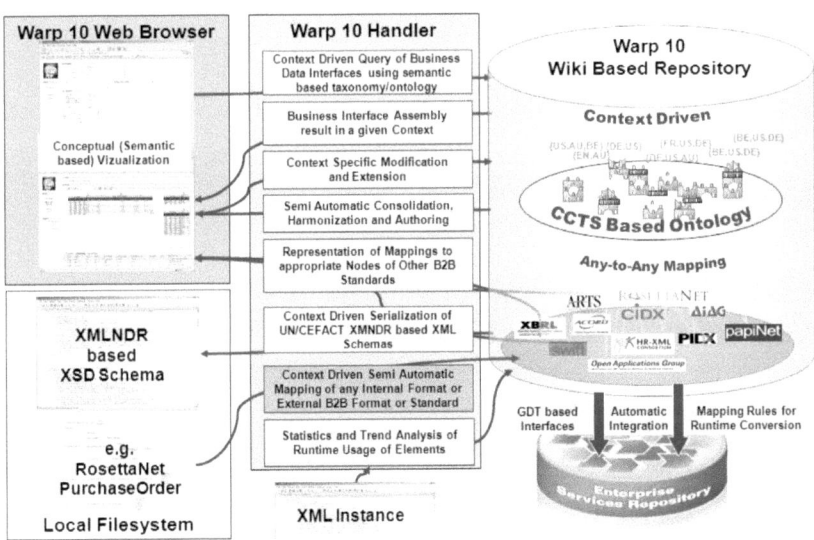

Figure 11.3: High-level architecture of the CCTS Modeller Warp 10.

Chapter 12

Conclusion

The two main contributions of this thesis are an ontology-based schema mapping approach and two novel approaches for the non-intrusive collection of integration knowledge from users. Both parts of the thesis have been applied and evaluated in industrial integration scenarios (cf. Chapter 10). On the one hand, the feasibility to collect integration knowledge using the two presented approaches could be proven in this evaluation. On the other hand, the evaluation showed that the proposed ontology-based mapping approach enables the automatic creation of high quality schema mappings.

Next, the research questions posed in the abstract are revisited and the proposed solutions are reviewed.

- *Which knowledge is necessary to create schema mappings?* The analysis in Section 6.1 showed that two types of knowledge, namely domain and integration knowledge, are necessary to create schema mappings. While domain knowledge is related to the relation of the real world entities represented by certain schemas or schema entities, integration knowledge is related to detailed knowledge concerning a specific implementation of a system or messaging standard.

- *How can the necessary background knowledge be collected?* In Section 6.2 two different approaches to collect required background knowledge, in particular integration knowledge were introduced. While the proposed approach to the collection of usage characteristics focusses specifically on one type of integration knowledge, the Example Data Injection can be used to easily collect knowledge regarding different implementation details. The goal of both approaches was to non-intrusively collect the integration knowledge from a user with no detailed implementation knowledge of the involved systems. The reason is that in industrial integration scenarios, e.g. in the area of Data Migration, implementation knowledge of the involved systems is usually not easily accessible (cf. Section 2.2). Consequently, approaches aiming at the collection of background knowledge should also be applicable in these cases.

The evaluation in Chapter 10 showed the feasibility of both approaches in industrial integration scenarios. While the collection of usage characteristics could be used to significantly reduce the complexity of the schema mapping problem, the Example Data Injection proved very successful for automatically creating schema mappings of high quality. Furthermore, the evaluation showed that both approaches could easily be used in situations where no detailed implementation knowledge of the involved systems or messaging standards is available.

- *How can background knowledge be exploited by an automated approach?* One of the key requirements of the different integration scenarios presented in Section 2 is the capturing and reuse of background knowledge. Section 6.3 showed how domain and integration knowledge can be modeled in an ontology enabling the usages of the captured knowledge by both, humans and machines.

  Based on the representation of background knowledge in a domain ontology the *O*ntology-*B*ased *M*apping (OBM) approach was developed in Chapters 7 and 8. The OBM approach divides the problem of developing a schema mapping for two schemas into two sub-problems: i) the lifting of the two schemas to a domain ontology and ii) the extraction of a schema mapping based on two liftings and a domain ontology. In both steps of the OBM approach, the background knowledge modeled in the ontology is exploited. During the lifting step it is exploited by the different matching algorithms (cf. Section 7.2)and the aggregation algorithm (cf. Section 7.3) to create a lifting between a schema and the domain ontology while during the mapping extraction step the background knowledge is used to identify the correct mapping category (cf. Section 8.3).

- *Can complex mappings be created automatically?* The analysis of different scenarios in the area of B2B integration and Data Migration showed that complex mapping expressions are very common (cf. Section 8.2.1). However, creating these complex mapping expressions automatically is not always possible. Therefore, the concept of mapping categories was introduced in Section 8.2. The idea underlying the mapping categories is to abstract from the details of complex mapping expressions resulting in two simplifications in the mapping process:

    – similar mapping expressions are grouped into one mapping category

    – mapping categories ease the development of the correct mapping expressions by a user.

The grouping of similar complex mapping expressions into one mapping category enables the automatic identification of the correct mapping category even in situations where the correct mapping expressions cannot be created. The identification of the correct mapping category is based mainly on the available background knowledge. The evaluation in Chapter 10 showed that the OBM approach is capable of identifying the correct mapping expression with very high precision.

In the case of some of the simple mapping categories, it is even possible to generate the mapping expressions automatically. In the case of the more complex ones at least templates of mapping expressions can be created automatically. These templates need to be completed by the user afterwards. In these cases the mapping category at least provides the user with additional information regarding the needed mapping expression consequently simplifying the development task of the user.

- *Can the mapping quality required for industrial applications be achieved?* The evaluation in Chapter 10 was performed using real world scenarios in the area of data migration. In these experiments the OBM approach was capable of achieving a average precision of ~ 0.97 and average recall of ~ 0.78 and consequently an average F-Measure of ~ 0.87. For each of the identified matches the correct mapping category was also identified in the experiments. The results presented are a significant improvement over the results achieved by existing approaches.

  The results achieved by the OBM approach show that by exploiting domain and integration knowledge, about 80% of the manual effort can be automated. As the overall approach requires an initial schema reduction and the maintenance and extension of the domain ontology and integration knowledge, this effort also has to be taken into account. However, as this knowledge can be reused across different projects, the initial effort for creating the domain ontology as well as the maintenance of the integration knowledge can quickly be amortized.

Put together, the results in this thesis show that the OBM approach is capable of achieving the mapping quality required for industrial applications. By exploiting domain and integration knowledge even the correct mapping category can be identified automatically. The collection of usage characteristics and the Example Data Injection enable the non-intrusive collection of integration knowledge. In summary, the results presented in this thesis achieve the ambitious goal of developing schema mapping to a new level where it can be applied in industrial settings, presented in the introduction.

Part V

Appendix

Appendix A

Questionnaire to Collect Usage Characteristics

The following questionnaire was used to evaluate the collection and exploitation of usage characteristics in the data migration to SAP Business ByDesign scenario. It is obvious that some questions of this questionnaire are closely related. If, for example, in a given integration project no address data should be imported for a certain object (e.g.. for the Customer object), the questions regarding address versions and phone numbers are not relevant. Consequently, only the relevant questions (according to previous answers) where presented to the user during evaluation.

- Which objects should be imported into the system? Possible answers: Customer, Supplier, Employee, House Bank, Clearing House, Tax Authority, Business Partner.

- Business Partner Questionnaire

    - Does the object business partner also cover persons?
    - Should time dependent business partner data be imported?
    - Should address data be imported?
    - Should different address versions such as "Kanji" be imported?
    - Should different address types or usages such as "delivery address" be imported?
    - Should notes for addresses be imported?
    - How should communication data such as phone numbers be imported?
    - Should phone numbers be imported?
    - Should fax numbers be imported?
    - Should email addresses be imported?

- Should URLs such as homepages be imported?
- Should contact person relationships be imported?
- Can the same person be the contact person for multiple business partners?
- Can a contact person have multiple workplaces at different locations of the same business partner?
- Should contact person calling hours be imported?
- Should contact person visiting hours be imported?
- Should contact person private address information be imported?
- Should service performer relationships be imported?
- Can the same person be service performer for multiple business partners?
- Can a service performer have multiple workplaces at different locations of the same business partner?
- Should service performer calling hours be imported?
- Should service performer visiting hours be imported?
- Should service performer private address information be imported?
- Should shareholder relationships be imported?
- Should other relationships such as "ship-to-party" be imported?
- Should bank account information be imported?
- Should payment card information be imported?
- Should blocks and blocking reasons for payment cards be imported?
- Should identification numbers be imported?
- Should tax numbers be imported?
- Should texts be imported?
- Should attachments be imported?
- Should address independent communication data be imported?

- Customer Questionnaire

    - Does the object customer also cover persons?
    - Should time dependent customer data be imported?
    - Should address data be imported?
    - Should different address versions such as "Kanji" be imported?

- Should different address types or usages such as "delivery address" be imported?
- Should notes for addresses be imported?
- How should communication data such as phone numbers be imported?
- Should phone numbers be imported?
- Should fax numbers be imported?
- Should email addresses be imported?
- Should URLs such as homepages be imported?
- Should contact person relationships be imported?
- Can the same person be the ontact person for multiple customers?
- Can a contact person have multiple workplaces at different locations of the same customer?
- Should contact person calling hours be imported?
- Should contact person visiting hours be imported?
- Should contact person private address information be imported?
- Should service performer relationships be imported?
- Can the same person be service performer for multiple customers?
- Can a service performer have multiple workplaces at different locations of the same customer?
- Should service performer calling hours be imported?
- Should service performer visiting hours be imported?
- Should service performer private address information be imported?
- Should shareholder relationships be imported?
- Should other relationships such as "ship-to-party" be imported?
- Should bank account information be imported?
- Should payment card information be imported?
- Should blocks and blocking reasons for payment cards be imported?
- Should identification numbers be imported?
- Should tax numbers be imported?
- Should texts be imported?
- Should attachments be imported?
- Should address independent communication data be imported?
- Should role information such as "customer is a prospect" be imported?

- Should industry sectors be imported?
- Should tax exemptions be imported?
- Should calling hours be imported?
- Should visiting hours be imported?
- Should goods receiving hours be imported?
- Should marketing data be imported?
- Should sales data be imported?

- Supplier Questionnaire
  - Does the object supplier also cover persons?
  - Should time dependent supplier data be imported?
  - Should address data be imported?
  - Should different address versions such as "Kanji" be imported?
  - Should different address types or usages such as "delivery address" be imported?
  - Should notes for addresses be imported?
  - How should communication data such as phone numbers be imported?
  - Should phone numbers be imported?
  - Should fax numbers be imported?
  - Should email addresses be imported?
  - Should URLs such as homepages be imported?
  - Should contact person relationships be imported?
  - Can the same person be the contact person for multiple suppliers?
  - Can a contact person have multiple workplaces at different locations of the same supplier?
  - Should contact person calling hours be imported?
  - Should contact person visiting hours be imported?
  - Should contact person private address information be imported?
  - Should service performer relationships be imported?
  - Can the same person be service performer for multiple suppliers?
  - Can a service performer have multiple workplaces at different locations of the same supplier?
  - Should service performer calling hours be imported?

- Should service performer visiting hours be imported?
- Should service performer private address information be imported?
- Should shareholder relationships be imported?
- Should other relationships such as "invoicing-party" be imported?
- Should bank account information be imported?
- Should identification numbers be imported?
- Should tax numbers be imported?
- Should texts be imported?
- Should attachments be imported?
- Should address independent communication data be imported?
- Should role information such as "supplier is a bidder" be imported?
- Should industry sectors be imported?
- Should tax exemptions be imported?
- Should bidding characteristics be imported?
- Should quality system information be imported?
- Should product category information be imported?
- Should procurement data be imported?

- Employee Questionnaire
    - Does the object employee also cover external employees?
    - Should time dependent employee data be imported?
    - Should address data be imported?
    - Should different address versions such as "Kanji" be imported?
    - Should different address types or usages such as "delivery address" be imported?
    - Should notes for addresses be imported?
    - How should communication data such as phone numbers be imported?
    - Should phone numbers be imported?
    - Should fax numbers be imported?
    - Should email addresses be imported?
    - Should URLs such as homepages be imported?
    - Should employee workplace address data be imported?
    - Should relationships be imported?

- Should bank account information be imported?
- Should payment card information be imported?
- Should blocks and blocking reasons for payment cards be imported?
- Should the employee ID be imported?
- Should tax numbers be imported?
- Should texts be imported?
- Should attachments be imported?
- Should address independent communication data be imported?

- House Bank Questionnaire
    - Should time dependent house bank data be imported?
    - Should address data be imported?
    - Should different address versions such as "Kanji" be imported?
    - Should different address types or usages such as "delivery address" be imported?
    - Should notes for addresses be imported?
    - How should communication data such as phone numbers be imported?
    - Should phone numbers be imported?
    - Should fax numbers be imported?
    - Should email addresses be imported?
    - Should URLs such as homepages be imported?
    - Should contact person relationships be imported?
    - Can the same person be the contact person for multiple house banks?
    - Can a contact person have multiple workplaces at different locations of the same house bank?
    - Should contact person calling hours be imported?
    - Should contact person visiting hours be imported?
    - Should contact person private address information be imported?
    - Should shareholder relationships be imported?
    - Should other relationships be imported?
    - Should texts be imported?
    - Should attachments be imported?
    - Should address independent communication data be imported?

- Should calling hours be imported?
- Should opening hours be imported?
- Should electronic banking hours be imported?
- Should working day calendar information be imported?
- Should payment medium format information be imported?

• Clearing House Questionnaire
  - Should time dependent clearing house data be imported?
  - Should address data be imported?
  - Should different address versions such as "Kanji" be imported?
  - Should different address types or usages such as "delivery address" be imported?
  - Should notes for addresses be imported?
  - How should communication data such as phone numbers be imported?
  - Should phone numbers be imported?
  - Should fax numbers be imported?
  - Should email addresses be imported?
  - Should URLs such as homepages be imported?
  - Should contact person relationships be imported?
  - Can the same person be the contact person for multiple clearing houses?
  - Can a contact person have multiple workplaces at different locations of the same clearing house?
  - Should contact person calling hours be imported?
  - Should contact person visiting hours be imported?
  - Should contact person private address information be imported?
  - Should shareholder relationships be imported?
  - Should other relationships be imported?
  - Should bank account information be imported?
  - Should texts be imported?
  - Should attachments be imported?
  - Should address independent communication data be imported?
  - Should calling hours be imported?

- Should opening hours be imported?
- Should working day calendar information be imported?

- Tax Authority Questionnaire
    - Should time dependent tax authority data be imported?
    - Should address data be imported?
    - Should different address versions such as "Kanji" be imported?
    - Should different address types or usages such as "delivery address" be imported?
    - Should notes for addresses be imported?
    - How should communication data such as phone numbers be imported?
    - Should phone numbers be imported?
    - Should fax numbers be imported?
    - Should email addresses be imported?
    - Should URLs such as homepages be imported?
    - Should contact person relationships be imported?
    - Can the same person be the contact person for multiple tax authorities?
    - Can a contact person have multiple workplaces at different locations of the same tax authority?
    - Should contact person calling hours be imported?
    - Should contact person visiting hours be imported?
    - Should contact person private address information be imported?
    - Should shareholder relationships be imported?
    - Should other relationships be imported?
    - Should bank account information be imported?
    - Should identification numbers be imported?
    - Should texts be imported?
    - Should attachments be imported?
    - Should address independent communication data be imported?
    - Should calling hours be imported?
    - Should opening hours be imported?

Appendix B

Implementation Details of the OBM Framework

The OBM Framework has been implemented using the Java[1] language. The functionality provided by the OBM Framework is solely available through an API. This API enables the integration of the OBM Framework into existing solutions that require semi-automatic schema matching functionality. Figure B.1 provides an overview of the packages comprising the OBM Framework.

The main package of the OBM Framework is the com.sap.research.obm_framework package. It contains the classes that form the public API offered by the OBM Framework. A description of this public API is given in Section B.5. Furthermore the main package contains the three sub-packages:

- com.sap.research.obm_framework.lifting
- com.sap.research.obm_framework.mapping
- com.sap.research.obm_framework.repository.

The first one contains all the functionality related to the lifting of XML Schemas to OWL-DL ontologies while the second one contains the functionality related to the mapping extraction on the basis of two liftings. The com.sap.research.obm_framework.repository package contains the functionality for accessing the schema, ontology, lifting and mapping repositories. A brief overview of these three packages is given in the subsequent paragraphs. In addition, Figure B.1 shows the main dependencies of the OBM Framework. The prototypical implementation mainly relies on the SecondString, the OWL API and the XML Beans libraries.

---

[1] http://java.sun.com

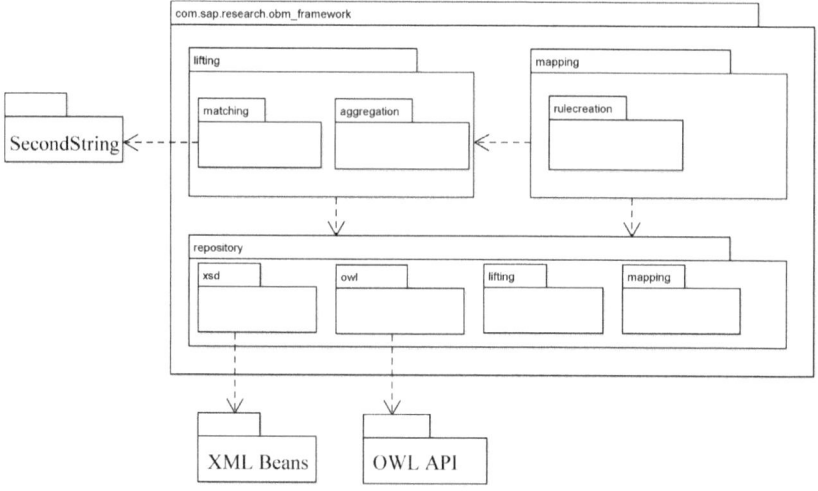

Figure B.1: Overview of the packages comprising the OBM Framework implementation.

B.1 The Lifting Package.

The lifting package itself consists of the following sub-packages:

- com.sap.research.obm_framework.lifting.matching
- com.sap.research.obm_framework.lifting.aggregation

The **matching** package contains the implantation of the distance metrics as well as the implementations of the matching algorithms introduced in Section 7.2.3. Additionally the matching packages also contains the functionality necessary for calculating the two-dimensional similarity matrix m'_{sim} based on m_{sim} as well as the implementation of the ontology-based aggregation algorithm presented in Section 7.3.

B.2 The Mapping Package.

The mapping package only consists of one sub-package, namely the package

- com.sap.research.obm_framework.mapping.rulecreation

Besides functionality for identifying matching schema entities based on two liftings also the rule responsible for identifying the appropriate mapping category for a matching element are implemented in this package.

B.3 The Repository Package.

The repository package consist of the following sub-packages:

- com.sap.research.obm_framework.repository.xsd
- com.sap.research.obm_framework.repository.owl
- com.sap.research.obm_framework.repository.lifting
- com.sap.research.obm_framework.repository.mapping.

The xsd packages encapsulates all functionality related to the handling of XML schemas. Besides functionality for parsing XML schemas into an internal representation it also provides functionality for parsing example instances for a given XML schemas. The package is implemented using the XML Beans package. Additionally this packaged also contains the implementation of the tree-like data structure used by the OBM Framework to represent XML schemas internally. Similar to this the owl package contains the functionality for parsing OWL-DL ontologies into the OBM Framework internal representation. The lifting and mapping packages contain the functionality for storing and parsing of liftings and mappings respectively.

Furthermore, the repository package contains functionality abstracting from a concrete repository technology. However, currently only the use of the file system as a repository is supported.

B.4 Used Libraries

As already mentioned above the implementation of the OBM Framework is based on a number of libraries providing different basis functionalities like XML schema handling, ontology handling or basic string matching algorithms. The most important libraries used by the OBM Framework are the OWL API together with the Pellet reasoner, XML Beans and SecondString.

OWL API: The OWL API[2] is an open source Java package for working with OWL ontologies. It is developed as part of the CO-ODE project.[3] It provides functionalities for in-memory manipulation of OWL ontologies compliant to the OWL 1.1 specification, parsing and writing of different serialization formats as well as an abstraction layer for accessing different OWL reasoners. In the OBM Framework implementation the OWL API was used in conjunction with the Pellet reasoner.

---
[2] http://owlapi.sourceforge.net/
[3] http://www.co-ode.org/

Pellet: Pellet[4] is an open source OWL-DL reasoner developed and supported by Clark & Parsia, LLC.[5] Like the OWL API the Pellet reasoner supports the OWL 1.1 specification.

XML Beans: XML Beans[6] are a set of tools and an API developed as part of the Apache XML Project.[7] As the previous two also XML Beans are open source. XML Beans allows the manipulation of XML documents through specialized Java classes generated on the basis of a XML schema. In the OBM Framework XML Beans are used for manipulating both, XML schemas and XML documents.

SecondString: SecondString[8] is an open source Java package for approximate string matching. It is developed at the Carnegie Mellon University and offers implementations of the basic string similarity metrics described in Section 7.2.2. In the OBM Framework the SecondString package has been used to implement the different string-similarity-based matching algorithms.

In the next section the public API that can be used to access the functionality of the OBM Framework is discussed.

B.5 Public API

The public API of the OBM Framework mainly consists of 4 classes:

- OBMFramework
- Lifting
- MappingExtraction
- Mapping.

The class **OBMFramework** encapsulates the functionality responsible for lifting a schema to an ontology. After the source schema, the target ontology and an optional example instance have been specified the doLifting(Matcher[] m, Aggregator a) method can be invoked. This method takes an array of **Matchers** and an **Aggregator** as input and returns an instance of a **Lifting**. Matcher is the common interface implemented by all matching algorithms. Similar to this **Aggregator** is the interface implemented by the aggregation algorithm. Once two liftings, one for the source and one for the target schema, have been created

---

[4] http://pellet.owldl.com/download
[5] http://pellet.owldl.com
[6] http://xmlbeans.apache.org/
[7] http://xml.apache.org/
[8] http://secondstring.sourceforge.net/

B.5 Public API

the method `extractMapping()` of the class `MappingExtraction` can be used to extract the resulting `Mapping` from these liftings.

Using this simple API the functionality of the OBM Framework is offered to other applications.

Appendix C
Evanto Details

This appendix provides some implementation details of the Evanto toolkit. As well, a detailed explanation of an example test script is given.

Evanto enables a user to easily specify test scripts that can later be executed automatically. These tests scripts are written using the Ruby[1] scripting language as well as some Evanto specific extensions to it. The interface between the Evanto test scripts written in Ruby and the Java implementation of the OBM Framework is provided by the JRuby[2] interpreter. The JRuby interpreter is an implementation of an Ruby interpreter using the Java language. In addition, it contains some specific extensions enabling a simplified access to Java classes from within Ruby scripts.

Figure C.1 again shows the Evanto script introduced in Section 9.2. Lines 1 – 19 of this script comprise the initial set-up phase which is part of every Evanto script. In this phase all required initialization steps are preformed. In the example script this step consists of initializing some variables (lines 2 and 3), initializing the two instances of the Java class **OBMFramework** that are required (lines 6 – 11), reading the master mapping from a file (lines 13 and 14) and initializing the matcher array (lines 16 and 17) as well the ontology-based aggregation algorithm (line 18).

Besides the initial set-up phase the example Evanto script contains one so-called **run**-method (lines 21 – 35). In an Evanto script each **run**-method encapsulates one evaluation step. The **run**-method in the example script is named OCRD_to_CUSTOMER_Mapping. It performs a lifting of the source and the target schema (lines 23 – 26), extracts the resulting mapping from the two liftings (lines 29 – 32) and finally stores the resulting mapping for later analysis (lines 33 and 34).

---

[1] http://www.ruby-lang.org
[2] http://jruby.codehaus.org/

```
 1  setup do
 2    # Set some variables that are used later
 3    set :result_target_dir, "./results/"
 4    set :domain_onto, "./IntegrationOnto.owl"
 5    # instanziate OBM Framework
 6    @source_fw = OBMFramework.new(File.new("./OCRD.xsd"), File.
 7                 new("./OCRD.xml"), File.new(domain_onto), nil,
 8                 true)
 9    @target_fw = OBMFramework.new(File.new("./d_CUSTOMER.xsd"),
10                 File.new("./d_CUSTOMER.xml" ),File.new(
11                 domain_onto), nil, true)
12    # read master mapping from file
13    @mastermapping = Mapping.deserializeFromXMLString(File.
14                 read(master_mapping))
15    # initialize the matchers and the aggregation algorithm
16    @matcher = []
17    @matcher << SampleInstanceMatcher.new()
18    @aggregator = OntoBasedAggregator.new(0.5)
19  end
20
21  run :OCRD_to_CUSTOMER_Mapping do
22    # lift the source schema and target schema
23    @source_lifting = @source_fw.doLifting(@matcher,
24                 @aggregator)
25    @target_lifting = @target_fw.doLifting(@matcher,
26                 @aggregator)
27    # extract the mapping from the two liftings
28    # and store it for later analysis
29    mapping_extraction = MappingExtraction.new(@source_lifting,
30                 @target_lifting, @source_fw,
31                 @target_fw)
32    mapping = mapping_extraction.extract_mapping()
33    result(:mapping, :list => mapping , :master => ".
34         /OCRD_CUSTOMER.xml")
35  end
```

Figure C.1: Example of an Evanto script.

References

[ABM05] Yuan An, Alexander Borgida, and John Mylopoulos. Inferring complex semantic mappings between relational tables and ontologies from simple correspondences. In Robert Meersman, Zahir Tari, Mohand-Said Hacid, John Mylopoulos, Barbara Pernici, Özalp Babaoglu, Hans-Arno Jacobsen, Joseph P. Loyall, Michael Kifer, and Stefano Spaccapietra, editors, *On the Move to Meaningful Internet Systems 2005: CoopIS, DOA, and ODBASE, OTM Confederated International Conferences,*, volume 3761 of *Lecture Notes in Computer Science*, pages 1152–1169. Springer, October 2005. ISBN: 3-540-29738-3.

[AFM+05] Rama Akkiraju, Joel Farrell, John Mille, Meenakshi Nagarajan, Marc-Thomas Schmidt, Amit Sheth, and Kunal Verma. Web service semantics - WSDL-S. Online, http://www.w3.org/Submission/WSDL-S/, November 2005. W3C Member Submission.

[Ame07] American Petroleum Institute. Petroleum industry data exchange (PIDX). Online, http://www.pidx.org/, 2007.

[BA05] Hannes Bohring and Sören Auer. Mapping XML to OWL ontologies. In *Proceedings of 13. Leipziger Informatik-Tage (LIT 2005)*, Lecture Notes in Informatics (LNI), 2005.

[Bat04] Steve Battle. Round-tripping between XML and RDF. In *Proceedings of the 3rd International Semantic Web Conference (ISWC)*, Hiroshima, Japan, November 2004. Springer. Poster.

[BCL+05] Angela Bonifati, Elaine Qing Chang, Aks V. S. Lakshmanan, Terence Ho, and Rachel Pottinger. HePToX - marryingXML and heterogeneity in your P2P databases (software demonstration). In *Proceedings of the 31st International Conference on Very Large Data Bases (VLDB 05)*, pages 1267–1270, Trondheim, Norway, 2005. VLDB Endowment. ISBN: 1-59593-154-6.

[Bec00] Kent Beck. *Extreme Programming Explained: Embrace Change*. Addison-Wesley, 2000. ISBN: 0-201-61641-6. Second edition 2005 with Cynthia Andres. ISBN: 0-321-27865-8.

[Bec02]   Kent Beck. *Test-Driven Development: By Example*. Addison-Wesley, 2002. ISBN: 0-321-14653-0.

[Ber96]   Philip A. Bernstein. Middleware: a model for distributed system services. *Communications of the ACM*, 39(2):86 – 98, February 1996. ISSN: 0001-0782.

[BGD97]   Andreas Behm, Andreas Geppert, and Klaus R. Dittrich. On the migration of relational schemas and data to object-oriented database systems. In J. Györkös, M. Krisper, and H. C. Mayr, editors, *Proc. 5th International Conference on Re-Technologies for Information Systems*, pages 13–33, Klagenfurt, Austria, 1997. Oesterreichische Computer Gesellschaft.

[BHHS06] Saartje Brockmans, Peter Haase, Pascal Hitzler, and Rudi Studer. A metamodel and UML profile for rule-extended OWL DL ontologies. In York Sure and John Domingue, editors, *The Semantic Web: Research and Applications*, volume 4011 of *Lecture Notes in Computer Science*, pages 303–316. Springer, June 2006.

[BM02]   Jacob Berlin and Amihai Motro. Database schema matching using machine learning with feature selection. In *Proc. 14th Intl. Conf. on Advanced Information Systems Engineering (CAiSE)*, volume 2348 of *Lecture Notes in Computer Science*, pages 452–466. Springer, January 2002. ISBN: 978-3-540-43738-3.

[Bus03]   Christoph Bussler. *B2B Integration - Concepts and Architecture*. Springer, 2003. ISBN: 3540434879.

[CDS+04] Emilia Cimpian, Christian Drumm, Michael Stollberg, Ion Constantinescu, Liliana Cabral, John Domingue, Farshad Hakimpour, and Atanas Kiryakov. Report on the State-of-the-Art and Requirements Analysis. Online, http://www.dip.semanticweb.org/documents/Deliverable1Wp5.doc, June 2004. Deliverable D5.1 of the DIP project.

[CID]   CIDX. Chemical industry data exchange (CIDX). Online. http://www.cidx.org.

[CRF03]   William W. Cohen, Pradeep Ravikumar, and Stephen E. Fienberg. A comparison of string distance metrics for name-matching tasks. In *Proceedings of the IJCAI 2003 Workshop on Information Integration on the Web*, pages 73–78, August 2003.

[DDH01]   AnHai Doan, Pedro Domingos, and Alon Y. Halevy. Reconciling schemas of disparate data sources: A machine-learning approach. In

Proc. of the ACM SIGMOD Intl. Conf. on Management of Data (SIG-MOD), pages 509–520, Santa Barbara, California, USA, 2001. ACM. ISBN: 1-58113-332-4.

[DFRW02] Mirella Dell'Erba, Oliver Fodor, Francesco Ricci, and Hannes Werthner. Harmonise: A solution for data interoperability. In *Proceedings of the IFIP Conference on Towards The Knowledge Society: E-Commerce, E-Business, E-Government*, volume 233 of *IFIP Conference Proceedings*, pages 433–445, Deventer, The Netherlands, 2002. Kluwer, B.V. ISBN: 1-4020-7239-2.

[Dig04] Digital Enterprise Research Institute (DERI). Web Service Modelling Ontology (wsmo). Online, 2004. http://www.wsmo.org.

[DK05] Christian Drumm and Philipp Kunfermann. Lifting XML schemas to ontologies - the concept finder algorithm. In Martin Hepp, Axel Polleres, Frank van Harmelen, and Mike Genesereth, editors, *Proceedings of the First International Workshop on Mediation in Semantic Web Services (MEDIATE 2005)*, volume 168. CEUR Workshop Proceedings (ceur-ws.org), December 2005.

[DLD+04] Robin Dhamankar, Yoonkyong Lee, AnHai Doan, Alon Halevy, and Pedro Domingos. iMAP - discovering complex semantic matches between database schemas. In *Proc. of the ACM SIGMOD Intl. Conf. on Management of Data (SIGMOD)*, pages 383–394, New York, USA, 2004. ACM. ISBN: 1-58113-859-8.

[DLN06] Christian Drumm, Jens Lemcke, and Kioumars Namiri. Integrating semantic web services and business process management: A real use case. In *Proc. of the ESWC 2006 Workshop Semantics for Business Process Management 2006 (SBPM 2006)*, June 2006.

[DLO07] Christian Drumm, Jens Lemcke, and Daniel Oberle. *The Semantic Web: Real-World Applications from Industry*, volume 7 of *Semantic Web and Beyond*, chapter Business Process Management and Semantic Technologies, pages 207 – 239. Springer, 2007. ISBN: 978-0-387-48530-0.

[DMDH02] AnHai Doan, Jayant Madhavan, Pedro Domingos, and Alon Halevy. Learning to map between ontologies on the semantic web. In *Proc. of the 11th international conference on World Wide Web (WWW)*, pages 662–673. ACM, 2002. ISBN:1-58113-449-5.

[DMR02] Hong-Hai Do, Sergey Melnik, and Erhard Rahm. Comparison of schema matching evaluations. In *Revised Papers from the NODe 2002*

Web and Database-Related Workshops on Web, Web-Services, and Database Systems, volume 2593 of *Lecture Notes In Computer Science*, pages 221–237. Springer, 2002. ISBN: 3-540-00745-8.

[Do06]　Hong-Hai Do. *Schema Matching and Mapping-based Data Integration*. Verlag Dr. Müller (VDM), 2006. ISBN: 3-86550-997-5.

[DR02]　Hong-Hai Do and Erhard Rahm. COMA - a system for flexible combination of schema matching approaches. In *Proc. of the 28th International Conference on Very Large Data Bases (VLDB)*, pages 610–621. VLDB Endowment, 2002.

[Dru04]　Christian Drumm. Finding Ariadnes thread in the data mediation maze. In John Domingue, Liliana Cabral, and Enrico Motta, editors, *First AKT Workshop on Semantic Web Services*, volume 122. CEUR Workshop Proceedings (ceur-ws.org), 2004.

[Dru07]　Christian Drumm. Challenges in automatic schema matching for data migration. In *Proc. of the Bertinoro Workshop on Information Integration (INFINT 07)*, 2007.

[DSDR07]　Christian Drumm, Matthias Schmitt, Hong-Hai Do, and Erhard Rahm. QuickMig - automatic schema matching for data migration projects. In *Proc. of the Sixteenth Conference on Information and Knowledge Management (CIKM 2007)*, pages 107–116. ACM, November 2007. ISBN: 978-1-59593-803-9.

[Ehr06]　Marc Ehrig. *Ontology Alignment. Bridging the Semantic Gap*. Springer-Verlag, 2006. ISBN: 038732805X.

[EIM+07]　Jerome Euzenat, Antoine Isaac, Christian Meilicke, Pavel Shvaiko, Heiner Stuckenschmidt, Ondrej Svab, Vojtech Svatek, Willem Robert van Hage, and Mikalai Yatskevich. Results of the ontology alignment evaluation initiative 2007. In Pavel Shvaiko, Jerome Euzenat, Fausto Giunchiglia, and Bin He, editors, *Proceedings of the 2nd International Workshop on Ontology Matching (OM-2007). Collocated with the 6th International Semantic Web Conference (ISWC-2007) and the 2nd Asian Semantic Web Conference (ASWC-2007)*, volume 304 of *CEUS Workshop Proceedings*, pages 96–132, Busan, Korea, November 2007. ISSN: 1613-0073.

[ES04]　Marc Ehrig and York Sure. Ontology mapping - an integrated approach. In *1st European Semantic Web Symposium*, 2004.

[ES07]　Jerome Euzenat and Pavel Shvaiko. *Ontology Matching*. Springer-Verlag, 2007. ISBN: 9783540496113.

REFERENCES

[Fel98] Christiane Fellbaum, editor. *WordNet*. MIT Press, 1998. ISBN: 0-262-06197-X.

[FZT04] Matthias Ferdinand, Christian Zirpins, and D. Trastour. Lifting XML Schema to OWL. In *Proc. of the 4th International Conference on Web Engineering (ICWE 2004)*,, pages 354–358. Springer, 2004.

[Gru93] Thomas R. Gruber. A translation approach to portable ontologies. *Knowledge Acquisition*, 5(2):199–220, 1993. ISSN: 1042-8143.

[Hai91] Jean-Luc Hainaut. Database reverse engineering: Models, techniques, and strategies. In *Proceedings of the 10th International Conference on Entity-Relationship Approach (ER 91)*, pages 729–741, San Mateo, California, USA, October 1991. ER Institute.

[Hep07] Martin Hepp. *Ontology Management: Semantic Web, Semantic Web Services, and Business Applications*, chapter Ontologies: State of the Art, Business Potential, and Grand Challenges, pages 3–22. Springer, 2007. ISBN: 978-0-387-69899-1.

[HHH+05] Laura M. Haas, Mauricio A. Hernández, Howard Ho, Lucian Popa, and Mary Roth. Clio grows up: From research prototype to industrial tool. In *Proc. ACM SIGMOD International Conference on Management of Data*, pages 805–810, New York, NY, USA, 2005. ACM. ISBN: 1-59593-060-4.

[HK03] Andreas Hess and Nicholas Kushmerick. Learning to attach semantic metadata to Web services. In *The SemanticWeb - ISWC 2003*, volume 2870 of *Lecture Notes in Computer Science*, pages 258–273. Springer, 2003. ISSN: 0302-9743.

[Inta] International Organization for Standardization (ISO). ISO 3166-1, codes for the representation of names of countries and their subdivisions. Online. http://tinyurl.com/32ezsm.

[Intb] International Organization for Standardization (ISO). ISO 8601:2004, data elements and interchange formats information interchange representation of dates and times. Online. http://www.iso.org/iso/en/prods-services/popstds/datesandtime.html.

[JHCQ05] Ningsheng Jian, Wei Hu, Gong Cheng, and Yuzhong Qu. Falconao: Aligning ontologies with falcon. In Benjamin Ashpole, Marc Ehrig, Jérôme Euzenat, and Heiner Stuckenschmidt, editors, *Integrating Ontologies '05, Proceedings of the K-CAP 2005 Workshop on Integrating Ontologies*, volume 156 of *CEUR Workshop Proceedings*, Banff, Canada, October 2005. CEUR-WS.org.

[KBS06] Dirk Krafzigand, Karl Banke, and Dirk Slama. *Enterprise SOA*. Prentice Hall PTR, reprint edition, 2006. ISBN: 978-0131465756.

[KGT06] Andreas Knöpfel, Bernhard Grone, and Peter Tabeling. *Fundamental Modeling Concepts: Effective Communication of IT Systems*. Wiley, March 2006. ISBN: 978-0-470-02710-3.

[KLW95] Michael Kifer, Georg Lausen, and James Wu. Logical foundations of object-oriented and frame-based languages. *Journal of the Association for Computing Machinery*, 42(4):741–843, July 1995. ISSN: 0004-5411.

[KS00] Vipul Kashyap and Amit P. Sheth. *Information Brokering Across Heterogeneous Digital Media - A Metadata-based Approach*. Number 20 in Advances in Database Systems. Kluwer Academic Publishers, 2000. ISBN: 978-0-7923-7883-9.

[Lar05] University of Georgia Large Scale Distributed Information Systems (LSDIS), Department of Computer Science. METEOR-S: Semantic Web services and processes. Online, 2005. http://lsdis.cs.uga.edu/projects/meteor-s/.

[LC00] Wen-Syan Li and Chris Clifton. Semint - a tool for identifying attribute correspondences in heterogeneous databases using neural network. *Data and Knowledge Engineering*, 33(1):49–84, 2000. ISSN:0169-023X.

[Lev66] Vladimir I. Levenshtein. Binary codes capable of correcting deletions, insertions, and reversals. *Soviet Physics Doklady*, 10(8):707–710, 1966.

[MIR93] Renee J. Miller, Yannis E. Ioannidis, and Raghu Ramakrishnan. The Use of Information Capacity in Schema Integration and Translation. In *Proceedings of the Nineteenth International Conference on Very Large Data Bases (VLDB)*, pages 120–133, Dublin, Ireland, August 1993. Morgan Kaufmann Publishers Inc. ISBN: 1-55860-152-X.

[MLM01] Murali Mani, Dongwon Lee, and Richard R. Muntz. Semantic data modeling using XML Schemas. In Hideko S. Kunii, Sushil Jajodia, and Arne Slvberg, editors, *Proceedings of the 20th International Conference on Conceptual Modeling*, volume 2224 of *Lecture Notes in Computer Science*, pages 149–163. Springer-Verlag, November 2001. ISBN: 3540428666.

[MLMK05] Makoto Murata, Dongwon Lee, Murali Mani, and Kohsuke Kawaguchi. Taxonomy of XML schema languages using formal language theory. *ACM Trans. Inter. Tech.*, 5(4):660–704, 2005. ISSN: 1533-5399.

REFERENCES

[MS02]   Alexander Maedche and Steffen Staab. Measuring similarity between ontologies. In *Proc. Of the European Conference on Knowledge Acquisition and Management (EKAW)*, number 2473 in Lecture Notes in Computer Science, pages 251–263. Springer, October 2002.

[MSZ01] Sheila A. McIlraith, Tran Cao Son, and Honglei Zeng. Semantic Web services. *IEEE Intelligent Systems*, 16(2):46–53, Mar./Apr. 2001.

[NHT$^+$02] Felix Naumann, Ching-Tien Ho, Xuqing Tian, Laura Haas, and Nimrod Megiddo. Attribute classification using feature analysis (poster). In *Proc.s of the 18th International Conference on Data Engineering (ICDE)*, page 271. IEEE Computer Society, 2002. ISSN: 1063-6382.

[Nie08] Frank Niemann. Projekt Galaxy: SAP baut Netweaver zur SOA-middleware aus. Online, February 2008. http://tinyurl.com/2q9p2n.

[NVS$^+$06] Meenakshi Nagarajan, Kunal Verma, Amit P. Sheth, John Miller, and Jon Lathem. Semantic interoperability of Web services - challenges and experiences. In *Proceedings of the IEEE International Conference on Web Services (ICWS'06)*, pages 373–382, Washington, DC, USA, 2006. IEEE Computer Society. ISBN: 0-7695-2669-1.

[PTU00] Luigi Palopoli, Giorgio Terracina, and Domenico Ursino. The system DIKE - towards the semi-automatic synthesis of cooperative information systems and data warehouses. In Y. Masunagam, J. Pokorny, J. Stuller, and B. Thalheim, editors, *Proceedings of the Challenges of Symposium on Advances in Databases and Information Systems (ADBIS-DASFA)*, pages 108–117, Prague, Czech Republic, 2000. Matfyzpress.

[RB01]   Erhard Rahm and Philip A. Bernstein. A survey of approaches to automatic schema matching. *The VLDB Journal: The International Journal on Very Large Data Bases*, 10(4):334–350, 2001. ISSN: 1066-8888.

[Ros07] RosettaNet Program Office. Overview - clusters, segments and pips. Technical report, RosettaNet, May 2007. Online, http://portal.rosettanet.org/cms/export/sites/default/RosettaNet/Downloads/RStandards/ClustersSegmentsPIPsOverview_UpdateFinal_May07_revised.pdf.

[SBF98] Rudi Studer, V. Richard Benjamins, and Dieter Fensel. Knowledge engineering: Principles and methods. *Data & Knowledge Engineering*, 25(1-2):161–197, 1998. ISSN: 0169-023X.

[SC07]   Gunther Stuhec and Mark Crawford. Accelerate your business data modeling and integration issues by CCTS Modeler Warp 10. Technical report, SAP AG, SAP Developer Network, November 2007. http://tinyurl.com/3boj5p.

[SEH+04]   Gerd Stumme, Marc Ehrig, Siegfried Handschuh, Andreas Hotho, Alexander Maedche, Boris Motik, Daniel Oberle, Christoph Schmitz, Steffen Staab, Ljiljana Stojanovic, Nenad Stojanovic, Rudi Studer, York Sure, Raphael Volz, and Valentin Zacharias. The Karlsruhe view on ontologies. Technical report, University of Karlsruhe, Institute AIFB, 2004.

[SK93]   Amit P. Sheth and Vipul Kashyap. So far (schematically) yet so near (semantically). In *Proceedings of the IFIP WG 2.6 Database Semantics Conference on Interoperable Database Systems (DS-5)6*, pages 283–312, Amsterdam, The Netherlands, 1993. North-Holland Publishing Co. ISBN: 0-444-89879-4.

[SO05]   Jens Stumpe and Joachim Orb. *SAP Exchange Infrastructure*. Galileo Press GmbH, 1. edition, 2005. ISBN: 978-3-89842-437-0.

[SPR07]   Fatiha Saïs, Nathalie Pernelle, and Marie-Christine Rousset. L2R: A logical method for reference reconciliation. In *Proceedings of the Twenty-Second AAAI Conference on Artificial Intelligence*, pages 329–334. AAAI Press, 2007. ISBN: 978-1-57735-323-2.

[Stu07]   Gunther Stuhec. Using CCTS Modeler Warp 10 to customize business information interfaces. Technical report, SAP AG, SAP Developer Network: Business Process Expert Community, November 2007. Online, http://tinyurl.com/34j7q2.

[SvH05]   Heiner Stuckenschmidt and Frank van Harmelen. *Information Sharing on the Semantic Web*. Advanced Information and Knowledge Processing. Springer-Verlag, 2005. ISBN: 978-3-540-20594-4.

[The02]   The Organization for the Advancement of Structured Information Standards (OASIS). RELAX NG compact syntax specification. Online, November 2002. http://www.oasis-open.org/committees/relax-ng/compact-20021121.html.

[The04]   The OWL Services Coalition. OWL-S: Semantic markup for Web services. Online, 2004. http://www.daml.org/services/owl-s/1.1/overview/.

REFERENCES

[The07] The Web Services-Interoperability Organization (WS-I). Basic profile version 2.0. Online, 2007. http://www.ws-i.org/Profiles/BasicProfile-2.0.html.

[Uni] United Nations Economic Commision for Europe (UNECE). United nations directories for electronic data interchange for administration, commerce and transport. Online. http://www.unece.org/trade/untdid/welcome.htm.

[Wac03] Holger Wache. *Semantische Mediation für heterogene Informationsquellen*, volume DISKI 261 of *Dissertationen zur Künstlichen Intelligenz*. Akademische Verlagsgesellschaft Aka GmbH, Berlin, 2003. ISBN: 978-3-89838-261-8.

[WMD07] Ingo Weber, Ivan Markovic, and Christian Drumm. A conceptual framework for composition in business process management. In Witold Abramowicz, editor, *Proceedings of the 10th International Conference Business Information Systems (BIS 2007)*, number 4439 in Lecture Notes in Computer Science, pages 54 – 66. Springer, April 2007. ISBN 978-3-540-72034-8.

[WMD08] Ingo Weber, Ivan Markovic, and Christian Drumm. A conceptual framework for composition in business process management. 2008.

[Wor99a] World Wide Web Consortium (W3C). XML Path Language (XPath). Online, 1999. http://www.w3.org/TR/xpath.

[Wor99b] World Wide Web Consortium (W3C). XSL Transformations (XSLT). Online, 1999. http://www.w3.org/TR/xslt.

[Wor01a] World Wide Web Consortium (W3C). Web Services Description Language (wsdl). Online, 2001. http://www.w3.org/TR/wsdl.

[Wor01b] World Wide Web Consortium (W3C). XML Schemas. Online, 2001. http://www.w3.org/XML/Schema.

[Wor03] World Wide Web Consortium (W3C). Extensible Markup Language (XML). Online, 2003. http://www.w3.org/XML/.

[Wor04a] World Wide Web Consortium (W3C). OWL Web Ontology Language. Online, 2004. http://www.w3.org/TR/owl-guide/.

[Wor04b] World Wide Web Consortium (W3C). XML Schema part 2: Datatypes second edition. Online, October 2004. http://www.w3.org/TR/xmlschema-2/.

[Wor06a] World Wide Web Consortium (W3C). Web services activity. Online,, 2002-2006. http://www.w3.org/2002/ws/.

[Wor06b] World Wide Web Consortium (W3C). Extensible Markup Language (XML) 1.0 (fourth edition). Online, August 2006. http://www.w3.org/TR/2006/REC-xml-20060816.

[Wor07] World Wide Web Consortium (W3C). XQuery 1.0: An XML Query Language. Online, Janurary 2007. http://www.w3.org/TR/xquery/.

[WSC[+]07] Jim Wilson, Gunther Stuhec, Mark Crawford, Mary Kay Blantz, Anthony Coates, Oyvind Aassve, Ed Buchinski, Michael Dill, Jostein Fromyr, Kenji Itoh, Garret Minakawa, Sue Probert, Nada Reinprecht, Jean-Luc Sanson, Fred Van Blommestein, and Sylvia Webb. UN/CEFACT Core Components Technical Specification. Online, April 2007. Second Public Review, http://75.43.29.149:8080/download/attachments/3801818/Specification_CCTS3p0+2nd+Public+Review+16APR2007.pdf?version=1.

[XE03] Li Xu and David W. Embley. Discovering direct and indirect matches for schema elements. In *Proceedings of the 8th International Conference on Database Systems for Advanced Applications*, pages 39–46, Washington, DC, USA, March 2003. IEEE Computer Society. ISBN: 0-7695-1895.

Index

Enterprise Application Integration, 13

SAP Business ByDesign, 151

A2A, *see* Application-to-Application Integration
Altova Mapforce, 146
Application Service Provider Integration, 14
Application-to-Application Integration, 14
Automatic Mapping Calculation, 56, 173

B2B, *see* Business-to-Business Integration
Background Knowledge, 67
Business Partner Ontology, 156
Business-to-Business Integration, 14
BusinessPartner, 23

Clio, 61
COMA, 62
COMA++, 62, 163
Complex Mappings Expressions, 6
Composite Matcher, 90
Conceptual Re-engineering, 64
Core Component Technical Specification, 180
Correction, 56, 175
Customizations, 72

Data Migration, 16
Data Model Heterogeneity, 26
Data Type Constraints, 72
DEBMAS, 23
DIKE, 60

Documentation Matcher, 103
Domain Knowledge, 68

Evaluation Ontology, 155
Evaluation Scenarios, 156
Evaluation Toolkit, *see* Evanto
Evanto, 142
Example Data Injection, 78
Extensions, 72

F-Measure, 157
Falcon-AO, 63
Finalization, 54, 56, 176

Galaxy, *see* SAP NetWeaver Composition Environment
Galaxy Workbench, 178

HepToX, 61
Heterogeneity Layers, 24

IBM WebSphere Message Broker, 146
iMap, 60
Implementation Details, 70
Import, 53, 56
Information Capacity, 65
Input Data Repository, 137
Instance Equality Matcher, 106
Instance Split/Concat Matcher, 106
Integration Challenges, 32
Integration Knowledge, 68
Integration Knowledge Ontology, 156
Integrity Constraints, 72
Iteration, 176

Knowledge Collection, 55, 171

Lifting, 48, 89

Lifting Extraction Algorithm, 108
Lifting Repository, 138

Manual Mapping Process, 53
MapOnto, 63
Mapping, 47
Mapping Development, 54
Mapping Extraction, 113, 137
Mapping System by Xu and Embley, 61
Master Data
    Basic Master Data, 17
    Dependent Master Data, 17
Master Mapping, 155
Matcher Repository, 137
Matching, 46
Matching Algorithm, 102
Matching Categories, 115
    Code-Value-Mapping, 119
    Complex, 121
    Concatenate, 119
    Create-Instance, 120
    Default-Value, 120
    Internal-ID, 120
    Key-Value-Mapping, 119
    Move, 117
    Query, 121
    Split, 117
METEOR-S, 177
Microsoft BizTalk Server, 146
Modeling, 80
    Code List Information, 86
    Conceptual Modeling, 80
    Default Values, 84
    Example Data, 88
    Global Identifiers, 86
    Integration Knowledge, 81
    Internal Identifiers, 86
    Technical Names, 82
Modeling Alternatives, 73

Naive Ontology Mapping, 63
Name Matcher, 102
Neighborhood, 128

Node-Path Matcher, 103
NOM, *see* Naive Ontology Mapping

OBM, *see* Ontology-Based Mapping
OBM Framework, 137
Ontology, 35, 44
Ontology Features, 93
    Attributes, 97
    Code Lists, 98
    Data Type, 97
    Default Values, 98
    Entity Documentation, 95
    Entity Hierarchy, 97
    Entity Name, 95
    Example Instance Data, 98
    Indentifiers, 98
    Relations, 97
    Technical Names, 97
Ontology Matching, 62
Ontology Merging, 62
Ontology-Based Mapping, 58
OWL-DL, 156
OWL-S, 177

Parametrisation, 173
Performance, 7, 168
Precision, 157
Preprocessing, 53, 56
Process Mediation, 15

QOM, *see* Quick Ontology Mapping
Quality, 6, 167
Quality Metrics, 157
Questionnaire, 77
Quick Ontology Mapping, 63
QuickMig, 62, 163

Recall, 157
Related Entities Matcher, 104
Repository Adapter, 137
Requirements, 6, 166
Review, 54, 56, 175
Root Entity, 40
Rule Creation, 138

INDEX

Running Example, 23

SAP CCTS Modeller Warp 10, 180
SAP Exchange Infrastructure, 146
SAP Migration Workbench, 148, 179
SAP NetWeaver Composition Environment, 178
Schema, 39
Schema Features, 93
    Cardinality Constraints, 95
    Children, 94
    Data Type Constraints, 95
    Entity Documentation, 94
    Entity Name, 93
    Example Instance, 95
    Parents, 94
    Siblings, 94
Schema Mapping, 19
Schematic Heterogeneity, 27
    Bilateral Heterogeneities, 27
    Meta-level Heterogeneities, 29
    Multilateral Heterogeneities, 28
Semantic Heterogeneities, 25
    Semantic Data Heterogeneities, 30
      Representation Heterogeneities, 30
      Scaling Heterogeneities, 30
      Surjective Mappings, 31
      Value Range Heterogeneities, 30
    Semantic Domain Heterogeneities, 31
      Aggregation, 32
      Incompatibility, 32
      Overlap, 31
      Subsumption, 31
Semantic Web service, 176
Semi-Automatic Mapping Process, 55
Similarity Matrix, 89
Similarity Matrix Aggregation, 107
Similarity Metrics, 98
    Dice Coefficient, 101
    Equality, 99
    Lexical Similarity, 99

Soft-TF-IDF, 100
SOA, 15
Structural Heterogeneities, 25
Stylus Studio, 146
Syntactic Heterogeneities, 25
System Heterogeneities, 24

Technical Names Matcher, 105
Testing, 54, 56, 175
Transactional Data, 17

Usage Characteristics, 73
    Collection of, 76

WSDL-S, 177
WSMO, 177

XML Document, 41
XML Schema, 40
XML Schema Lifting, 50
XML Schema Mapping, 48

VDM Verlagsservicegesellschaft mbH

Die VDM Verlagsservicegesellschaft sucht für wissenschaftliche Verlage abgeschlossene und herausragende

Dissertationen, Habilitationen, Diplomarbeiten, Master Theses, Magisterarbeiten usw.

für die kostenlose Publikation als Fachbuch.

Sie verfügen über eine Arbeit, die hohen inhaltlichen und formalen Ansprüchen genügt, und haben Interesse an einer honorarvergüteten Publikation?

Dann senden Sie bitte erste Informationen über sich und Ihre Arbeit per Email an *info@vdm-vsg.de*.

Sie erhalten kurzfristig unser Feedback!

VDM Verlagsservicegesellschaft mbH
Dudweiler Landstr. 99
D - 66123 Saarbrücken
www.vdm-vsg.de

Telefon +49 681 3720 174
Fax +49 681 3720 1749

Die VDM Verlagsservicegesellschaft mbH vertritt

Printed by Books on Demand GmbH, Norderstedt / Germany